Pilgrimage
of a **Pupil**
Preacher
and **Pastor**

For Ria –

with love and every blessing

for the future –

John Bell

Pilgrimage

of a Pupil

Preacher

and Pastor

The Mystery and the Miracle of the Church

REVD H W M CANT

Foreword by Very Revd Dr Gilleasbuig I. Macmillan
Minister of St Giles Cathedral, Edinburgh

Bellavista Publications - 1999

ISBN 0 9525350 4 1

Published by Bellavista Publications, Bellavista, Carness Road,
Kirkwall, Orkney, KW15 1TB. Tel./Fax. 01856 872306

Printed by Cromwell Press,Trowbridge,Wiltshire

Contents

Foreword

by the Very Revd Dr Gilleasbuig I. Macmillan

Minister of St Giles Cathedral, Edinburgh

The pleasure and sense of privilege in writing a Foreword to this book come partly from an admiring friendship with the author, partly from the recognition that we all stand on the shoulders of our predecessors and that there is nothing new under the sun, and partly from the awareness that Bill Cant's ministry has been exercised during a period of great change and development, heights and depths, unlikely to be repeated in the same ways in the future, inasmuch as we can reasonably predict.

The grounds of admiration are his holding together things which are too often found separately: devotion to the church and appreciative identification with the community; respect for the past and eagerness for the future; commitment to the core of the Gospel and energetic willingness to discover forms of believing fitted to the circumstances of time.

What he has written expresses one gifted Scotsman's engagement with more than a half century of a changing Scotland, demonstrating faithful and creative witness to a constantly adaptable Christian religion, the identity of which is much more like that of a river than that of a monument in stone.

Gilleasbuig Macmillan

Dedication

For Margot, my Wife

For the Family - Children and Grandchildren

For the Churches and Parishes where I have been Minister

Acknowledgments

The thanks of the author and publishers are due to the following, for permission to quote extracts: to the late G M Brown for quotations from *An Orkney Tapestry, Magnus, The Golden Bird* and *For the Islands I Sing;* and for two stanzas from 'Christmas' by John Betjeman in *Church Poems;* and to John Murray (Publishers) Ltd; to those authors for making quotations from their books published by the SCM, and for permission to do this given by the SCM Press, London; also for permission of Oxford University Press to quote from their books, mostly by the late Professor J Baillie; permission was also asked to quote from books by the late Revd Professor John Knox of Union Theological Seminary, USA, especially from *The Church and the Reality of Christ;* and from Bloodaxe Books Ltd to quote from 'The Minister' by R S Thomas - *Selected Poems 1946-68;* permission was granted from Hodder and Stoughton, to quote from the late Professor W. Manson's books, not least from *The Way of the Cross*, and from his commentary on *The Gospel of Luke.*

Thanks are also given to John Macquarrie in *God Incarnate - Story and Belief* (Editor A E Harvey) allowance to do this was given by the SPCK; in addition we are grateful to Donald Reeves to quote from his book *For God's Sake,* permission being given by Harper Collins Publishers to do this. Further the author and publishers are indebted to the Very Revd R S Barbour, to Elizabeth Templeton and to the Revd Dr J P Newell for permission to quote from their writings.

I am further much indebted to Mr Stewart Davidson and Mrs Leslie Davidson his wife, of Bellavista Publications, Orkney, for great care in preparing this book for publication. I'd also like to thank Mrs Eileen Sabiston for her considerable help in the initial typing.

Introduction

I have much appreciated the support and guidance of all the Parishes where I have served. I especially remember the joyful and generous celebration given to me and my wife, Margot by St Magnus Cathedral Congregation, when I retired in September 1990.

The origin of this book comes from the First Service in the Cathedral at 9.45 a.m., when on one occasion the different groups then were asked by the present Minister, the Revd Ron Ferguson, to consider how they would spend the last six weeks of their life. I was with a few people to think about this. One of these was the Orkney Islands Council Convener, Mr Hugh Halcro-Johnston. He said he would use the time to tell his children what things he had thought important, and which had motivated his life.

I thought this a very good answer, and felt I could well do something similar myself. I could write down something of the story of my life as well as of the ministerial training I had received, and of the Churches and Parishes where I had served. It was in remembering the assistance and help I had received from parents, relations, teachers, fellow soldiers and countless other people that I finished this book.

In addition to all these I wish to thank two friends particularly. First, there is the Very Revd Professor John McIntyre, CVO, DD, DLitt, formerly of New College, Edinburgh University, and a Past Moderator of the General Assembly of the Church of Scotland. He had the goodness and the patience to read what I had written, and gave me much help in putting it together, and in his wise suggestions on its Theology.

I would also wish to express my gratitude to the Minister of St Giles Cathedral, Edinburgh, the Very Revd Gilleasbuig I. Macmillan, MA BD DD, Dean of the Order of the Thistle, who, despite a very busy life and ministry, has generously written a Foreword.

Chapter I

The Early Days - At Home and at School

1. A Home in Edinburgh

Every Cathedral has its distinctive features. This is certainly true of St Magnus Cathedral in Orkney. The visitor to it is made quickly aware of the rose coloured beauty of its stones, of its splendid proportions enhancing both its height and length, of its fascinating Norwegian origins, and not least of its magnificent West and East windows. Your eyes are drawn to the East window as soon as you enter the West door. This window has four lights below and a wheel window above; these lights depict Jesus Christ crucified on the lower part, and higher up, our Lord ascended. The ascended Christ calls for recognition that he is victor over sin and death, and is now set free to travel over the world, invading both individual lives and groups of all kinds, nations, communities and families. He is the world ruler who invites all those committed to him to enable him to reach out to others. This may well have been the insight of Stephen in the Book of Acts (Acts 7.56) who said, "Behold, I see the heavens opened, and the Son of man standing on the right hand of God". "But whereas the original Apostles and witnesses thought that Jesus would come back to them, - 'Lord, is it at this time that You restore the Kingdom to Israel?' - did Stephen say that they must go out and, so to speak, anticipate the Son of Man's coming by proclaiming Him to every nation and people of that larger world which was now included in His dominion?"[1]

No limit in space or time can be placed on the work of the ascended Christ. He is constantly moving forward from place to place in century after century, searching and knocking at the door of human hearts. Western society has certainly been long aware of his presence, "but He has been standing at Europe's door for almost two thousand years; so that you and I were born into the long heritage of that knocking".[2] Families have surely shared in this, and I believe that in my own family, the lives of my parents had been penetrated by the knocking of this same cosmic Christ. By his Spirit he entered their minds and hearts and enabled them, slowly or quickly, to decide for him, and to become members of his Church, and witnesses for him in the world. It is then his gracious will to break down the barriers of disunity and separation and to reshape the members of a family so that they can become sons and daughters of God, and be bound together by his Spirit of forgiving love.

This leads on to the nature of my family home. I was born in 1921–an only child–in a village, outside Edinburgh, called Juniper Green, one of many villages in those days near the banks of the Water of Leith. After some years there my parents changed their home to Colinton, a little nearer Edinburgh, where a new house was built in Bonaly Road, within fifteen minutes walk of the Pentland Hills. Another early memory–I would be about four years old at the time–is of a horse and plough coming in to the field around the house to plough up the ground. My parents had married in 1914, just before the Great War began, but, like so many others then, they were soon separated when my father was posted to France. He served initially as a private, then as an Army Officer. After the Armistice he resumed his work as a civil servant, eventually becoming Assessor of Public Undertakings (Scotland). My father had been born in Glasgow but had moved to Edinburgh, where he went to school, and later met my mother who was a Primary School Teacher. In the biography of the late Bishop J A T Robinson, there is an early interesting chapter called 'Inherited Blessing' in which tribute is paid to what he received from his parents and forbears. One of the greatest of these blessings was the gift of the Christian Faith. It was in large measure from his family that he learned that - "the Lord is good; his mercy is everlasting; and his truth endureth to all generations".[3] I too feel how fortunate I was in my family, and that it is right to say, at this beginning stage, how I learned from them the mediated goodness of God and of the Christian Faith. I hope I may be able to say to my children - "I delivered unto you first of all that which I also received. . ."[4] The signs of Christian Faith are to be seen in certain of my grandparents in word and deed, though I can speak with specific details only in relation to my parents. Edwin Muir in his fascinating autobiography tells us how he felt about the family home in Wyre, Orkney. There were good relationships with the neighbours who helped one another when required, and the culture and life within that home was indeed happy. Muir wrote of these neighbours and of the people who shared his home. . . "they had a culture made up of legend, folk song, and the poetry and prose of the Bible; they had customs which sanctioned their instinctive feelings for the earth; their life was an order, and a good order".[5] It would be true to say that the culture of my home had similar elements in it. It was my mother who taught me "legend" in the sense of great stories and poetry and who opened the door for me into fascinating books. For example from an early age she told me the story of Robert Louis Stevenson, and she led me on from *The Child's Garden of Verses* to *Treasure Island* and *Kidnapped* and to so much more. I can also still see one of Stevenson's prayers in a frame in one of the rooms in my family home. I can still delight in RLS describing so accurately the stream and banks of the Water of Leith as it swings round below Colinton manse: 'Dark brown is the river, Golden is the sand . . .' What he had to say about Swanston Cottage and the Pentland hills, 'The hills of home', also comes vividly to mind, and·

the people whom he sees among them at different periods, including Covenanting and Victorian times. Despite the cynical views which have sometimes been taken of the writings and life of RLS, I have derived much benefit from contemplating his stories, and from recalling his courageous life in so many travels and places. But I owe to my mother so much more than 'legends', and doors opened into famous stories and books. She left to me and to so many others the splendid example of a persistent compassionate care for others, not least for those in physical need. I can vividly remember,–though this provision is often disapproved of today–how often I would come home from school in the late 1920s and 1930s, to find, at the door, or sitting in the garden, a man or a woman, sometimes with a child, eating the sandwiches or drinking the hot soup prepared by my mother. She came from a large family, as did my father, she had two sisters and three brothers, and as the eldest of the family she gave them much care and attention. The oldest brother was in a reserved occupation, but the 1914-1918 War saw the youngest brother killed–a private in the Royal Scots, while the other in the Services, survived the war as an officer in the Gordons. She always had the best of relationships with her brothers as with her sisters–with Nell, a nursing sister for most of her life in a hospital in Johannesburg, South Africa, and not least with Jean, who lived near us in Colinton, and with whose family I had a very happy companionship. Both these aunts were delightful people, and I have splendid memories of them, as of two of their brothers. The music in our home was provided by my father who was able to play the piano by ear, and at weekends he and his sister were able to play for us and friends the hymns and popular songs of the day. Perhaps it was my father who encouraged me many years later to take a part in one of the Gilbert and Sullivan Operas at secondary school. I regret that I did not persevere with music lessons, though it is a great comfort to me that some of my family, particularly my son Andrew, has inherited his grandfather's gift for and love of music.

"The poetry and prose of the Bible" was another element in Edwin Muir's family culture and this took the form, in part, of the practice of the presence of God in the home. It may surprise some that I speak much of Edwin Muir, but you cannot have lived in Orkney for more than 25 years and not know something about Edwin and his remarkable poems and autobiography. So I don't apologise for giving these further words of his concerning his father in Wyre: 'Every Sunday night he gathered us together to read a chapter of the Bible and kneel down in prayer. These Sunday nights are among my happiest memories; there was a feeling of complete security and union among us as we sat reading about David and Elijah'.[6] And Muir remembers clearly a constant phrase in the prayers, "an house not made with hands, eternal in the heavens". By way of contrast we did not regularly have family prayers, though occasionally after the war, I led these, with my parents' encouragement. Yet my father always studied his *Daily Light*, and said grace before meals. Corporate worship was a feature of family life however, within the United Free Church in

Juniper Green, in the early 1920s, and that was continued in the same Church, St Andrew's, once it became Church of Scotland in 1929. In this Church my father was for many decades a very active elder–as Sunday School Superintendent, then Bible Class Leader, Treasurer, and last, but not least, in the evangelical role of acting Session Clerk in one of Edinburgh's new Church Extension Charges–Sighthill. I have interesting memories of sitting in the family pew in St Andrew's Church both before and after the 1939-45 War. On one occasion–there was a cushion on part of the seat only–my father needing more comfort in sitting, probably without thinking, pulled the cushion away from the two ladies further along during a hymn, with the result that they sat down astonished, cushionless, and with quite a noise! That was a good service! I believe I resented the Church going for quite a while as a teenager, but I was willing to go to an enquirer's class, and eventually, but questioningly, became a full member of the Church in the time of a very highly thought of minister–George Reid, later a Queen's Chaplain, and a Moderator of the General Assembly of the Church of Scotland. Without the example and help of my parents in word and deed in the fellowship and worship of the Church, it is very doubtful whether I'd ever have become an active member of it, far less a minister of the Gospel. When I came later to learn and understand more of the Christian Faith it had been rooted without doubt, not only in my home culture, but in the worship and fellowship of the Church where I became a member.

Muir's home and his neighbours in the Orcadian island of Wyre "had customs which sanctified their instinctive feelings for the earth". They were very much aware of the seasons of the year. For many months of winter the land had to be left alone in those times; the cattle were drawn into the byres and the farmers and their families were brought together often into one place; "The winter gathered us into one room as it gathered the cattle into the stable and the byre; the sky came closer; the lamps were lit at three or four in the afternoon, and then the great evening lay before us like a world: an evening filled with talk, stories, games, music and lamplight".[7]

Then with the release of the cattle from the dark byres and their rushing into the fields, and the sowing beginning in the fields, the spring time had begun. The pattern of life was ruled by what had to happen in the various seasons of the year, and farmers and their families lived close to the earth and to their animals, always aware of the gift they had been given of their land and of its potentiality for life and fruitfulness. They had their regular days of rejoicing when the Lammas Market was held annually in Kirkwall, or when the crops were ultimately ingathered, or when in the New Year they saw the start of sowing - "My father," wrote Muir, "took a special delight in the sowing, and we all felt the first day was a special day".[8]

In my home in Colinton we could not have the same agricultural customs as those in Wyre, but, because the house was literally only a few minutes walk from Bonaly Farm and its open fields beyond, we had great delight in the countryside. Weekends saw us taking the opportunity of refreshing walks to the Pentland Hills and to the reservoirs that lay close at hand–Torduff, Clubbidean, Bonaly, within an hour or so, and Glencorse further away. Sledges came out in the winter, and the fishing rods and golf clubs in the spring, and in the summer my parents greatly enjoyed the proximity of the fields and hills around them, but even more the customs that bound them to the garden round the home. These altered with the passage of the years, for it took some time to change the plot of land round the house–about one third of an acre–into a garden. I can remember well my mother buying the trees and the bushes and the rhododendrons and the roses for various parts of the garden, and my father sowing the seed in the lawns. We had a large roller and at one stage I needed all my strength to move it. It did not take many years before the trees were growing tall–chestnut trees, holly trees, cherry trees, apple and crab apple trees–and before we had what my mother particularly delighted in–glorious red and pink and white rhododendrons as well as beds of roses. I remember thinking how beautiful these roses were, in the same places where I'd seen them five years before, after my return from the Army. Soon too the grass could be cut, and there were lawns where there was enjoyment to be had in a cricket pitch or on a bowling green. Friends and neighbours or family could be invited in to such games. For many years my father delighted to share in these, as also with me and others on the golf course, especially on holiday.

Edwin Muir, you will remember, further spoke of the life of his home and neighbours as "an order, and a good order". That seems to me a fitting way of describing both the relationships within my home, and without. My mother kept not only an attractive home but a hospitable one. Most weekends there were present members of her relatives or my father's. They visited us from Edinburgh or from further afield; our Sunday lunch was often shared with others, and was especially good and enjoyable. Relationships with the neighbours were almost always mutually enriching, both for adults and young people. Families on either side of us shared in a common interest in their growing gardens, and the young people found time, especially in summer days, to play cricket and other games in the gardens. It would be wrong to say that the neighbourly relations were always intact. I recall one occasion when my cousin and I were playing tennis. By mistake the racquet slipped out of my hand and flew over to the next garden. The neighbour was angry, not so much because it might have landed on his roses, but on one of his small children. To make him angrier still we climbed the fence and tried to get back the racquet. But the neighbour had taken it indoors and then phoned the house. We were sent round to apologise though my father thought that it was a bit of a storm in a tea cup!

Once the 1939-45 War started most of the happy garden games stopped. Young neighbours were called up to the Forces. On the whole our immediate neighbourhood did not loose too many killed in the war, though one of our neighbours, early on, sadly lost one of his sons, shot down while flying a fighter plane. My closest friend and companion and cousin in Colinton–an officer in the REME and a Paratrooper, after being in the Royal Scots–managed to come through the war unscathed, and was able in 1946 to return to Edinburgh University. Why one was taken and another survived will always remain a mystery, known only to God.

My parents struggled to keep good order in the garden during the war years. My father was an Air Raid Warden, along with many others, yet still kept up his work for the Church and the Community–in different societies and in relation to the welfare of Service people. He retained his interests in the Burns Club, the Bowling Green, the Literary Society and in the League of Nations, while at the same time continuing in a job that, with short staff, made quite heavy demands upon him.

2.   *Life at School - A Story of Failure and a Second Chance*

I have said nothing so far about my schooling, but this is certainly something usually very important to parents. My mother was particularly interested in education, not least in that of her only child. Nowadays parents often consult their children about which secondary school they would like to attend. But this was probably unusual in the early 1930s. I was never asked about this matter though some points could have been made to me about the possibilities, for some secondary schools were quite near to where we stayed; it was not essential to travel into Edinburgh for schooling, either by train or by bus. At any rate, it was my mother who enquired about schools and who decided that when I left Primary School–Gillsland Park School–where incidentally we were taught the game of rugby by a young man by the name of R Selby Wright–I should go at 12+ to the Edinburgh Academy. This was a different decision from that of the parents of my nearest male cousins on both sides of the family, who were sent to George Watson's College. I have to say that I found the change to the Academy very disturbing; I knew of no other boy of similar age with whom I could travel, and in whom I could have a class-mate. It took me quite a long time to settle down and to cope with the work and the sport opportunities. Standards in both spheres were high, not least to me in cricket and in rugby. The sports grounds were either Raeburn Place or Newfield–mostly Newfield, near Inverleith. Often I didn't get back from there to Colinton by train or tram till 5.30 pm or 6 pm, when there was usually plenty homework to be done. Especially from 4th Classical to 5th Classical I did not do very well in comparison with some other pupils to whom everything seemed easy. However I can say that in the first year at the Academy I greatly enjoyed the school sports, on the rugby field, on the cricket pitch, on the running track (and even in the boxing ring!).

Yet there was, to me at any rate, a major catastrophe to come in my school career. It happened at Newfield, one summer evening, quite unexpectedly, when we were practising for the sports day. I can remember very clearly what happened: the boys of my age had taken part in a number of short races, and were then requested to cover longer distances. Ephors (school prefects)–perhaps it was only senior boys–were there to encourage younger people, though they could not necessarily be blamed for what was to follow. At the close of one event I collapsed, and woke up in one of the Academy Boarding Houses which overlooked Newfield. There I was well taken care of, and eventually sent home in a taxi. The result of all this was that the family doctor decided that I was to be kept back from all school games for an indefinite period. This seemed to me then a complete disaster. If at one time I had been wisely drawn out of the water–my mother rescuing me when I plunged too far on one occasion into the sea–I felt I was being very unwisely drawn out of the enjoyable waters of all physical school games. But the medical decision had been taken, and I could not alter it.

But some few years later, there was, in my mother's eyes at least, much worse to come. My next two years were not very happy for I felt cut off from the rest of my friends, who were able to continue their games and also share in the activities of the OTC. I had to watch my class mates, now in uniform, doing their drill or their piping each Friday afternoon after 3 pm to 4.15 pm or later. I had to content myself with chess or golf or play reading, which were to me poor alternatives. It was in 5th Classical that along with others I sat for the Oxford and Cambridge Certificates. I recall exactly where I received the results, and this was 'the worst to come.' We had gone as a family with cousins on my mother's side, for the month of August that particular year to Kinloch Rannoch, where we had the let of a pleasant house, with fishing rights in the Tummel. I was down at the river when my mother came to speak with me telling me bluntly how poorly I had done in the exams. I tried not to allow what I'd been told to spoil the holiday. At least it didn't spoil the fishing, for we managed to catch a good number of trout! However the exam results brought the family, and myself, in particular, to a serious decision. Should I continue to carry on at school with a classical course? Would it not be better to try some less demanding course and leave as soon as possible? Should I be drawn out of the water of school life altogether? The alternative would be to move on to 6th Classical when opportunity was given to the pupils who wished, to sit 'Highers' for entrance to the Scottish universities. I was truly uncertain what to do, realising that I had been kept off games, and, as it appeared then, a failure also at school work, certainly in terms of the recent examinations. My parents were very good at this time encouraging me to go ahead. My mother especially believed I should try once more to make something of my school work even though I could still receive no affirmation of myself (possibly!) in school games. One or two of the masters at the Academy apparently also felt I could do better. I realise that this is a pretty gloomy story so I quickly bring it to an end by saying that with help from home and from school I made surprising progress on my return to school, passing the necessary exams in 6th Classical for the Scottish University Entrance. One further difficulty was presented to my school career. The school authorities thought that it would be wise to retain me for a second year in the

6th form. This was the only occasion I can recall my mother seeing the Form Master, and asking that I be allowed to go to 7th Classical. It gave me much encouragement that this was allowed, as the friendship of my class-mates meant very much to me. It also gave me the opportunity to learn more in challenging company, the company of nine to ten boys, most of whom were very bright, some of them being prepared to sit for Oxford or Cambridge exhibitions and scholarships. I quickly realised that I certainly didn't belong to this academic league, but I somehow felt liberated to do more school work in Latin and Greek and English and Ancient History, and at the same time I believed I must take steps to seeking full entrance, once more, to all physical games and to the OTC. This was duly done. So I stayed one further year at Edinburgh Academy. I felt I had been given a second chance to have a full share in the life of the school in 1937-39, and in that I found much fulfilment and happiness.

I made some small progress in the OTC, receiving my Certificate 'A' and becoming a lance corporal! These matters may seem very insignificant but they were not to me at the time! Nor was the fact that in cricket I received my 2ndXI colours, with a trial for the 1stXI, and got a rugby sweater! I am very much aware of how trivial my problems were at school in comparison with so many others who had major learning difficulties, or whose parents had a big crisis in providing the school fees, but I have tried honestly to describe my school days at the Academy, and I can recognise the anxieties which some things must have caused my parents.

It is more than 60 years since I left school, and since then I have met a good number of Academicals. Only a small number of them viewed their school experience as sad and depressing–one or two of these may have had, in their view, an unfortunate time in a school boarding house. The vast majority tell of good times and have carried into their lives many excellent school memories. They speak of blessings and not cursings, of how they found help through the companionship of boys or masters, or of how they discovered the wisdom and patience to plod on and try again, or of how they found the treasures ultimately of some achievements in the playing fields and in their studies which became part of self affirmation and acceptance and became to them a pledge of what they might yet achieve. Many grasped that life was more than some personal accomplishment, for it had to do with seeing something of the huge disadvantages of others, at home or abroad, and of acting with others about this. In my last year I certainly learned something of this in the Academical Boys' Club in Henderson Row.

In George Mackay Brown's book, *Pictures in the Cave*, shadowy figures appear to old Sigurd, looking back at what happened in the past. Throughout the centuries it was clear to him that different individuals got great blessings, not harm, from having been in that rocky cave. They come before his eyes: for example there was Robert the Bruce who found the patience of wisdom and new inspiration as he watched there the persistence of the spider; Pedro, who escaped from the wreck of a Spanish Galleon, found healing and care through it; a boy Eric, who, with courage searching the cave, found there a precious pearl which was soon sold, and was the means of saving the family croft and his life in the future; and there was the German lieutenant who discovered reconciliation there: "There's no enemies here, now or ever. We're a band of brothers–the knights of the cave".[9] And old Sigurd, who had been made the recipient of the splendid stories of those blessed, not cursed by the cave, was resolved to hand over these treasures to the young girl who was his companion, so that she could pass them on to others. These were the pictures and the real treasures of the wrongly called witches' cave.

I have my own 'Pictures in the Cave' of my secondary school. It was not a witches' cave; we could have been a better "band of brothers", and certainly we were no knights in shining armour, but we had been given valuable blessings and ineradicable memories. I am no Sigurd with a wonderful memory: others, like Magnus Magnusson can tell excellent stories of the school, and of how, over a century and a half, it has helped and shaped and guided the lives of so many who passed through it. Only a few fellow pupils in that 7th Classical flash through my mind's eye. Some of them were tragically killed in the war like Michael Blair, Head Ephor, Dux of the school, and Captain of the 1st XV, and another young man also with a bright future ahead of him. Others returned to civilian life–Harry Keith (judge), Vaughan Shaw (business man), G S S M Walker (Minister), Ian Baillie (diplomat), John Forrester (doctor). My final memory of the school is of the last day when there took place the speech making and the prize giving, with many parents present. An Admiral addressed the school and its guests. I was given a Greek prize, and with many more pupils went off to OTC camp. We had sung, or recalled for the last time, the school song:

> "Floreat Academia,
> Mater alma, mater pia:
> Huic paremus, hanc amamus,
> Ergo fortiter canamus
> 'Floreat Academia' "[10]

Notes

1. W. Manson - 'The Epistle to the Hebrews' - Hodder and Stoughton Ltd - pp32-33.
2. John Baillie - 'Christian Devotion' - Oxford University Press (1962) - p56.
3. Psalm 100 v.5.
4. I Corinthians 15 v.3.
5. Edwin Muir - 'An Autobiography' - The Hogarth Press - p63.
6. Ibid - p26.
7. Ibid - pp30-31.
8. Ibid - p32.
9. George Mackay Brown - 'Pictures In The Cave' - Canongate Publishing Limited - p135.
10. Magnus Magnusson - 'The Clacken and the Slate' - Collins - p241.

Chapter II

Edinburgh University and the War Years

Many people have a clear memory of where they heard that their country was at war with Germany in September, 1939. This happened for me while on holiday. It was the custom of our family to spend time in September, after some weeks elsewhere, in a small village called Kinnesswood, in Kinross-shire. Here in earlier centuries most houses had their loom. Its most famous literary inhabitant had been Michael Bruce, the poet, who has been credited by some authorities with writing Paraphrases. You can still visit his home in one of the side streets leading up to Bishop Hill, overlooking the village. In 1939 we were as usual staying in the cottage, whose windows, on one side, looked across the fields to Loch Leven, and which had been renovated about 1933, the original building having been built with the help of my maternal great grandfather. There had been little new building, or transport change, after the 1914-18 War, and I can recall being taken by pony and gig from Mawcarse station to the Kinnesswood cottage. In the 1920s and early 1930s there were few cars in the village street; butchers and bakers called at the houses with their horse drawn vehicles, while in the fields the crops were stooked, and then carried back to the farm in a cart drawn by a Clydesdale. I enjoyed sharing in this farm work even into the late 1930s. It was in a house across the village street where, along with my mother, I heard the Prime Minister say that Britain was at war with Germany, its Government having failed to withdraw its troops from Poland.

1. Army Enlistment, University Life, and Angling Days

Almost immediately, even in this small rural area of Scotland, changes began. One of the first of these was the 'blackout' and soon came the arrival of evacuated children from urban areas. I was part of a group of people who awaited a number of buses, packed with children and mothers. They were to go to certain village homes and nearby farms. But it was not long before we had to return to Edinburgh and get accustomed, along with neighbours and fellow citizens to war time life. How often young people are influenced by their peer group; this was true in my case regarding volunteering for service in the Forces. I heard that my cousin had joined the Army by going to the High School yards, Infirmary Street in Edinburgh. I felt it right to do the same, and as I had had some previous cadet experience at school, it was natural that I should offer for Army service. So after interviews with various Army Officers and a medical examination, I received a day's pay, and was told that I was enlisted, and would hear when I would receive my call up papers, though it might be some time. Meanwhile I was encouraged to join the University OTC while I was attending University classes at the beginning of October. For many students the move from school to University is a difficult one. I cannot say that this was my lot as what I had been given at school enabled me to follow with understanding and interest the teachings I received in my first year classes of Latin and Greek and Ancient History. Had I been asked at that time what I was going to do in life, I couldn't have given an answer. However I might with truth have replied that I did have two priorities–to pass whatever exams I could, prior to my call up, and to make vigorous effort to obtain Certificate 'B' from the Army authorities which, I was told, would give me entrance to an Officer Cadet Training unit. This was the target suggested to many of us who had already had cadet experience. By the year 1940 I had managed to achieve this, even being promoted to the rank of Corporal! This was partly to help with the instructing of others in weapon training and other duties. Many of us became quite knowledgeable about weapons, including the Vickers Machine Gun. The mysteries of platoon and company tactics were explained to us in TEWTs (tactical exercises without troops).

I did not spend time in those university years in too many societies, though I attended some university debates and occasionally attempted to contribute there. But the university group, besides the OTC, which particularly interested me was called the Student Christian Movement. This was the place where my mind was stimulated to think who I was, what is a University, and who is a Christian student. I had never heard of this group of students until I entered the old quad of the University. However I soon came to appreciate that there were Student Movement Secretaries–usually ministers of the Church of Scotland. I shall always be indebted to the Revd Ian Fraser, for drawing me into the SCM study groups, and its meetings and conferences. Ian, at that time, was the Scottish Secretary and good at raising fundamental questions in student minds about the meaning of life, about Christian beliefs, and about major ethical and political issues of the times. I learned, particularly from these SCM study groups, where there was open discussion of such themes. I was instructed often by fellow students as to their aims in life, and in relation to their basic commitments in the light of their self knowledge, and in the light of Scripture and the claims of Christ. I learned that the living God speaks not just in Scripture but through persons. My eyes were opened to what prayers meant to my contemporaries as they led the worship at SCM meetings. By the time I was called up in 1941, I had been made aware that I had so much more to grasp regarding Christian Faith and Life, and that other students, not just divinity students, had so much more understanding and conviction of how the Word of God had been made flesh in Jesus Christ. My mind had been stimulated to think deeper about the mystery of Christ and of his Church and the world. It would be very wrong, it should be said, to think that the students of my time, or indeed of any time, thought that the SCM had all the answers to their problems, or that their leaders had infallible wisdom. In truth there were always those who delighted to make fun of the Movement. They used to sing with great gusto *Poisoning the Student Mind*:-

> 'The SCM has found its true vocation
> In poisoning the student mind,
> Its leaders by astute manipulation
> Are poisoning the student mind,
> And pure souls are sure that we will go
> To toast our toes at furnaces below,
> If we persist in listening to leaders that we know
> Are poisoning the student mind'.

Chorus

> 'Poisoning the student mind, poisoning the student mind,
> Bold men, bad men, villains double dyed,
> 'neath their smiling countenance hide
> Spiritual arsenic and moral cyanide -
> Poisoning the student mind, poisoning the student mind,
> Poisoning the student mind.'

Verses were changed as the years passed, and various students, or teachers of note were included. For example, after the war, Robin Barbour's name figured (later he became Professor of New Testament at Aberdeen University):-

> 'We've been to school where Mrs Barbour's Robin
> Is poisoning the student mind,
> Where priest and layman really are hob nobbin,
> Poisoning the student mind,
> The eschaton is coming, Fenn has said,
> But look out for the judgement if you're a nasty red,'
> Chorus–'Poisoning the student mind.' etc.

Whatever was put into the verses, that last verse was always the same (at least at some conferences):

> 'There's just one thing that I forget to mention
> The student hasn't got a mind,
> That's why its safe to hold this great convention
> For poisoning the students mind,
> But if its leaders heard this awful news
> In rank despair they'd take at once to booze,
> So let them go on thinking if they choose
> That they're poisoning the student mind.'

The years 1939-41 soon passed by. I gave much time to the OTC and became involved in the LDV (Local Defence Volunteers) with others, seeking to guard the old quad building against the threat of fire bombs etc. I was told that if I took six academic subjects in two years I could be awarded a War MA, and I managed this, taking in English, Moral Philosophy and Second Year Greek in the next year. My call up papers came in June, and I was away to a new world in the Malvern hills in England where there was an OCTU (Officer Cadet Training Unit).

Before passing on to the army days this could be an appropriate point to speak of another area of life in which I spent much time enthusiastically, and where I was often renewed in body, mind and spirit–the sphere of nature. Countless people have discovered enormous delight in this. There are those who have always seen nature, whether its mountains or seas or valleys or streams or birds or animals or flowers as a wonderful gift. In George Mackay Brown's story *The Golden Bird*, John Fiord came back from Aberdeen to be schoolmaster in the Orcadian rural valley where he grew up. He was disappointed in love, and returned to his home one weekend very disconsolate. But he was excellently cared for by a disabled girl called Sunniva. She had cleaned up his old croft home and went there to make his supper, though she was both very deaf, and dumb. Soon John Fiord began to read to her after the evening meal. These are some of the words spoken:

"Your enjoyment of the world is never right, till every morning you awake in Heaven; see yourself in your Father's Palace; and look upon the skies, the earth, and the air as Celestial joys: having such a reverend esteem of all, as if you were among the Angels. The bride of a monarch, in her husband's chamber, hath no such causes of delight as you.

You never enjoy the world aright, till the Sea itself floweth in your veins, till you are clothed with the heavens, and crowned with the stars: and perceive yourself to be the sole heir of the whole world, and more than so, because men are in it who are every one sole heirs as well as you. Till you can sing and rejoice and delight in God, as misers do in gold, and Kings in sceptres, you never enjoy the world". . .[1]

Particular parts of this beautiful world appeal to different people. John Fiord read to Sunniva of how "you never enjoy the world aright, till the Sea itself floweth in your veins . . .", for others it is the rivers and the streams that do this. David S Cairns, a great Scottish theologian in the early part of this century (Professor of Dogmatics and Apologetics in 1907 in the United Free Church College in Aberdeen, known later in 1929 as Christ's College, where Cairns became Principal) was fascinated by a particular stream near his home–the river Eden. He fished it day and night for many years. "I went on fishing", he wrote, "and so the Eden in many of its reaches flows though my memory and, when I wish, I can hear its music and the roar of the Linn and see its high set 'scaurs' against the green of the trees and meadow and the "ripples of the rising trout" in the long, still reaches on many, many glorious summer days. I am very thankful for the Eden".[2] Cairns also wrote: "I shall never forget my unalloyed delight in capturing my first trout in the Linn Hole . . . a grand pool on the Eden". Mine was caught, not in the Borders but in one of the burns which flow down from the north side of the Pentland Hills, and I can identify with the Professor's passion for country streams and burns and for trout fishing. It is interesting to find these Pentland Hill burns mentioned in *Memorials of His Time*, by Lord Cockburn. These burns met together in the grounds of what is now called Bonaly Tower, but which was then "a scarcely habitable farm house". Lord Cockburn writes:

"In March, 1811 I married, and set up my rural household gods at Bonaly, in the parish of Colinton, close by the northern base of the Pentland Hills. . . Everything, except the two burns, the few old trees, and the mountains are my own work, and to a great extent the work of my own hands. Human nature is incapable of enjoying more happiness than has been my lot here . . ."[3] This is yet another Scot wonderfully aware of the beauty of the nature, and of that little corner of the earth which was God's gift to him, and where for Lord Cockburn, "There is not a recess in the valleys of the Pentlands, nor an eminence on their summits that is not familiar to my solitude".[4]

From fishing with worms the burns of the Pentland Hills–not least the burn within the grounds of the present Bonaly Tower–and the reservoirs from which they tumbled, I moved on later in my teens to the art of dry fly fishing. But I learned this initially in the Borders not in the Eden, on the Blackadder and the Whiteadder, tributaries of the river Tweed. My tutor in this gentle art had had some grim experiences in the 1914-18 War where at a very young age he had fought in the trenches, and later required time to recover from his bayoneting episodes there. My parents had looked after him for some time, and I believe he was grateful for this. At any rate by the 1930s he was a school master, and used to come to Edinburgh by car, and on certain weekends in spring and summer, took me to his delightful home in the village of Gavinton, outside Duns, and within easy reach of the rivers Blackadder and Whiteadder. I have golden memories of fishing with him in the dawning of a day, when light was coming out of darkness, and everything seemed to be awakening to life, and when the flies began to settle on the waters and the fish started to move about at the dawn rise. What I learned on these expeditions to the Border streams I continued to practice on the Water of Leith in Colinton, and higher up at Juniper Green and Currie and Balerno, and in the river's upper reaches, while waiting for my call up papers, in the summer months of 1941. After finishing university exams, I had the opportunity to practice fly fishing skills in Loch Leven and on the River Leven, from the village of Kinnesswood. Looking back it seems so amazingly cheap–7/6 for the evening loch fishing without a boatman. Occasionally, on a very good night, there could be two dozen fish or more in the bottom of the boat when we rowed home, all about 1lb each or over. Fishing in the River Leven cost nothing, but you had to be extremely good at dry fly fishing, able to use very fine gut casts of 4x or 5x, to be able to catch anything where your fellow anglers were Lochgelly or Lochore miners–sadly often unemployed, but experts in the dry fly art, and splendid companions by the bank.

2.   A Short Army Home Service Rollercoaster

My first posting in the Army was to an OCTU in the Malvern Hills. But almost at once many of us were moved out to the Salisbury plain, and then up to Scotland, to the Bellevue Hotel, which was part of the OCTU there in Dunbar.

It did not take long to realise that a number of us were ill prepared for this course. We were surrounded by many fellow cadets who had done six months or more in different army units. Others around us had seen active service at Dunkirk and elsewhere. I have few clear memories now of our instructors but they were mostly experienced sergeants, sergeant majors, and officers, and there was also a Guards regimental sergeant major, well able to make sure that we became efficient at drill on the barrack square. We had of course our stories about some of these senior officers or NCOs. When asked by phone by an officer if he had seen his great coat around in a certain quarter, the NCO had held it up and said. "Is this it, Sir?"

I was interested to read recently of how in the 1914-18 War cadets were treated in the "officers school" in their "house". The "house" was overcrowded and although the cadets had such officer comforts as batmen, and a Mess Room with table cloths, there was no bathroom and they had to sleep on the floor. Their work was hard with drill or a lecture at 6.30 am and the day ended with a period of cleaning, polishing and preparation for the next day. So much for the condition of Wilfred Owen, the poet, in his OCTU in 1916. In 1941 we certainly had a bathroom but no Mess Room with table cloths, yet at least we had beds, and very reasonable rooms. Looking back on this part of my time in the Army, I can see how fortunate I was in two cadets with whom I shared my room. Both were English. One was looking forward to joining an infantry battalion, the other was a linguist and very much hoped to get entrance to the Intelligence Corps. None of us got into difficulties with the instructors, though no doubt we each had some problems with a part of the course.

Each cadet had a spell in charge of a platoon for a week or longer, and sharing in its different activities was assessed for his attempts at taking command. He was also reported on by NCO or officer in those many other areas which included a good deal of physical training, outdoor tactics, map reading, weapon training, driving army trucks and riding motor bikes. I was far too inexperienced to make any assessment of the instructors. I could not have said of them what Brigadier Frank Coutts said, no doubt correctly, of those who sought to train his OCTU of 1941: "The staff were only fair to middling; some of the lecturers were charming 're-treads' (retired officers, re-employed) but the tactical training was years out of date . . . We actually spent days constructing a First War trench system, which would have done credit to the Battle of the Somme".[5] I am sure our training was a lot better than that, but then it was being done across the border, and not in the Malvern Hills! My memory of our instructors is that they were approachable and humane and on the whole knowledgeable and intelligent, though they certainly didn't have time to do what "the Beloved Captain" did as described in the book of that name: After he watched his men at drill, "he picked out some of the most awkward ones, and, accompanied by a corporal, marched them away by themselves. Ingeniously he explained that he did not know much himself yet; but he thought they might get on better if they drilled by themselves a bit, and, that if he helped them, and they helped him, they would soon learn. His confidence was infectious . . . Very soon the awkward squad found themselves awkward no longer; and soon after that they ceased to be a squad and went back to the platoon".[6] Some of us no doubt appeared to the RSM a very awkward squad, but in the end, with thanks to him in great measure, we survived the passing out parade, finished the course, and were sent off to our various units. Cadets often wonder to which regiments they will be sent. Each of us was invited to state a preference. I had had uncles in the Gordons and in The Royal Scots and my father had been in the Cameronians, and I put down for these if my memory is right–but instead, I found myself commissioned into the King's Own Scottish Borderers. They were originally raised in 1689 as the Edinburgh Regiment for the defence of the Capital City, and to secure the Protestant succession to the throne of Scotland. I was soon to learn something of the Regiment's history. It was raised by David Leslie, Earl of Leven, wears the Leslie Tartan and had fought with distinction in many parts of the world. In early times it was known for its outstanding conduct at the Battle of Killiecrankie, after which the Scottish Capital honoured its Regiment by giving it permission to recruit in the city, excepting Sunday, without getting council authority. The badge of the KOSB has on it, upon a saltire the Castle of Edinburgh with mottoes: 'In Vertitate Religionis Confido' and 'Nisi Dominus Frustra', all ensigned with the royal crest.

3. Service in the 9th Battalion of the King's Own Scottish Borderers

After a short leave I was posted to the 9th Battalion KOSB, in Ulverston, Lancashire, where Lt. Col. W A H Maxwell was the Commanding Officer. He had been a good athlete in his earlier days, but this had not apparently helped him in the difficult inter-war years when there was slow promotion. At any rate he was a kindly CO to a newly joined officer. I well remember my first Sunday with the Battalion, I was asked to inspect the Company, prior to going to the Church Service. One or two men were not too well turned out, and I recall the Sergeant Major rebuking me in a kindly way for not putting them on a charge, but I didn't think a soldier would have liked his place of worship after that. Some years later I might not have been so generous. At any rate, this episode reminded me of the story of a group of men being sorted out on a Church Parade. Anglicans were moved to the right, and Roman Catholics to the left, but a soldier was left standing in the middle, and not belonging apparently to either denomination was given some work to do in the latrines while his comrades worshipped. The next Sunday they were on parade again, but this time no soldier was in the centre. The sergeant major spotted him among the Anglicans: "Why have you today become an Anglican?", was the question; to which the soldier replied: "I didn't like my place of worship, sir".

We had a good Church of Scotland padre in the 9th KOSB, but even if we had had the Archangel Gabriel, some soldiers would never have appeared to like their place of worship! Anyhow I liked my initial job of a platoon officer and realised something of the responsibility of trying to get to know, and understand, and learn from the different characters and backgrounds of the NCOs and men; some of them came from Edinburgh and the Borders and were conscripts; others had a long service background, like my batman; Macbeth–an old soldier with many years service in

India, and a loyal friend to me over the time I knew him. Once posted to a company, I soon got to know my fellow officers and other senior NCOs. As I had really very little experience in many areas of training, I was put down for a Mine Course. Just before going off to this, the Company Commander sent for me and informed me that he'd decided to attend this himself. He was killed by a mine soon afterwards, a sad loss to us all. Soon after this, I was detailed for a Battle Course at Llanberis, in North Wales. The exercises covered the area around Mount Snowdon, including an attack near its highest point–all these were done with live ammunition, and all platoon weapons, as well as full kit per man, were carried. I remember clearly an officer instructor near the top of Snowdon shouting rude comments at our attempts to struggle upwards, as light was breaking. The angry and weary course member next to me muttered: 'If he doesn't shut up, I'll shoot the bugger, he's forgetting we've live ammunition'! It was a tough course where some people didn't manage to finish or were wounded. This was because it included members who had escaped from Europe, but did not always understand the commands, and their covering fire on one occasion landed amongst some of the others, causing casualties. All participants in the course came away with a good idea of fire and movement, some of us knowing what it was like to have the mortar bombs dropping near, with detrimental results.

Before being posted on the next spell away from the battalion, we were moved to different camps–to Sale, near Manchester, and to Worstead Park Camp, near North Walsham, where we did long and exhausting route marches of up to 40 miles. Usually hutted camps were provided for billeting troops but we were fortunate in Sale, where some soldiers were accommodated in empty houses with fine rooms and washing facilities. But we never reached the privilege of a billet in such a school as Roedean, where, according to 'One Blue Bonnet', there was "a bell in each room which invited us to 'Ring if you require a mistress in the night' ".[7]

I was fortunate about this time to be sent on a long course of several months, to Catterick Camp, Yorkshire. Why I was selected for this I don't know, but it was a refreshing change, and I was soon involved in the details of how communications worked within a battalion, from platoon to company, to Battalion headquarters and from there to Brigade. We learned to communicate by flag and lamp and heliograph, but most of all by wireless using either speech or morse. During the initial months I had to work hard to pick up morse and become proficient at a reasonable rate.

On my return to the battalion I took over the signal platoon and was very content with this new role. This led to an opportunity to work more with the Adjutant and Second-in-Command and CO, while it also brought me an increasing comradeship and knowledge of the HQ company officers. Their names come back to me–eg Tony Gossage (Carriers), Walter Ballantine (Mortars), Ronnie Bannatyne (Anti-Tank), Ted Brough (Signals), (before me). These were splendid friends always supportive of others. Yet this job didn't last long, for we had by now been designated a Training Battalion. One day the Second-in-Command told me I was to become one of the officers who had to put recruits through a weapons course with live ammunition. He felt my Battle School experience had given me some preparation for this. This proved to be my last energetic job prior to leaving the 9th KOSB, for I was soon called to the Adjutant's office, and told I was to go on embarkation leave, destination unknown. It was something of a shock, yet many of us had known it would come one day. It was what we had been training for all these months and years.

We had experienced many Officers' Mess Guest nights as well as memorable visits to the Sergeants' Mess on festive occasions, but when a good number of us were leaving for overseas, or for another battalion of the regiment, there was a special farewell party. It was a happy and yet sad occasion, for you were taking leave of so many friends among officers, NCOs and men. One consolation for me was that I was soon to go off from Waverley station to London in the company of two other 9th Bn. KOSB officers from Edinburgh. Other friends were soon posted to the Airborne Division preparing for the Arnheim battle. Most of these were either wounded, captured or killed. At any rate I will always be grateful for the good comradeship and genuine friendships of the 9th Bn. KOSB and for all I learned from those who shared these years with me–men of all ranks.

4.   Posted Overseas: Service in The King's African Rifles

When we embarked on the Dutch ship in November, 1943, most of us were unaware of where we were going. The voyage turned out to be longer than we had expected, the troop ships in the convoy went out almost to the Azores before they turned back, and eventually, via the Spanish coast, entered the Mediterranean Sea at Gibraltar. It was a new way of life for so many of us. We were four to six in a small cabin in double bunk beds, and were given a great deal of physical training, lectures and opportunities for getting to know others from the different services–including a detachment of the WRNS! If we had a long voyage it was at times dramatic, as when, just through the straits of Gibraltar, we were attacked by torpedo carrying German aircraft off the coast of Southern France. The convoy lost at least one ship and our own troopship had some people killed by machine gun fire. Yet we had been let off lightly in comparison to the huge losses suffered by other convoys in earlier years. If there were those seeking to destroy us from without, there was those seeking to defend us from within. Here I refer not only to the men who manned the anti-aircraft guns, but to a group of people who sought to engage themselves and others in prayer and Bible study. I had never thought of having this experience on a troopship. I discovered that an RAMC Major, a surgeon, was at the back of it all. He had a strong conviction that there were Christians on board, other than himself, and that he should bring them together. Most of us saw around us on the ship our fellow servicemen and women, doing the kind of things that went on in such a situation–submitting to the activities required, playing endless games of cards, chatting up girls when they were around, finding ways of keeping fit–but this Major saw those about him, not only as his comrades, but as all sons and daughters of God, capable of a joyous companionship with him and one another. Here was a man living out his faith on a troopship. I recall him praying for and being given a room on the crowded ship where he and any others who wished, could meet together to hear God's words in Scripture and pray for others. Later on he conducted a Service which was well attended and much appreciated by many. Though I did not expect this at that time, here was a man possessed by the Holy Spirit, a person intensely alive, amazingly aware of and sensitive to the needs of others, but also alive to God, to the God revealed in Jesus Christ, whom he called 'Father'.

I am indebted to Bishop John V Taylor for quoting this story of institutional life. "They were all sitting half dead in their wheel chairs, mostly paralysed and just existing, they didn't live. They watched some television, but if you had asked them what they had watched they probably would not have been able to tell you. We brought in a young woman who was a dancer, and we told her to play beautiful, old-fashioned music. She brought in Tchaikovsky records and so on and started to dance among these old people, all in their wheel-chairs, which had been set in a circle. In no time the old people started to move. . ." The Bishop comments on this story: 'I am struck by that story not merely as an account of a remarkable therapy, but as an instance of the effect of the really alive upon the half-dead or upon lifeless situations. And, in particular, it throws light on the impact of Jesus Christ upon his contemporaries".[8] The Bishop saw this story as a parable of the transmission of life from Jesus Christ to those who come under his spell and to those who shall do so. The name of this Major on our troopship escapes me, but he was certainly one of those to whom Christ had given life, and who had made him a transmitter of this life to others, even on a troopship in the Mediterranean Sea. How many people were deeply influenced by him–I took along some friends to the meetings–I don't know, but he certainly helped one soldier to come more alive to other people, to the reality of self, and to the Scriptures and the life of prayer; he helped one pilgrim to be more aware of the presence of Christ and of the mystery of God the Father.

One of his 'remarkable sayings remains with me "I pray that I may be strengthened to share Christ's Cross." I did not grasp his meaning then, but I take him now to have meant that he wanted to stroke out self and let the serving and forgiving and, if need be, suffering love of Christ for others shine through him, such life being God's eternal life.

The journey was by no means over when we reached Alexandria, for we had some time in a camp in the desert outside Cairo. Then we were taken by train to another ship, which took us down the Red Sea to be landed at last at Mombasa. Thence we were moved to the Transit Camp near Nairobi, Kenya. I little knew then that I had still had thousands of miles to go. However another convoy was being prepared–this time of lorries–and we set off on the road to Northern Kenya and the Somalilands, bivouacking in the bush, and having opportunities to watch the wild game. In this way I experienced my first African Christmas in 1943 in a small bush camp. One of the company there was another medical officer–this time a doctor but a very different character from the surgeon of the troopship. He seemed to be a frustrated man, with a lima which kept jumping around during the Christmas meal, landing on one's shoulders or among the plates, but the owner was soon too happy to notice. It wasn't a particularly joyous Christmas! Eventually the convoy moved into Jig Jiga, just inside Abyssinia, where the 24th Uganda Battalion of the King's African Rifles was camped. I was the only new arrival and this was to be my new home for some months.

I quickly discovered my fellow officers–a few of them belonged to the Oxford Group–were a welcoming and friendly crowd. Many of them had had battle experience in the war against the Italians; some of them were Kenyan farmers. One such was the Commanding Officer, an able and popular Colonel. I was given command of the signal platoon, and was helped by the Second-in-Command who knew much about this battalion's way of life. It was in reality for me a new culture. There was a new language to learn–Swahili–otherwise there would be little or no communication with the Askaris–the African soldiers from different tribes; there was a new discipline to experience in terms of the daily routine–an early start at 6 am, often in the form of a company run in the bush to see how fit we were, and how able to hunt down the quails–birds that could only fly for so long, followed by breakfast, and longer hours of daily work than in Britain. There was further a new understanding to be grasped of the background training and discipline of the African NCOs and soldiers. I had scarcely got used to this Abyssinian camp when the battalion was moved south to a camp outside Nairobi and from there to Moshi, in what was then Tanganyika, at the foot of Mount Kilimanjaro. After some months we were moved on yet again, this time out of Africa altogether, to Mauritius. This meant another troopship and the voyage to this small island in the Indian Ocean, to the East of Madagascar, and a good way south of the Seychelles. By this time my fellow officers were all good friends, and I had come to speak comfortably with the Africans, and to appreciate many of their fine qualities as well as those of the British NCOs. On this delightful island there was more time for some platoons and companies to be on their own, in idyllic camps by the seas where there was opportunity, gratefully accepted, to swim each day. Near the main camp there was a sports and social club where the Officers' Mess was given membership. Soon the battalion had both a cricket and rugby club. I was fortunate to be able to play in both of these, and greatly enjoyed doing this. I still have a small medal presented to the members of the battalion rugby team which defeated the French team from the island! Whether it had to do with my efforts at cricket or rugby, it was at this time that I was promoted Captain! It was not all sunshine however on Mauritius, for here we experienced a severe cyclone. There was some damage to the camp building, but there was a great deal of destruction to the dwellings of the Creole population. This led to an outbreak of polio in which the battalion lost its excellent Medical Officer for he went to help the civilian authorities and caught the disease. I shared the room next to him, and was quarantined for a time.

"In the ninth year of our service in Uganda, an unexpected change in our family situation made it necessary for us all to return to this country. This was a reversal of all we had planned and hoped. . . I felt absurdly angry with God, and took it out on my innocent family in a nasty, prolonged grouchiness".[9] In these words, Bishop Taylor tells how an unexpected move had upset him. That is very much what happened to me when suddenly I was posted to a different battalion back in Kenya. This hadn't been my plan at all, and I loathed leaving all my friends behind in Mauritius, as I flew off one morning, in a Catalina flying boat, to Mombasa. My CO had done his best to stop the posting but Company Commanders were required for the 6th Tanganyika battalion which was getting ready for the war in Burma. In my new battalion there was little spare time, and while I was befriended by many in HQ company, where I became Company Commander, life wasn't the same as in my former unit. And so, with so many others, I was delighted when VJ Day came, and there was the prospect of the voyage back to Britain, and the opportunity of demobilisation and of a return to civilian life, possibly to a resumption of study at University or Divinity College.

Notes

1. G M Brown - 'The Golden Bird' - Grafton Books (Collins Publishing Group) - p115.
2. David Cairns - 'An Autobiography' - S C M Press Ltd (1950) - pp55-56.
3. Lord Cockburn - 'Memorials of His Time' - Robert Grant and Son Ltd - p153.
4. Ibid - p154.
5. Brigadier F Coutts - 'One Blue Bonnet' - B & W Publishing - Edinburgh - p42.
6. Donald Hankey - 'The Beloved Captain' (Edited with notes by R S Wright) - Geoffrey Bles - p34.
7. Brigadier F Coutts - Ibid - p41.
8. John V Taylor - 'A Matter of Life and Death' - S C M Press (1986) - pp35-36.
9. Ibid (1986) - pp63-64.

Chapter III

Training for the Ministry of the Church of Scotland

1. Entry into the Divinity College: The Sub-Wardenship of New College Settlement and New College

The biographers of Sir Walter Scott tell us how much he was influenced by the community life in which he shared. His character and destiny was moulded strongly by his parent's home, and by that of his paternal grandparents at Sandy Knowe Farm, in the Borders. But we hear too of how greatly life in Edinburgh, 'his own romantic town', especially the Old Town, left its mark upon him. "It was in the Old Town on the slopes of the Castle Rock, in the Edinburgh 'Golden Age' that, as a boy, he become strongly conscious of his own nationality and of his nation's past".[1] There Scott was made aware of that town's companionability and friendliness, and there he grasped a great deal of Scotland's language and ballads and poetry, so that, in later life, he was able to make the past live in his books with his own unique imagination and powers of expression.

Ordinary people have also been repeatedly moulded by the communities in which their lives have been set. I had been demobbed at Redford Barracks, only a mile or two from my home in Colinton, and I believe that I was conscious then of how strongly I had been influenced by the different communities of the war years. It was the corporate nature of life at OCTU, or in the 9th Battalion KOSB, or on the troopship, or in The King's African Rifles battalions, which had powerfully shaped me. Service experiences moved some people away from religion and from the worship of the Christian God, but others were pushed towards a greater understanding and service of Him. I was among the latter, though I wasn't at all sure that I should take up training for the Church of Scotland Ministry, nor if I did this, of how I could cope with academic lectures, and with a possible return to the study of Greek and to starting Hebrew.

However I was very fortunate, once a civilian again, of having those around me who gave me encouragement to read Scripture more, and to take the step of becoming a student at New College, the Divinity College in Edinburgh. I had the necessary interviews there, and began attending classes in the spring and in the early summer of 1946. About this time, I remember I was asked to speak at a social in St Andrew's Church, Juniper Green, for ex-Navy, Army and Air Force personnel. I had been looking afresh at the New Testament and said I felt not at all sure of what I had to offer as a divinity student, but in the Gospel there was the story of a young person who gave all he had at the feeding of a great crowd, and that Jesus had used his offer in a wonderful way. After this, with support from my minister, the Revd George Reid–himself a returned Army Padre with a distinguished war record–and from my parents, I committed myself to training for the Ministry, and decided not to do the shortened course for servicemen, but to attempt the three year course for the Bachelor of Divinity Degree.

In this year, 1946-1947, I had envisaged enjoying the comfort and fellowship of my home in Bonaly Road, Colinton, but this was not to be. I was asked by the late Professor W S Tindal, who had been Montgomery's Chaplain in the 21st Army Group, to go as Sub-Warden to New College Settlement in the Pleasance, Edinburgh. It was made clear to me that this would mean residence in the Settlement with a group of students, not all divinity students; it also meant Boys' Club work, as well as taking responsibility for getting speakers at the brief evening worship in the Chapel. The job further meant being the Assistant Minister in the Pleasance Church, where the Revd Dr Bernhard Citron was the Minister (he was also the Warden of the Settlement). This invitation to me proved a bit of a crisis in my family. It was pointed out to me that I had only been out of the Army for a few months, and now I was proposing to leave again and stay in a strange place at the other end of the city. And what about my studies? Could they be done as well as, not just an assistantship, but the role of being to some extent in charge of some other students who would share life in the Settlement with me? Surely this was not a wise move! Whatever I decided could be seen as selfish. I was an only son and I hadn't seen my mother for years, and I was proposing to go off to live in an extended family which I was suggesting would benefit my ministerial training! I well understood her resistance to this new venture, though my father was more accommodating.

In the end I thought I should accept this new job, and I hoped that I might be able to cope with the college studies as well as find life in the Settlement a window into the ideas and convictions of my fellow students, and into a beginning in the work of an Assistant Minister–in the conduct of Christian worship and in pastoral work, including the conduct of funerals, and into service again in a Boys' Club. In the end, my parents supported me, and I came out from town to see them when I could. They believed that in taking the role of Sub-Warden, I was doing so in the trust that, with God's help, I would be able to make a contribution to the Settlement fellowship and to its ongoing work there, and to the work of the Parish.

My time in the Pleasance Settlement brought me into close relationships not just with the students, but with the lay superintendent, Miss Colvin, who was a kind and competent person, always considerate of the needs of her 'boys'. They responded, on the whole, to her requests, but sometimes were idle about coming down to meals in the morning. I remember on one occasion saying that there were to be no more late comers in the morning. They would all be on parade at the proper time for breakfast. Someone must have complained to Professor Tindal, for he gently said to me: "You are not in the Army now, Bill". My other close relationship was of course with the Warden and Minister.

Bernhard Citron, who was a theologian with a profound experience of conversion–his pilgrimage at that time was from being a wandering German Jew to a Church of Scotland Minister and College Lecturer. This conversion had in no way narrowed his life but rather had given him a new awareness of so many areas of vitality. It had made him wonderfully sensitive to the needs of other people, both in New College where he lectured, and in the Pleasance Church Parish, and not least to his new Sub-Warden Assistant. Theologian, Bernhard certainly was; his book *The New Birth* reveals all this, but my most vivid memory of him is not only of his teaching or preaching, but of his struggle to take suitable gifts to so many people, children and adults, when he went visiting. He lived out so well the text: "Freely you have received, freely give". He was a Minister greatly beloved by many both in congregation and parish. He was further gracious to his assistant in his stumbling efforts at the conduct of worship and in pastoral work, including the taking of funerals. I still recall my first sermon in the Pleasance Church. Whatever else it was, it was christological, about Christ and one of his great challenges, and it had as the text; (St Luke 8 v.50). "But when Jesus heard it, he answered him, saying 'Fear not, believe only, and she shall be made whole'. I tried to say that that meant "believe in my unchanged love and in my saving power".

Bernhard overlooked the inadequacies and said that he thought part of it 'pure gospel'. I didn't really know what he meant by that, but I felt he intended to support and encourage me in my effort at preaching. Besides learning something about the conduct of public worship and preaching, there was given too the opportunity of getting to know students from different years in New College. I was able to invite them down to take Chapel prayers in the Settlement. All of them made excellent contributions later to the Christian Ministry, whether as a Parish Minister or as a University Chaplain, or a Missionary. I have often wondered how they thought about those early years, when they too were learning their trade in many places, but sometimes also in the New College Settlement.

I was ready to do a second year as Sub-Warden and Assistant Minister, but once again I was unexpectedly moved out. I had not been feeling well for some months and had eventually to go to the Edinburgh Royal Infirmary where I had an appendix operation. It took me quite a while to get fit again, and I had also got far behind with college work. So, somewhat reluctantly I gave up the Sub-Wardenship, and was given a new assistantship in my home Church–St Andrew's, Juniper Green. This was a very different kind of Church; I didn't experience there Boys' Club work, or the kind of poverty and bad housing and injustice which were so evident in the Pleasance. There were no doubt deeper kinds of poverty, well known to George Reid, the Minister, and probably to some of his Elders. I was asked to teach as best I could the Bible Class, and found this no easy task.

2. New College - Learning from John Baillie - 'Our Knowledge of God' and the Church

I must now turn to some experiences in New College, the Divinity College in Edinburgh. Ex-Servicemen, particularly, were learners who had to struggle in different spheres. There may have been a few who had to make a constant effort to keep financially solvent, but there were certainly many who wrestled with the difficulties of belief, of scriptural interpretation, of public worship, preaching and prayer, of relationships, personal and communal, and above all of the Gospel of unconditional love. We were, I believe, profoundly aware of our ignorance in most of these subjects, so we were conscious of how little we knew of the tradition of Faith, of what the Old Testament had to teach of this, of the Gospel tradition, of the Early Fathers' teachings, and of Reformed and Modern Theology. At any rate, we all had to grapple with the knowledge of God, and with the Trinitarian Faith. But there were those at New College well equipped to provide us with information and help.

Some members of staff made it known how pleased they were to teach ex-Servicemen, for they were so ready to learn and delighted to take seriously their classes. However the truth was that there was another side to a number of us. There were those who slipped out to the Princes Street coffee shops or elsewhere, when they could not take any more of the late Professor G T Thompson's lectures on Dogmatic Theology. In his class it was once said: 'Excuse me, Sir, you gave us that lecture yesterday!' Then the monocle would fall out of the former Colonel's eye, and 'G.T.' would say - 'Oh hell, so I did'. He was a learned man and we came to see that he had much to teach us not only about what reformed theologians had said in the past, but about what Karl Barth was teaching at that time. 'G.T.' had translated the first volume of Professor Barth's Dogmatics called 'The Word of God', and also a huge book called 'Reformed Dogmatics' by Heinrich Heppe on which many of the lectures he gave us were based. All our teachers had good things to say to us but some were outstanding lecturers, and men recognised outwith the Church of Scotland as persons of great distinction. Amongst these I must first mention John Baillie, Professor of Divinity at the College.

Like so many other students, I owe a great deal to this Professor. He helped so many of us to know about God and to know him. He did this not only in the lectures he gave but in the books he wrote; their names are well known to many Ministers.[2]

'Our Knowledge of God' was the first of these given for study in our initial year. It was from what he said to us, and from this book and others that many of us came to understand something of how we know and respond to God, and something of the paradox of Grace, human and divine in the Church. We were led to see God as seeking, and demanding, and giving, and indwelling in his Church, the people in Christ.

In more than one place Baillie told us of how he himself came to believe. It was through the "embrace of God", through God's reaching out to him in certain ways. At a very early age God broke into his consciousness in his home, where he felt that his life, like that of his parents, was under the transcendent claim. Of his family he wrote: "What was this constraint that was laid on us? Whose was this greater will that we were both called upon to obey? . . . Once again, I have no memory of a time when I did not know the answer. From the beginning I knew that it was God".[3]

I and many other fellow students could not share such an early conscious divine awareness, but we came to see that this seeking God could come to people in many different ways–in a family, or in all the varied events and meetings of life. Baillie helped us to recognise this, for he taught that God was searching for him in a wider context than that of his home, in what he called his "life and history". He wrote these words which describe wonderfully well a question some of us had on our return from the Services: "Can I, looking back on my own life and history, truthfully describe it as an eager quest? Was it I who was all the time seeking an elusive Good, or was I the elusive one, artfully evading a Good that was seeking me? And if haply there had been a finding, is it I who have at last found Him whom I sought, or is it He who has found me? Was I all that time knocking at His door or He at mine? . . . And shall the glory now be mine or His? Shall I sing of my achievement or of His gift? For me at least there can be but one answer -

I sought the Lord, and afterward I knew
He moved my soul to seek Him, seeking me;
It was not I that found, O Saviour true -
No, I was found of Thee".[4]

But we were soon up against the question: "What does this seeking and knocking God want of us"? We learnt that in the Middle Ages it had been taught that God wanted his people to know him, and to reach this knowledge by reason and revelation. So Baillie introduced us to the Medieval Synthesis which for some centuries influenced theological thinking, and had much demand in it. According to St Thomas, we were to use the light of unaided reason, and by inference rise up to God from "those things which have been made". This would tell us 'that God is and what he is not". If we wished to know 'who God is', then we must listen to the revelation of God in his Word, to the Scriptures of the Old and New Testaments. There we would find the prophetic and apostolic testimony to the living God in his mighty acts in Israel and in Jesus Christ his Son. But our teacher was concerned that we should not see the revelation of God as unqualified demand, (he also pointed out to us the inadequacy of knowing the Father of Jesus Christ by inference from the world of his creation). To use some words of Baillie's written in the 1950s: "For the demand that is here spoken of is a demand of a very specific kind–it is a demand that we should accept a gift. What God asks of us is not that we should do anything for ourselves but that we should allow all to be done for us by Him. Just because this offer is so stupendous, and we have the taking or leaving of it in our own hands, the demand it makes upon our wills is the most solemn to which we can ever be subjected. As Dr Brunner says: 'God is revealed to me as <u>demanding</u> us for Himself in that He is revealed as the <u>Giver.</u> His willing something <u>for</u> us is at the same time a willing something <u>of</u> us. He demands us for His love. That is His commandment. It is the New Commandment, but only now is it properly conceived as the commandment of Him who gives before He commands and commands only in giving'."[5]

It is so easy to see God's coming to us only as a simple demand. Baillie liked to put this point in a story of the preacher Spurgeon. The Minister one day went to the door of a poor woman with money towards the payment of her rent. He got no reply at her door, but later, when she met him, she said: "I heard the knocking well enough, but I believed it was the man come to collect the rent".

What then is this gift which is involved in God's demand? It is the gift of God Himself in his mighty rescuing acts made known in the Old and New Testaments, these actions being spelt out in the deliverance from Egypt and in the law and the prophets in the Old Testament, but supremely in the life, death, and resurrection and ascension of Jesus Christ his Son, and in the bestowal of the Spirit to the Church. This might seem as though this action of God is all in the past, but that is not so, for God comes to his people in the community of the Church which, by the Spirit's power, becomes in every age the story telling community–ie it bears testimony to what God has done for us, and wills to give to us, above all in Jesus Christ. Christians tell the story of the Gospel, the Good News of the revelation of God in Christ, of his victory over sin and death, and of his continuing life, to one another within the fellowship of the Church in song, in reading and preaching the word of God and in the sacrament of Baptism and Holy Communion. Hence the <u>community of the Church</u> was for Baillie part of the Gospel; for it is there that God wills to show himself: "The Christian Revelation was not addressed to a number of disparate individuals, but to a community. Only within the <u>koinonia</u> has it any reality. It is in fellowship, and only in fellowship, that God reveals Himself. 'For where two or three are gathered together in my name, there am I in the midst of them'. . . On the other hand, the revelation vouchsafed only to the fellowship is capable of authentication, only so far as, through the fellowship, it reaches the individual".[6] Thus Baillie found God initially in the community of his home, also in the wider sphere of his varied "life and history"; yet more and more he came to know God through the community of Christ's Church, whether in Scotland or Germany or Canada and America. In these different Churches he found God's unique revelation in Jesus Christ's life and divine love, and that life and love came to him through the persons who were its members, whether Ministers, leaders or people: "Just then, as in ancient Hebrew times religion meant membership of the Israelite community, so now Christian religion means membership in the Church of Christ. . . Christianity is essentially a community affair. This does not mean that it is not at the same time a personal affair; on the contrary, it is just because it is a community affair that it is a personal affair, for it is only in community that personality can be born and developed".[7]

When Baillie told us about the God who was seeking for us in the family and in "life and history" with their changing situations, that was acceptable and helpful, but when he went on to say that "Christian religion means membership in the Church of Christ", this raised a big question in the minds of many of us from the Services. To countless men and women from the 1939-45 War, the Church could be side stepped, and religion privatised, kept to oneself. It should also be noted that this hostility and indifference to the Church was clearly felt as well in the 1914-18 War,[8] and awareness of this is still now prevalent amongst high ranking Churchmen. A former Archbishop, William Temple, wrote in "The Church: Its Scandal and Glory" . . . "I know that the Church repels. You look at some of its members, and you see complacency, censoriousness, division, vacillating leadership. I feel that, too, for I do not live in a sort of haze of purple! I see and I feel the defects of the Church acutely. Now, it is a very old problem".[9]

How then were we to react to this very old problem–to the scandal of the Church, obvious to many within her, and to many returning Servicemen who were largely indifferent to her, if not sometimes contemptuous of her, though they were honest enough to say that, prior to the war, they had only infrequently attended any services of Christian worship? How could we be enthusiastic about giving leadership in such a community, and in encouraging others, our former comrades of war-time days, to enter into it? Yet we were being clearly told that "the Christian religion means membership in the Church of Christ" . . . Here was the agony and struggle with the Church, not just for returned ex-Service people, but also for those of us back from the Forces, who were training to be Ministers within her in the future.

Some of us remembered the communities in which we had lived for the last five years or so. These Army battalions in which our lives had been set had had both scandal and glory on them–the scandal of a few who always wanted not to obey orders, or wanted to cause divisions, and be censorious, and yet, very importantly, the glory of so many, who were wonderfully loyal to genuine leadership and who gave again and again magnificent examples of sacrificial service in the course of what they saw as their duty. And so, if we clearly could see the scandal of the Church, should we not also grapple with what was called its "glory"? Only so might we be able to hold on to the community of the Church for ourselves and for others, including our ex-comrades. The glory of the Church, we learned, was the presence of God in the midst of it - "and glory both in the later Old Testament and in the New is really only another word for presence".[10] This glory or presence then, had been made visible in Jesus Christ, the Word made flesh–"The Word was made flesh, and dwelt among us, (and we beheld his glory, the glory as of the only begotten of the Father), full of grace and truth". So the glory of the Church is Christ, present among his people. With other believers, Baillie knew and taught us that Christ "loved the Church and gave himself for it" and that he had risen and ascended to come and be in his Church, working in it through the gift of the Spirit. This gift was his greatest legacy and promise to his community of the Church: "Nevertheless I tell you the truth, it is to your advantage that I go away; for if I do not go away, the comforter will not come to you but if I depart I will send him to you".[11] So we cannot think of Christ's glory and presence in the Church without thinking of his pouring out the Spirit upon all its members willing to receive him. And this Spirit is our Lord's life and love, the reality of his risen self.

Could we then take courage and invite people to see the glory that lies beneath the surface of the Church, and urge them to enter into it and participate in its life and witness? We felt we could, but we had to be clearer about what was meant when it was said that Christ was in the Church constantly pouring out there his Spirit, his risen life. How was he doing that? In the Reformed Tradition, in which the Church of Scotland shared, he was doing this by the reading and the teaching and the preaching of the Word, and by calling people out to hear and respond to this, and to pass on what had been heard. Was this not part of the real Church which lay beneath all its ritual and its choral music and beneath all the great Festivals of Christmas, Easter, and Pentecost? Words spoken and heard certainly lay beneath the surface of things in a battalion's life, beneath its spit and polish, and its parades and inspections and exercises and barrack room life. The battalion's real life found its spring, it could be said, in the Commander's orders being given and heard and obeyed by certain leaders at his 'O' Group (Order Group). The Company Commanders were regularly called forward to hear these and then they passed them on to the Platoon Commanders, who did likewise to their men. Many of us felt that the spring of the Church's life was similar, and I was delighted to find that the great theologian, Karl Barth, had had a like thought. "The Church" he wrote, "is the assembly called together, united, held together, and governed by the Word of its Master–or it is no real Church at all. A commander calls his officers and NCOs to the front, to make certain communications to them and give them their orders. It is in this act of calling, this reception of communication and command that the real Church exists. Thus and in no other way!"[12] Sometimes Platoon Commanders did not personally hear their Commanding Officer's words, but they heard the testimony to these words given them by the Company Commanders. So in the Church we do not always hear the words of our Commander ringing in our ears, but we hear the testimony to them passed on to us in the words of Scripture, read or preached or sung or made sacrament.

Yet words or commands alone in a Battalion were not enough to carry the men along in devoted service; there also had to be deeds, and that is what in any good unit they received. For the CO or his representative, regularly came down among them to see their company lines, or their meals, or the condition of their barrack rooms, or the state of their uniforms and weapons. This was the Army form of pastoral care, and it was just as vital and important as the words of command and the teaching. Without this, Army leadership could become unreal and hypocritical and enlarge the gap of ignorance and suspicion between the leaders and the led. So with Christ, he was not only the leader who spoke to his people, ruling and ordering their life, but he was the leader who acted for his people and towards his people invading their lives, seeking to act out in them his perfect love to God and humankind, the life he demanded of them.

It is significant that Baillie ends his book *Invitation to Pilgrimage*, published first in 1942, with the chapter called 'Invitation To Church' where he sees this community, both human and divine, as being the necessary fountain for giving strength to the ideals of fraternity and equality and justice, and as being creative of a new humanity in which humankind is bound to God as Father, and to one another. He taught us to see this same Church as open to all races and nations, as indeed universal, and yet also more than human, for it was and is and ever will be the creation of God through his Son. It was the place for John Baillie where humankind must come to repent and confess their sins and receive pardon and hence be renewed in body and mind and spirit. For it was Christ's will no longer to dwell in a single physical body but in the Body of the Church; his mystical Body. For John Baillie this was a wonderful challenging thought: "The immensely solemn and moving thought which St Paul suggested to his converts was that we who are Christians are the limbs and organs of this mystical Body. We are Christ's hands and feet, His eyes and ears and mouth, through which He now continues to do His work in the world".[13]

Despite its scandal, ministers in training must focus on the glory of Christ's forgiving love and renewing power within his Church, and have confidence that, through the working of his invading Spirit there, operating through the lives of its members, the ex-Servicemen, now often the man in the street, can be invited into its fellowship. "You and I owe all the knowledge of God that we have to our upbringing in the one tradition and our reception into the one fellowship of the Church of Christ, and the only way that is open to us whereby we should bring to others the blessings of that knowledge is by initiating them into the same tradition and receiving them into the same Church".[14]

3.   New College - Learning from William Manson: Jesus - The Son of God: The Mystery of the Kingdom of God: The Norm of the Christian Life

I must now speak of one other New College teacher–Professor William Manson. He was Professor of New Testament Language, Literature and Theology in 1925, and later in 1946 succeeded Principal Curtis in the Chair of Biblical Antiquities and Biblical Criticism.

William Manson's successor was the late Professor J S Stewart who wrote: "Manson was one of the most erudite Biblical interpreters of his time; but he was the humblest of men for he was other worldly in the true sense of that much misunderstood word, carrying with him everywhere the mystic's sense of the divine presence, and always helping duller minds to apprehend that unseen world of which he himself was so vividly aware".[15] Some of New College Staff saw him as their spiritual tutor; he was certainly that to so many of the students. In particular, he was a badly needed tutor to ex-Servicemen after the 1939-45 War, who if they found a problem with the nature of the Church, found often a stumbling block with the Gospel of the Resurrection, as they tried to grasp that "The Resurrection" (referring to Christians of New Testament days) "was not an article of their creed, but the life of it".[16]

The Son of God

I well remember a Captain in the 9th KOSB telling me that in his view Jesus Christ was a wonderful human person, who had used his free will to obey God, and who gave his life in the service of others. So he and his comrades had to follow the principles of Jesus, to the utmost of their ability, in truthfulness, humility and compassion. This Captain was a good humanist, like so many of his fellow soldiers, genuinely concerned for the well being of his men, and willing to die, if need be, for his comrades. He understood Jesus when he said "greater love hath no man than this that a man lay down his life for his friends", yet the Resurrection he could not accept. That to him was an imaginative dream. I believe my Army friend was speaking for the vast majority of his men who were now demobbed, and for some of these ex-Servicemen, divinity students, soon to be asked to preach. Had we the confidence to do this? Had we the sure conviction that Jesus Christ had risen, not to stay away from his people, but to encounter them, and give them his risen life, thus continuing his work of reconciliation, winning over men and women into the Father's company and into fellowship with one another? It was well for us that William Manson had a powerful undying conviction that the crucified Christ was alive, raised up by God and that he was continuing his reconciling work, sharing his Sonship of God with his followers, restoring in them the image of God and reversing the work of Satan: "But as many as received him, to them gave he power to become the sons of God, even to them that believe on his name" (St John I v 12). God for Manson, was the lifting up God, who had raised up his Son to new life, and his purpose was, by the power of the Spirit given by that same Son to the Church, to lift up, not just Israel, but all humankind into eternal life.

But if we were to find more in Jesus than the inspiring example of a dead Jewish leader crucified by his enemies many centuries ago, we had to look at his teaching and life and at the testimony of the New Testament. Manson helped us to see who Jesus was. In the Gospels Jesus is called by many names, for example: 'Son of God', 'Servant of the Lord' and 'Son of Man'. These are titles or categories which show how he was understood or interpreted. Manson called these "The Messianic Categories in the Tradition"[17] (The tradition of Matthew, Mark and Luke). We had to grapple with the meaning of all of these, but before we left college, I and many others, had firmly grasped the Son of God category. For William Manson had the very deep assurance that our Lord's messianic consciousness–his conviction that he was God's choice to save his people and unite them in fellowship with God as Father and with one another–was rooted in his filial consciousness, by which is meant his constant awareness that he was the Son of God, the Father's Son. And Jesus knew that he was called not only to live in this awareness, but also to bring it to others, though he felt that they showed little consciousness of this, for they were "as sheep without a shepherd", wandering in the desert and darkness of their world. However for Manson, consciousness of Sonship and Messiahship did not exist in Jesus together from the start: rather "the Messiahship of Jesus comes as the final seal or imprint upon that sense of revealing the Father which had carried him into all his work for men".[18]

When the awareness of Sonship came to Jesus, we can never be sure, but the New Testament bears witness in the Epistles to this Sonship, but also in the Gospels, eg at his temptation, transfiguration, and at the Cross and Resurrection. Even as early as his baptism, there is witness to it. Then the voice of God spoke to Jesus saying: 'Thou art my beloved Son in whom I am well pleased' (Mark I v 11). Manson taught us that there were two main interpretations of 'Son of God' here. It could be explained as equivalent to Messiah, or it could be traced to Jesus' unique sense of filial consciousness and fellowship with God. Manson made the second choice, and makes this comment on this 'Son of God' title in his commentary on the Gospel of Luke, at the point of the baptism: "In view, however, of the uncertainty whether 'son of God' was in Jewish usage synonymous with Messiah, and of the fact that none of our Gospels gives the voice heard by Jesus in the form 'Thou art the Messiah' but all in the form 'Thou art my son, the Beloved', it seems best to adopt the second alternative, and to conclude that the Christian title 'son of God' while it includes

Messiahship with reference to Jesus, has its origin and primary ground in the filial love toward God which possessed Jesus, and which at his baptism became charged with the quality of a supernatural revelation".[19]

The Mystery of the Reign of God - The Norm of the Christian Life

But another important question we were taught to consider was how was Jesus to exercise his reconciling role, how was he to win over the hearts and lives of his people to their God and Father? He refused to attempt this along the lines suggested to him at his temptation and resolved to attempt it through teaching and preaching. This meant not only the proclamation of a message, but also the gathering of a fellowship or band of people to whom he might give his teaching and the knowledge of his way of life.

This brings us to the message of the kingdom or reign of God, with which Jesus came into Galilee, soon after his baptism and temptation. Jesus said "The time of your waiting is over, and the reign of God is at hand: repent and believe in the good news" (St Mark 1 v15).

Manson was well aware, like all New Testament scholars, of the complexity of the meaning of the reign of God: "The reign of God was a conception which varied with the quality and degree of the individual's religious insight. For some it signified merely the national glorification of Israel. For others it implied an apocalyptic event in the far future. For Jesus it derives it's character and immediacy from the filial joy in God which is his possession. To make men sharers in his experience, to discover God afresh to their souls, to call Israel to an absolute acceptance of the Rule of God in the heart–this is the task to which, as by a rending of the skies, Jesus is called".[20]

And it was within the fellowship of the disciple band, that they experienced what "Fellowship with Christ" meant, being learners in his school–what Manson called, in more than one book or article, "the first stage" in the "Norm of the Christian Life". There too an exciting new life was to be experienced. And the life Jesus was offering, was new as over against the Jewish religious life of his time. So it was an enormous privilege to be brought within this disciple band. There his men were given to know "the mystery of the reign of God". There this mystery, or open secret, of the reign of God took the form of a new life of freedom and joy which was an essential part of "the curriculum of Fellowship with Jesus Christ" (Manson). Jesus, present to his disciples, opened the door for them into becoming sons of God by a rebirth of spirit, offering to them a distinctive kind of prayer life to God as Father, and a new openness to his Word to them; the door was also opened to them for a distinctive love for all men and women, not just for Jews but for Gentiles (including love for enemies) while at the same time this new love reached down to 'publicans and sinners', for salvation was to come in Jesus' understanding, not by segregation but by association. Yet again a great door of faith was opened up for them for they were called to see God doing his saving work, not only at some future time, but <u>now</u> in Christ, in his words and actions, in the midst of their life together and beyond it; not least, Jesus turned the key for all his disciples into a fellowship of joy, into mutual celebration of him and of one another. They were given the opportunity to celebrate him as they made room for his works and watched his actions, but they were also taught to remember that he willed to celebrate them. "Jesus on one occasion alludes to these disciple-followers under the figure of the 'friends of the Bridegroom', guests invited to have part in a wedding-feast (Mk 2 v19). That is a very remarkable privilege. It means that, because they belong to Jesus, these followers enter with Him on the freedom and joy and on all the conditions of the <u>Messianic time</u>".[21]

Yet within the fellowship of Jesus, Manson reminded us that all was not freedom and joy. Though the disciples had come to know a new kind of corporate life in prayer and love and faith and hope and joy, they had also been given a new perception of themselves. In thought, word and deed, they were continually found wanting, living as they were in the presence of Christ the disciples found it both joyful and hard to live with Jesus. His truth, and teaching, his mind and heart, contained in the Sermon on the Mount, again and again judged them, and they must have wanted to get out of his light. Yet this deep down they knew they could not do: "To avoid the light is natural and instinctive to men, and to face into it is hard–but it is <u>Life</u>!"[22]

But the disciples had to learn that there was more in the Christian life than having the privilege of being with Christ in the band of the disciples, they were asked to move forward with their Master to the Cross and to share his forgiving and suffering love there in the world. This taking up of the Cross, this overcoming of self, Manson called 'the second stage' in 'The Norm of the Christian Life'. This call to accompany Jesus to his Cross, to deny self, to give up their lives in his service was too much for the disciples. They were made more aware of the gap between themselves and their Master. Peter, who told Jesus that this kind of thought and movement forward was not the right thing to do, was told bluntly that he had a radically ungodly mind. So the disciples were now confronted with the thought of a suffering Messiah, and told: "whosoever will come after me, let him deny himself, and take up his cross and follow me" (Mk 8 v34). And Manson made plain to us what all this meant for modern disciples and wrote this clearly in these words: "it is not <u>things</u> that a man has to stroke out of his life, but the personal principle of hesitation, weakness, fear, clinging, evasion, reservation, refusing to share with Christ, not merely in mind, but in fortune".[23] And Manson took the view that the necessity of our appropriating not only the mind but the fortune, the very life of Jesus, brings home to any person who tries to do this, the immense gap between himself or herself and the Saviour, Jesus Christ.

Manson saw the disciples, the followers indeed of Jesus in any age, as those "standing afar off from Jesus, discovered to themselves, and in effect saying, as all in such judgement-hours must say:

'My sins have taken such a hold on me,
I am not able to look up to thee;
Lord, I repent; accept my tears and grief'.[24]

But our teacher did not leave the Norm of the Christian life at this hard stage, his thought regularly moved on to a third stage–that of <u>Sacramental Life.</u> This was the place to which the broken disciples, only too aware of their disunity with Jesus and one another and with God their Father, (and soon to be more aware of their need for forgiveness as betrayers) were led by their Master. He had his plan for his men; he was going to give his life in perfect obedience to God for them–'Thy will not mine be done'–and then this righteous life would be given to them, with the assurance of forgiveness for all that they had or had not done.

He planned in the bread and wine of his own institution, of the Lord's Supper, to materialise grace–his undeserved forgiveness and his new life for them. So Jesus took bread and, having blessed, broke it and gave it to them. "The meaning is: This, the thing proferred, is I, Myself, My person, My life, which is being given for you. Take me to yourselves".[25] In the same way the cup, which Jesus also took, was, he said, 'My blood of the Covenant' which brought to all who received it in faith, his sacrificial life, poured out for many for the forgiveness of sin, and now given to them.

In his words, spoken and written, William Manson brought home to his students, certainly to many of his ex-Service students their weakness and sin, and the way they constantly wounded Christ, their living Saviour. When asked one day at a New College retreat: "What is our sin?" He replied bluntly, 'you crucify Jesus Christ'. And yet our teacher took us forward to the Sacramental Life through the Lord's Supper "Jesus had said 'Follow Me!' He had said 'Deny thyself!' Now he says 'Take, this is My Body!' He is by this act bridging the gulf, closing the gap between Himself and us, between our guilt and powerlessness and His own perfect offering of His life to God".[26]

Whatever else William Manson gave us to carry eventually into the work of the Ministry in parishes or elsewhere, he proclaimed to us the Gospel of Jesus, the Gospel of the Kingdom of God, of the Reign of God over evil. He placed deep within us the message of Jesus, 'The reign of God is at hand', or in the NEB version (Mk 1, all the words of v.15) "The time has come; the kingdom of God is upon you; repent, and believe the Gospel". He brought to us his own abiding conviction that these words meant that the reign of God was near, that it was not confined simply to the future, as it often was in the apocalyptic vision. It was really present in this world–in Jesus himself, and among his men, and in days to come would be more fully among the Apostolic Band, and in the Church, and within each follower of Jesus. "The "mystery" of the Kingdom, lay in the paradox involved in supposing that the

Kingdom of Heaven itself was already existent on earth"[27]. . . "it is already cast into the processes of history as the seed is cast into the ground. The event, the harvest will inevitably come".[28]

The way the reign of God was to come dawned on us slowly. I had heard the late Dr George MacLeod preaching to the students of Edinburgh University at the start of the 1939-45 War in the Men's Union, and telling them that they each were made for the Cross, to carry it in all their ways, for it was an 'I' with a line through it. They would rise to this, as they went on contemplating Christ's Cross where there was the full revelation of God's own perfect forgiving love for the world. I fear I heard the words but did not grasp their meaning. It has often taken a long time for the followers of Jesus to grasp that they have to take up the Cross. I had yet to learn that the struggle to incarnate the Cross in the Parish in the company of leaders and people, awaits every genuine minister of the Gospel.

And if there is truly no reign of God over us without Christ's Cross, so there is no reign of God over us without faith. In his Introductory Note to Manson's book, *Christ's View of the Kingdom of God*, H. R. Mackintosh wrote: . . . "God enables us to see, more clearly than before, that just because God is Holy and Almighty Father, the coming of the Kingdom is relative to the Cross in Jesus' experience and to faith in ours".[29] Faith for Manson meant "trust in the present power of God, appropriation of that power as put forth for man's salvation now. It is intelligent subordination to God" (cf Matthew 8 v10f)".[30] So, when we do receive the will of God for us, for example in prayer and in serving and forgiving love, we believe we become recipients of God's renewing power but also that the power of God is released for others, so that they too overcome evil and are brought nearer to God. This is what I now understand Manson to mean in his Preface to his Commentary on Luke's Gospel where he gives this excellent summary of the Kingdom of God: "Jesus offers to his nation, not a new doctrine of the Kingdom, but a conception of the will of God which, if received, brings the goal indicated by the Kingdom into measurable, and indeed, immediate relation with the lives of men. On close approach we find that loving enemies, meeting evil with good, dying to self and becoming by a new birth, sons of God, constitute the central and vital datum, 'the mystery' which Jesus reveals to men".[31]

In all my parishes I endeavoured to work out with others the practical stages which could convey this mystery to the people to whom I was called to minister.

Notes

1. Moray McLaren - Sir Walter Scott, 'The Man and Patriot' - Heinemann - p16.
2. These are listed at the end of Baillie's 'Christian Devotion' - Oxford University Press (1962).
3. J Baillie - 'Invitation to Pilgrimage' - Oxford University Press (1942) - p39 (also Our Knowledge of God, (1947) - pp4-5).
4. Ibid - p85. 'Invitation to Pilgrimage' (1942).
5. J Baillie - 'The Idea of Revelation in Recent Thought' - Oxford University Press (1956) - pp84-85.
6. Ibid - p108.
7. J Baillie - 'Invitation to Pilgrimage' - Oxford University Press - p118.
8. J Baillie - 'Roots of Religion in The Human Soul' - James Clarke and Co Ltd - Passim (1937).
9. A M Ramsay - Introducing the Christian Faith 6. 'The Church It's Scandal and Glory' SCM Press - p69.
10. J Baillie - 'The Sense of the Presence of God' - Oxford University Press (1962) - p260.
11. St John 16v.7.
12. Karl Barth - 'Against the Stream' - SCM Press (1954) Editor R. G. Smith - p67.
13. John Baillie - 'Invitation To Pilgrimage' - Oxford University Press (1942) - p121.
14. Ibid - p123.
15. J S Stewart in the Foreword to 'The Way of the Cross' by W Manson - Hodder and Stoughton - p3.
16. Quotation from Bishop Westcott's 'The Gospel of the Resurrection' in H A William's 'Jesus and the Resurrection' - Longmans, Green and Co - p3.
17. See W Manson - 'Jesus The Messiah' - Hodder and Stoughton - pp103-120.
18. Ibid p109.
19. W Manson - 'The Gospel of Luke' - Hodder and Stoughton - p32.
20. Ibid - p32.
21. W Manson - 'The Way of the Cross' - Hodder and Stoughton - p43.
22. Ibid - p45.
23. W Manson - 'The Norm of the Christian Life' - Scottish Journal of Theology - Vol 3 No1 - March, 1950 - p41.
24. W Manson - 'The Way of the Cross' - Hodder and Stoughton - p72.
25. Ibid - pp73-74.
26. Ibid - p74.
27. W Manson - 'Christ's View of the Kingdom of God' - James Clarke & Co - p95.
28. Ibid - p96.
29. Ibid - Introductory Note - pp7-8 - H R Mackintosh.
30. Ibid - 'Christ's View of the Kingdom of God' - pp88-89.
31. W Manson - Commentary on The Gospel of Luke - p.viii Preface.

Chapter IV

Post Graduate Ministerial Training in America and Aberdeen

Union Theological Seminary, New York, and
The West St Nicholas Assistantship, Aberdeen

1. The Seminary   ·

The journey to this Seminary founded in 1836 to train students for the Christian Ministry of all Protestant denominations, had been travelled by many, both students and teachers, before my time. Such famous names as George MacLeod, John Baillie and John McIntyre are to be associated with it. I do not know for certain how they found it, but I believe they would see it as an exciting and stimulating place in which to stay and study or teach. Those of my year, 1949-50, in which some of us worked for the Degree of STM (Master of Sacred Theology), certainly saw it that way.

Here was an interesting international fellowship. Our fellow students came from different continents–some from Scandinavia, and from other parts of Europe, some from the Far East and India, and, as one might expect, many from different parts of the United States and Canada. It was indeed an energising experience to meet and talk with such men and women, and to receive from them insights, not only theological, but also social and geographical. A photograph of our year brings home clearly the world wide nature of its membership.

Here too there was a new kind of service, not only from student to student reaching across the nations, but from staff to students. I was not long in the Seminary before I was asked by Professor John Knox to go to his house, and have a talk with him about what I studied in New College, Edinburgh, and about what I'd like to do in Union. I went to this New Testament Professor's home somewhat on edge, feeling pretty ignorant, but I was received as a very welcome student brother from Scotland, who had been taught by William Manson, "one of Europe's famous New Testament scholars". In meeting John Knox I realised I'd met someone, not only supremely able to guide my future study, but a wonderfully gracious Christian man, whose spirit reminded me very powerfully of William Manson.

Yet again here was probing but stimulating worship and preaching in the James Chapel. In my year we soon came to recognise what a galaxy of teaching and preaching stars were on the staff of Union at this period. How beneficial it was to listen to the words of professors Reinhold Niebuhr or Paul Tillich, or Paul Scherer, or James Muilenburg or Fred Grant, and not least of John Knox, as they spoke in Chapel as well as in the lecture room.

From a physical point of view also we were well looked after. The College building of the Seminary may not have had a beautiful campus like Princeton, or some other American Divinity Colleges, but students' rooms were to us spacious and comfortable, even though it took some time to get used to the rumble of tube trains going underground nearby, and to the traffic on Broadway, just below one's window on the 7th floor of Union. And my memory of the food in the dining hall was that it was excellent, far beyond the expectation of an ex-Service student.

However it quickly became clear to those of us from Scotland that it would be hard to survive on the money provided by our Travelling Scholarship, so we had to find an assistantship, reasonably near to the Seminary, which would help us financially. I thought I was fortunate to be offered one on Long Island at 15 dollars per Sunday. This meant on Sundays being present at morning and evening services, as well as at the meeting for teenagers later in the same day. The minister of the charge to which I went had been once a saddle back preacher in Canada, but had come to the USA and settled in this Congregational American Church. He was a hard working minister and a good pastor to his people and was ably supported by his wife. He could however be very demanding on his assistant. He assumed that I could preach a sermon at any time. One Christmas Sunday morning he suddenly announced to the congregation that his young friend from Scotland would now give the Christmas message. After that I always had a spare sermon with me somewhere! But I did find the Church leaders and people friendly, and I was given insight into American Church life through having to share in the services and work with the young people. However I can see now that this assistantship eventually proved detrimental to the academic work I sought to do in Union, for the minister fell ill, and I was asked to take many more services than was wise and I found myself writing sermons for Sunday when I was finishing my thesis on The Kingdom of God - (That is my excuse anyway!).

It is time now to go back to what I learnt at the Seminary. Just because we had so many fascinating teachers around us it was difficult to decide which classes to attend. It seemed obvious to take a course with Reinhold Niebuhr,[1] probably the best known in America of all the Union staff. I still have one of my better efforts in terms of essays which was written for him on his course, "The Christian View of Human Nature". It was called "The Biblical Doctrine of Redemption in the Old Testament, in the Synoptics, in St John, and in St Paul, with special reference to the Structure of Human Nature and Existence". The great man wrote on it 'A–Very Good indeed'. In those far off days that helped me a great deal! It was in contrast to some of my poorer essays for others on the staff. I learned much also from courses I took on preaching from Professor Scherer, and about the Old Testament from a dynamic and illuminating lecturer by the name of James Muilenburg. Looking back at the

Seminary, I feel it was an unforgettable experience in different areas of ministerial training, and in very happy student fellowship, both male and female. Not least I was given so much more understanding of the Christian Faith from the gifted teachers there, for me in particular, from the late Professor John Knox.

2 Learning from Professor John Knox - Baldwin Professor of Sacred Literature in the Seminary

a) Faith in Christ in Relation to Historical Fact

I can recall something of the teaching of John Knox. He made clear to us many things and here is one of these. It had become for him a passionate conviction–namely 'The Miracle of the Church' in which the meaning of the Resurrection was certainly to be found. This for me was badly needed teaching, for despite what I'd been taught by John Baillie and William Manson, and some good experiences within congregations, I still had the soldier's nagging scepticism about the Church, along with doubts sometimes about the Resurrection. The Church, whether in America or in Scotland or in England after the war, seemed hopelessly far away from the reign of God, from the new conception of the will of God revealed in Jesus in which William Manson had so eloquently instructed us. Yet here was another distinguished New Testament scholar, far away from Scotland, who so clearly had seen this very important Church problem for many years. He tells us about this in many places but he puts it clearly in the Foreword to a book published about a decade after my time at Union, called *The Church and the Reality of Christ*. Here are Knox's words: "It was more than 40 years ago that I first became acutely aware of the problem the present discussion is concerned with–the problem of how faith in Christ can be essentially related to historical fact and yet be as sure as faith must be–and I do not think I have since felt the problem in any greater depth that I felt it then. My first impulse was to say: 'If we have only the Church, we have nothing'. It took more than twenty years for me to reach the point of seeing that in having the Church we have everything".[2] The last part of that sentence I still needed to know and understand and when at Union Theological Seminary to have the grounds for it made clear. And that is what John Knox did. We can only understand that in "having the Church we have everything", Knox said, if we come to understand the mystery of Jesus Christ within her.

b) St Paul's View of Christ and the Early Church

Knox believed that St Paul was the best New Testament interpreter of who Jesus is and was. In lectures and in a book called *Chapters in a Life of Paul*, revised when

I was at Union, he explained that the thoughts of Paul moved back from Christ risen and exalted to Christ crucified: "Paul's thought about Christ the person always moves from the 'Christ who lives' to the 'Jesus who died', always from the one known to the one remembered. It is the present living reality which comes first to his mind when he speaks of Christ"[3] (this movement of Paul's thoughts, he pointed out, can be seen also in Galatians 2 v 20 and in Philippians 3 v 10). This same Christ not only met Paul (Saul then) on the Damascus road, he met him earlier among the Christians whom he had persecuted. It was in the The Early Church, persecuted, that Saul saw Christ, for example in Stephen, who showed in his death the kind of love shown on the Cross, being filled there with forgiving love even to his enemies. In this way Christ risen and ascended, or the heavenly Christ, was operating in his Spirit and was reaching out to Saul in grace, in undeserved love, prior to his confronting him on the Damascus road. Knox puts this clearly in these words "Christ had begun to make himself known to Paul–perhaps against the latter's will–as the Spirit of the persecuted Koinonia (fellowship) before he made himself known in the visual experience in which Paul's conversion culminated".[4] And yet it was in the Damascus experience that Saul, remembering probably what he had seen of Christ's spirit in persecuted people such as Stephen, heard Jesus say: "Saul, Saul, why persecutest thou me". The living Christ had indeed been there in the Spirit among his persecuted people, and when Saul asked, 'What shall I do?', he was told: 'Arise, and go into the city, and it shall be told thee what thou must do' (Acts 9 v6) - that is, meet there your enemies, those you have been against, in forgiving love, and learn from their Christian fellowship. So Saul obeyed and went to Damascus, and was baptised and became Paul, the new man in Christ. Thus St Paul grasped the mystery of Christ's saving presence in the early Church of his day. The Christ who can be known through the Spirit among his people where he still prays and loves and speaks and rescues from sin and death, is the same Christ as was crucified, and revealed on the Cross the forgiving love which was God's love, and which blots out the guilt of sin and gives deliverance from its power. So for Paul, the Christ who is known is also remembered, and he who is remembered as the crucified Christ is still known by his people and at work in their midst and he continues to speak to them, heals and feeds them, and transforms them in the Church, the community of his Spirit and love.

c) *Knox's Conviction about the Significance and Miracle of the Church*

But what about the post 1939-45 War Church? Is Jesus Christ with his gift of the Spirit also to be found there? Has it a similar significance? Is this where faith in Christ can be related to historical fact? Is there in this Church also the same kind of generous and forgiving love, even for enemies, just as it was on the Cross? And is there still in the Church of our time the kind of passionate believing prayer such as Jesus prayed to the Father? Does Christ, through the Spirit, inspire such prayers in ministers and people, so that they feel the living Christ lives and prays in them? And does Christ by the same Spirit still preach and teach there? John Knox believed these were urgent and deep questions, for if this Spirit of Christ was there in this Church, then God's action, his saving activity in Jesus Christ, was shown to be real, then Christ truly lives, though once he died upon the Cross, and the empty tomb or the resurrection appearances in the past, testified to in Scripture, would not be seen as so important for persuading Christians of Christ's risen power. Nor would Christians require the subtle interpretations of New Testament scholars to help their belief in the Resurrection. At any rate John Knox had a perceptive view of the Church for the students of his day. He wrote: "the valid evidence of Jesus' Resurrection was the realised presence and power of the Christ they remembered, alive after his passion. This evidence was provided only within the Church's existence. To share in that existence is, for us also, 'to know him and the power of his Resurrection', and thus to possess the only possible reason for believing in the resurrection at all".[5]

And if the life of the Church has deep significance for the resurrection, it also has profound significance for what Knox called the Christ Event, that is, of his life and teaching and healing, of his death on the Cross and of his rising again and of the gifts and recognition of Christ's presence and Spirit. Knox was particularly persuaded that in the complex reality of this event, it is the coming into being, or emergence of the Church, which has the priority. This takes place when the risen Lord bestows the Spirit upon his people, his Spirit of perception responding to himself, and of obedient and serving and reconciling and forgiving, and if need be, of suffering love, and when, as in the case of Paul, this Spirit is recognised as that of God and Jesus Christ, then people feel his judgement and say 'what shall I do?', and come under the orders of Christ, their living Lord and Commander.

It is interesting to find that a distinguished theologian, Professor John Macquarrie, whom I remember as a lecturer at a Bagshot Army Chaplains' course, wrote about 'The Concept of a Christ-Event' in a book called *God Incarnate: Story and Belief*. He compares what Bultmann and Knox have to say about it. For Bultmann the Christ Event was primarily the word of preaching, there is little about its social character. This is what Knox takes up; yet Macquarrie does not think their views are conflicting "Both men are agreed in seeing the Christ-event as something larger than the career of the man Jesus of Nazareth, and both are agreed in making that larger reality the centre of faith".[6] The Church's beginning "certainly included the more limited event of the career of Jesus of Nazareth and Knox accords to that a normative value for the subsequent life of the Church,[6] but 'The event has no historical reality except within the history of the Church' (Knox words)."

Yet again Knox saw clearly the significance of the Church for God's love within her . . . "we do find the reconciling love of God in the Church" . . . "There is great evil–appalling evil in the Church" . . . "But faulty and partly evil as it is and has always been, it has actually proved to be the carrier of a love of God which cannot be known except through participation in its life–a love which seems to those who receive it as alone adequate to cover our sins and the sins of the whole world, and as alone able eventually to redeem us from their power. I have said that membership in the Church is a sharing in memory and the Spirit; it is also a sharing in love, that is, a sharing in the <u>receiving</u> of love, a sharing in <u>being</u> loved–and being loved in a unique way, which overcomes our loneliness and estrangement, and with our brethren makes us sons again in our Father's house. We are speaking of this actual experience of sharing in love when we speak of the Atonement".[7]

So in the Church Knox believed he had everything, though the Event of Christ for Knox was not to be identified with the Church. He wrote and spoke of what he called the miracle of the Church "The miracle, the only miracle, was 'Christ crucified'–the identity of the risen exalted 'Christ' with the remembered one on his Cross. The only 'glory' of the human life was the love willing and able to bear the burden of our sins and griefs".[8] There in the Church he was the same crucified Christ pouring out his forgiving love upon those who were against him or indifferent to him; here was the divine love willing and able to carry and bear human sins and grief. Knox's miraculous view of the Church is best put in his own words: "The Church is the corporate reality of Christ, the body of Jesus' Resurrection, the locus of God's presence and saving action! The Church is God's deed, wonderful beyond our understanding! 'Thanks be to God for his unspeakable gift!' One who so speaks about the Church regards it as a 'miracle' in the only true sense of that term. This is what a 'miracle' is–a reality to which (however 'natural' it may seem to others) one finds oneself responding in some such way". [9]

If Knox had been asked to point to a Scriptural passage which made clear what he called the meaning of the Christ-Event as the coming into being of the Church, he certainly would have pointed to St John's Gospel chapter 21 v7. "It is the moment when <u>after Jesus' death</u> a group of his Disciples recognise in a divine Presence wonderfully new and strange, the very one they have known and loved: 'It is the Lord' (John 21 v7)". "In this moment of recognition", wrote Knox, "the Resurrection (whatever it may be conceived to have been in and of itself) became for the first time a historical fact, and the Church, which had been in process of "becoming" since Jesus' first disciples were gathered about him, came finally into actual being".[10] And it can be noted further that once the disciples recognised Jesus they came under his orders and went and had breakfast with him, being fed by him with bread and fish.

Yet this discussion of Christ in the Church might seem to suggest that it is the only place of his dwelling. Knox vigorously denied this: he well knew that Jesus is at the right hand of God, and also that he is at work in the world, as he had been on the Cross on a hill outside Jerusalem. Christ crucified may indeed be found again and again in the corporate Church, but Christ also, though he may be so often unrecognised, is in the world, pouring out his seeking love upon all, people of all the nations, so the Christ whom we come to remember and experience in the Spirit in the Church is the One sent by God into the world, who now sends us into the same place - 'As the Father sent me, so send I you'.

My time in Union Theological Seminary, New York, was over, and I was soon on my way back to Scotland to be a minister in the Church of Scotland, yet somehow to be a bearer of Christ's love in its crucial form among the people of my day and generation.

I shuddered at this challenging thought, for the problem wasn't just the Church, and whether Christ was in it and recognised there and responded to there, the problem for the minister also was the world which was so unbelieving and where so many people were lost. Yet here again John Knox had something to say of great help. He spoke about "the foolishness of God"[11] being so hugely lavish and prodigal. He knew about the weakness and lostness of his people; but let them return to God, and they would not only find acceptance with him, but they would be trusted again to do his work. The story of the prodigal son was the story for Knox of two prodigals and one was the father who poured out his love.

And Knox saw this same prodigal love on the Cross which had immense power in it to draw human hearts to it, though they might try to escape from the magnificence there of an ageless love. Even if there be great resistance in the world to this Cross and the mysteries of divine love there, it is God's gift to us, and we have to show it forth in deeds in the world. "And the Cross, wherever it is found, whether in Golgotha or on our own street, speaks only more eloquently of the deep, firm grasp God's beauty and love have, and have always had, on our hearts for showing as well, what brutal blows we have dealt in our ruthless effort to get free of it. But this last we cannot do–we cannot escape our nature and destiny. Our wisdom must finally yield to the wisdom of His Glory, and our proud strength to the relentless pressure of His love".[12]

3. The West St Nicholas Kirk Assistantship, Aberdeen

I wondered what I should do when I returned to Edinburgh from Union Theological Seminary, New York. I felt I wanted to become a Parish minister, yet I knew I was ill-equipped to do this work, despite four years of academic training, as well as some practical assignments. However I received a letter just shortly after arriving home, from the Minister of the West Church of St Nicholas, the Revd Anderson Nicol, asking me to come to Aberdeen and be his Senior Assistant there.

After seeing Mr Nicol, later Dr Nicol, I was happy to accept the job, and set off for Aberdeen, and for the experience of Church life in a busy city centre charge, the congregation numbering at that time about 2,700 souls.

The Church team consisted of the Minister, an excellent Deaconess–Miss Currie, a Junior Assistant, a Church Secretary and myself. The Minister and his charming wife Jean were extremely helpful to me in countless ways, and I was given a warm welcome into the congregation. In many spheres I learned a great deal from Anderson Nicol. He was an outstanding pastor and administrator, dedicated to the well being of all who belonged to the West Church, as well as playing a considerable part in the General Assembly Committees and in Ministry to the Town Council of Aberdeen, and to the Town.

I was given work to do in the Youth Fellowship, where there were many talented young people who had genuine questions to ask about the Christian Faith, and I was given also a share in the Sunday Services. In relation to pastoral work, 25 visits were required each week. These had to be written down in a book which was handed to the Minister prior to the staff meeting the following week when the visits were gone over, and the member's card was marked.

I mention only one of the many things, not to be forgotten, in relation to pastoral visiting. It may seem trivial but it opened a door for me into the minds of what I thought were a number of the congregation. I was asked by the Minister to go and visit quite a proportion of members who had shown, for some time, little or no interest in the Church. One of these asked me why he should come back into the fellowship of the West Church. My reply was not only I felt he would be welcomed, but that the risen living Christ was there, and by the Spirit he could share in forgiveness and in the new life and love offered by his Lord. His reply will always be retained in my memory - "So they say, sonny, so they say".

In the West Church I had come up against disbelief in the Resurrection, and against the stumbling block of congregational fellowship. This old man in no way believed that Christ was in the Church in his Spirit of reconciling and forgiving love. I was back with the problem of John Knox, my teacher at Union, "The problem of how faith in Christ can be essentially related to historical fact". I had been looking for the miracle of the Church - 'Christ crucified' - the identity of the risen, exalted 'Christ' with the remembered one on his Cross" - and in that visit, and in many others I did not find it. Yet Knox's words came back to me, "we do find the reconciling love of God in the Church. We would not belong to it, if that were not true; indeed we do not really belong to it except insofar as this is true". I realised that I could not judge West St Nicholas on the basis of these visits. I could not ignore that there were many leaders, elders, teachers, Guild ladies in the congregation who were showing that, perhaps often in stumbling ways, they were the carriers of a love of God which was growing in them because in the Church they had learned, with those around them, to experience the risen Christ through his Spirit and to remember the same Christ crucified in history. Whatever could be said about those I had been sent to visit, there were those in the West Kirk whom I believed to be 'in Christ', in the new existence of reconciliation within the body of Christ, reaching out to others in cherishing and forgiving, and sometimes suffering love. This was the sharing in the new humanity created by God, enabling them to be, with countless gone before them, people 'in Christ'. "I am sure", wrote Knox, "we are expected to take the preposition 'in' more strictly and naturally, to indicate a place–its object being an actual body in which we can be located, to which we can belong as parts to a whole".[13] If we are all 'in Adam' alienated from God our Father and from one another, then in the Church, 'in Christ', we can more and more become re-united with the Father and with those who are our brothers and sisters there. All this is to be given a glimpse and first fruit experience of that ultimate reconciliation including God and our neighbours and everything in heaven and on earth. At any rate I hoped that I might have experience of the new humanity and of many 'in Christ' in the particular Church to which, it was probable, I would be called soon.

The months at West St Nicholas passed quickly, during which I received great kindness and hospitality from the manse family. The Minister's wife was always to me, as to so many other assistants, a very generous hostess and a loyal friend. About this time the Minister offered to write to certain vacancy committees on my behalf, but I felt I should go to the pulpit supply agent in 121 George Street and enquire about vacant charges. He suggested I might be interested in Fallin Parish Church, near Stirling. It had been a charge closely associated with the Iona Community and one which the late Revd Dr George MacLeod had often visited. I had never heard of it, but there was much youth work done there and a Church House filled with young, each evening of the week. The Parish was principally a mining parish, though the community of Throsk was also part of it, having a naval armament depot nearby. It seemed it could be a good place to go, and I agreed that my name could be given to the Vacancy Committee. I eventually preached in Fallin Church on Palm Sunday of 1951 and was elected its minister, though I was not the vacancy committee's first choice.

Notes

1.   Charles A Briggs Professor of Ethics and Theology at Union Seminary.

2.   John Knox - Foreword - 'The Church and The Reality of Christ' - Collins - London - p10.

3.   John Knox - 'Chapters in a Life of Paul' - Abingdon - Cokesbury Press - p130.

4.   Ibid - p126.

5.   John Knox - 'The Church and The Reality of Christ' - Collins - London - p68.

6.   Harvey (Editor) God Incarnate - 'Story and Belief' - Chapter on 'The Concept of a Christ-Event - p77.

7.   John Knox - 'The Church and The Reality of Christ' - Collins - London - p109.

8.   Ibid - p75.

9.   Ibid - pp73-74.

10.   Ibid - p79.

11.   John Knox - 'The Foolishness of God' - Union Seminary Review Vol XIX - (November, 63).

12.   Ibid - p4.

13.   John Knox – 'The Church and The Reality of Christ' - Collins - London - p105.

Chapter V

Ministry in Fallin Parish Church, Stirling

I looked forward, after leaving West St Nicholas Church in Aberdeen, with great expectation and pleasure to starting a Ministry of Word and Sacrament in the Parish of Fallin and Throsk. This Ministry included a pastorate of over 300 in the congregation, apart from those in the Parish. I never thought that it would be an easy ministry for I was well aware of my own inexperience, as well as my ignorance of what life in a mining community would be like. However I became quickly conscious that the Minister before me had been a gifted and industrious man, with a particular concern for the young people, and with a genuine concern for the community and for all who were in need, both old and young. He had a secretary, a talented lady, and also the backing and interest of the late Revd Dr G F MacLeod himself. With the help of certain elders and young men and women in the Parish, he had co-operated with the Iona Youth Trust in setting up a Church House, next to the Church and Manse, which was filled with young on most evenings, and with older people as well, on many Saturday nights. There was a strong and creative link between the Church and Community; at any rate, the Community was, to a considerable extent, in the Church House, if not in the Church. Indeed I found that I wrote in the first edition of the Fallin Church Magazine (Price 4d!) since becoming Minister: "As everyone knows the Community is not too much in the Church, or it is not in the Church at present, but there is nothing like high hopes and a reminder to ourselves that the Lord is not done with Fallin or Throsk by any means!"

But I must go back to the day of my induction and ordination in Fallin Church in May, 1951. I have said that I looked forward with great expectation to this day but it exceeded all my expectations, and indeed astonished me. The service still stays with me, not only in the sense that there was a very good attendance of the congregation and parish, but also of the Presbytery. I was fortunate also in the Ministers who shared in the principal parts of the Service. The sermon was preached by the Minister of Logie Church, the Revd J Hunter, and the Moderator of the Presbytery, who spoke to me and the congregation, was the Revd Joseph Lynn CBE, who had been a long serving Service Padre. I can still remember their texts: 2 Timothy 3v5 - "Having a form of godliness, but denying the power thereof: from such turn away" (Hunter); and I Timothy 1 vv18 and 19 - "This charge I commit unto thee, son Timothy, . . . that thou mightest war a good warfare, holding faith and a good conscience" 'So fight gallantly, armed with faith and a good conscience' (NEB) (Lynn).

That service was very helpful to me then and often since that day. But it was what happened afterwards that surprised me even more. For the Interim Moderator (or it may have been the Presbytery Clerk) came up to me and handed me an envelope of which he told me to take good care, and read afterwards. This I did, and was astonished to find that it contained a cheque for £5,000. I learned soon that this was part of a much larger amount given to George MacLeod, by the late Lord Lithgow, to help the work of the Church in certain areas. The £5,000 gifted to the Fallin Minister was to enable the youth work in Fallin Parish to continue. The Church House had been formerly set up and administered by the Iona Youth Trust; now with this generous gift of £5,000 it would in future be looked after by the Fallin Church House Trust. A new club leader was to be appointed by this Trust with the approval of the Leaders Youth Council and the Kirk Session.

It was not long before a club leader was appointed but the lady found the job very difficult for her, and soon afterwards a second leader was chosen, this time a man, who had remarkable gifts, and an excellent background to handle those he had to work with, and to take the strain involved in Church House. He was Herbert Christie, a former Sergeant Major or Senior NCO in the Army (Argyll and Sutherland Highlanders) and someone who had a splendid musical gift, especially when working with young people in a club, or with a choir in the Church. A Minister usually requires elders and leaders who will be responsible in the duties they have accepted, and who will be loyal to the Minister of the time, which does not exclude being honest with that Minister; I always felt that Herbert Christie, along with the elders, were really God's gift to me all the years I was Minister of Fallin Parish Church.

1. Visiting, Worship and the First Communicants' Class

I will say more of the Church House youth work later, but now I turn to the situation within the congregation. Attendance at the Church was not really very good, and offerings were low. There was clearly the requirement for a careful visitation, by the new Minister, of the whole congregation. I remember thinking that by the start of September, when I was to be married in Cramond Kirk, it might be possible to have visited every home–every congregational home. Whether I achieved this or not I cannot now remember, but I had at any rate visited most of them by then. I went with the District Elder round each District and found this to be a good idea, as he was able to show me where to go, and give me valuable information about most of the families.

I had to think carefully about what I was going to do on these visits, were they to be more than social calls, and if so, what 'more' was to be done? It was clear to me that I must try to listen to what was said to me in each home about the members of the family there, or the person there, and about the local Church and Community. There would surely be tragedies or joys in many homes, though I would not necessarily be told of these at this stage.

Were I not to be told about the family, it could be helpful sometimes to ask. But if I was to listen, I thought I should also feel free to <u>invite</u> all in the family to attend the Parish Church, where I felt they would be welcomed, and where the contribution of their presence and worship and relationship with others was important. Some of the elders, perhaps all of them, had already given this invitation, but I still believed I was there in each home also to do this. I further believed that at least in some of the homes, there had been for many years a deep spirituality; that in these there had been men or women of prayer, and of continuing compassionate and forgiving love, and that they would know that filial joy in God their Father, and that love for their brothers and sisters in the fellowship of the Church and for those outwith it, of which I myself had come to know a little. These would be people of the Kingdom of God, or people of the Spirit, or people 'in Christ', who had prepared in different ways for a new Minister coming, and would rejoice if I took time to pray, and to lift up their family and the local Church to God the Father, for his Blessing. Such people would already know about the Resurrection; they would be aware that Christ was in the Church, speaking and serving or forgiving and renewing, and that some days, at any rate, he lived in them, in their homes and relationships. And they would surely be right to think that their new Minister should also know about these things, and should believe in them, and need not be ashamed of them. So I decided that while I would not be able in every home to pray, it would be right to do this where possible, with their permission; also the members of that family would sometimes, contribute to the prayer I offered, by what they told me about themselves.

In all these visits, in this Parish, as in my other Parishes, I was always aware of the huge opportunity which was again and again presented to a Minister of affirming the reconciliation of the members of a family to God their Father, and to one another in the mystery of Christ's love.

So, many visits could become the place where a separation from God the Father or from some person, was broken down and a new unity suggested or enacted; it could become a place where an individual became aware afresh that he or she was truly a son or a daughter of God the Father, through Jesus Christ, his living Son. It could be that in these often today despised visits, Professor William Manson's words could be acted out, for I have often come back to his statement about the Kingdom of God (made more than once in his commentary on St Luke and elsewhere): "Jesus offers to his nation not a new doctrine of the Kingdom of God, but a new conception of God's will which, if received, will bring the goal indicated by the Kingdom of God into measurable, indeed into immediate, relation with the lives of men. This revelation the disciples have received but others do not comprehend it. They do not see that loving enemies, meeting evil with good, putting away selfishness, becoming 'sons of God' by a rebirth of the Spirit (vi. 27-36), represent the mode in which the Reign of God actualises itself in human life".[1]

And this actualising of his reign can be done in simple acts of prayer as also in repeated specific acts of love. Such costly acts bring the goal of the Kingdom, the destruction of evil, the destruction of apartness from God or man into vital relationship with human lives (even in a home!).

I shall return soon to the amazing results of these visits to the homes of the congregation as far as I could see them, for I was quite sure I could only recognise a few things. Now I must say a little about another very important area of a Parish Minister's work–namely his conduct of worship. This has to do with leading the prayers, or co-operating with the prayers of the people, but it also has to do with teaching and preaching the Gospel, the Good News of what God has done, for both Minister and people, in Jesus Christ, whereby the door of reconciliation with God their Father has been opened for them, and whereby they can become brothers and sisters of one another, and servants of others.

I had not been a few months as Minister before I realised the huge trust which had been placed in me, and any Parish Minister, not only to meet and try to get to know, and understand, and love and pray for and with the people of the congregation and Parish, but also Sunday by Sunday, to preach to them and help others to teach them. Yet certain resources were available for these high duties, the primary one being the Word of God, and week by week I would need to find a message which the living God wanted me to proclaim to those who came to worship him; and behind me, in seeking to do this, I knew I had the prayers of at least some members of the congregation and my own family's prayers, as well as so many more. Another resource which I found invaluable was the Book of Common Order 1940, which not only contained specimen Orders of Service, with prayers for morning and evening Services, but also a Lectionary–Readings, both from the Old and New Testament, for each Sunday. Yet again I had some commentaries on books within Scripture which could help me to understand the particular scripture passage from which I might preach. At any rate, throughout the summer months of 1951 I tried to prepare the Word of God for the people Sunday by Sunday, always remembering that God could speak to those who were worshipping, through the hymns or the prayers or the readings of scripture, or their meeting together, as well as through the preaching. I also realised that the visiting I was doing could feed the preaching, and give me valuable illustrations.

I well recall one home in which the husband did not appear, but I was invited to come into the back room to see him. It was late on Friday evening, and he had had too much to drink and he was asleep in his chair. His wife told me it was always that way at week-ends, but she had carried this through many years, and she would go on doing it to the end, for she would never leave him. It was her form of the At-one-ment. I got to know him afterwards; he was in many ways a good man.

I now come back to one result of the many visits I had made to homes within the congregation. I had always in each home given a warm invitation to come to the Church Services, but also, where suitable, had invited any in a family, who were not members of the local church or of another, to come to a Communicants' Class, probably to meet in September. I thought I might well have difficulty in gathering together people for this, so I was astonished to see an enormous class of over 80 people who wished to consider becoming members of the Church. It may have been hard to make a plan for visiting the congregation, it was now just as difficult to make a plan as to how I meant to communicate the Christian Gospel to so many men and women, both young and old. I wished I had had more experience, and more training in teaching a class of communicants. My only experience of such a class had been my own class with George Reid my Minister, in 1938 or 1939. I fortunately remembered that he based his talks on the questions put to those wishing to join the full membership of the Church. It seemed sensible that I should do the same. So I tried my best to give talks to those who came to Fallin Church on the questions for Communicants in the Book of Common Order, 1940.

It seemed right that a Minister should endeavour to say what he understood such questions to mean. They were:

1. Do you confess your faith in God as your heavenly Father, in Jesus Christ as your Saviour and Lord, and in the Holy Spirit as your Sanctifier?
2. Do you promise, in dependence on Divine grace, to serve the Lord and to walk in His ways all the days of your life?
3. Do you promise to make diligent use of the means of grace, to share dutifully in the worship and service of the Church, and to give of your substance, as the Lord may prosper you, for the advancement of His Kingdom throughout the world?

Looking back now, I can see that it would have been wise to obtain some help, either from other ministers, or elders as I did later, and to divide such a large class into smaller groups, and to have taken more time to give better instruction. However this was not done, and I went ahead to give the talks I had prepared, giving opportunities for questions as I went along.

It is not possible to say much about the content of what was said to these communicants. But I knew that I was on firm ground when I spoke to them about the deep need for all of us for reconciliation to God our Father, to one another and within ourselves. As all my principal statements were biblically based, I was able to refer them to the story of Adam in Genesis. What happened to Adam, his separation from God, having rebelled against him, was true of each one of us. We were each separated from God and man, and what we required was reunion with him and others. Put biblically, we were sinners who required grace–the undeserved goodness of God in action. So I told them of the Gospel, of how God came in his Son Jesus Christ and in his own person on earth reunited humankind to God, such was his perfect obedience to the Father's will. Reconciliation therefore is in Jesus Christ before it is through Jesus Christ, who, as risen Lord, gives to each believer his own Spirit, God's Spirit, and it is by this Spirit that the believer is bound to God as Father and to other people. I did my best to stress that it was God who had raised his Son, Jesus Christ from the dead, and that this risen Lord had not risen to stay away in heaven, from people in any age or country, but to come close to each person, seeking entry into their life, their everyday life. It was here that I endeavoured to confront each communicant with the wonderful promises of Christ. Such as 'I am the Good Shepherd' or 'I am with you always'. No one in the class was not being sought by this seeking shepherd; there was no one in it with whom he did not wish to share his life–abundant life, overflowing with an indestructible forgiving and unchanging love, and with steadfast believing prayer to an ever gracious Father. Each communicant had to be aware of Christ's gracious encounter with him or her. This awareness would bring both shock and amazing delight, shock because they would suddenly see that for long they had wounded and refused his love, but despite feeling judged, they would be able to make room for the great gift of Jesus Christ to every Christian–the gift of the Spirit from Christ crucified which would enable each one "to repent and believe the Gospel". It was Jesus Christ's will to make his dwelling within the life of every person, and to guide their path in all relationships. No communicant could truly live apart from Christ; each was bought with a price, the price of Christ's life and death on the Cross, and of his rising again and the gift of the Spirit. The Good Shepherd wanted to be their guide and guard always, but also wanted to bring them into the fold of his new community, the Church, where they would discover increasingly, Christ and him crucified, - 'Christ in you (plural) the hope of glory', within the fellowship of the Church, where quarrelling with others and blaming others could be destroyed, and his given love established.

After some of these talks in the Church to this large, and, in age, very varied class, I felt quite depressed. I believed that on occasions they had become inattentive; for my teaching was not really reaching the minds and hearts of this invited gathering. I was only too aware of the weakness of my thoughts and words. However rather than give up, I realised that I had to hold fast to "faith and a good conscience", and I said to myself at this time, what I'd told the class - "faith cometh by hearing, and hearing by the Word of God". And that Word of God was not only something written or spoken but something lived, not just by Christ's people but by Christ himself; he could be pleased to create faith in the hearts and minds of members in that class, through the stumbling words and thoughts of a young and inexperienced minister.

2. Loving One's Neighbour in the School and Parish

But faith in Jesus Christ means that the person who begins to receive it and act upon it, starts to pray daily to God the Father–that is "The natal cry of Christianity" as William Manson often said; he also starts to love his fellow man or woman, whoever they are.

From an early time in New College these words of Emil Brunner printed themselves on my mind: "God will not bind me to himself on any other terms than these, that he bind me at the same time to my brother". So it was not enough to give all one's energies to the membership of the congregation, or of a communicants' class. There were community relationships which required attention. Across the road from Fallin Manse, there stood the School–Primary, and Junior Secondary) - and the School House. Here was another very important area of work for the Parish Minister.

In my time, the Head Teacher was an ex-army officer, and a man still closely associated with his comrades in the Services in the local branch of the British Legion. He was a strong disciplinarian but I believe he was genuinely concerned for the School, the staff and the pupils. I will always be grateful to him for welcoming me as the School Padre, and for allowing me to conduct services of worship in the School. I clearly recall one morning when the turn out of the pupils in the hall irritated him. There were no seats in the hall, and the pupils stood in row after row. He shouted 'hands' and he went round some rows to see if they had washed, and then he also looked to see if the buttons on their jackets were sewn on. He was not pleased, and told them that many were unwashed and untidy. "They deserved to be dropped in a jungle but they are here to worship", and turning to me, said 'And, by God, they will worship; carry on Padre! It wasn't the best 'Call to worship' I had heard!

It hardly needs to be said that I found this area of Parish work extremely difficult, as I had never attempted before either to talk to children in a school, or to lead their worship. I was thankful that the school services weren't the only place where I encountered the children, for many of them came to the Church House Clubs, if they didn't appear in the Sunday School, or Church.

Further up the long village street and on the same side as the School and the Pit, stood what was known as 'The Blocks'. I had already, by the time I first visited these 'Blocks', been round many of the council houses both in Fallin and in Throsk. Some of these were overcrowded with young married people waiting to be allocated a home of their own. Yet 'The Blocks' were much worse; in them there were far too many people packed together in inadequate accommodation. 'The Blocks' had been built prior to, or shortly after the First World War. They were built of brick. They had been the property of the Pit, but now they belonged to Stirling Council. There was very poor washing and laundry provision; washing had to be done in large steamies–wash houses–and there were lavatories, often out of action, for three homes. Houses were entered from the back and you had to climb upstairs to reach the houses on the floor above. I marvelled at the patience and good humour of so many of those who lived in them, though there were those who couldn't stand the cramped conditions and spent their evenings, or some of them, in the local pub, or were hooked by the pitch and toss schools, some distance from their back doors. The more I came to understand the conditions in which those, almost across the road from my own manse and house, were being asked to live, the more I realised that it was profoundly wrong, especially as so many urgent repairs required to be done. Some phrases of George MacLeod came to my mind–for I had sat at his feet in 1948 in Iona, and later, and I now found myself in one of those parishes in Scotland in which he was taking a particular interest–The Church must show to others an "Incarnational Faith", she must not just talk about the love of Christ, but clearly reveal this love in acts. Yet "Love in practice" he used to say, quoting Dostoevsky, "is a harsh and terrible thing compared to love in dreams". How were the people of 'The Blocks' to be loved and cared for in a way that their appalling housing conditions might be immensely improved? But another quote of MacLeod's entered my mind; "Christianity begins in mysticism and ends in politics". Could this be a possible way of helping the neighbours of 'The Blocks'? At this point I was given a further kick to do more about this by one of those often regarded as an enemy of the Church, though I had already been given cause in Fallin to see their positive side. One communist heard of what he interpreted as an attack by me on communists, and he wrote me a letter which revealed the passion of the communist to change the social conditions of the people:

"Sir, I note the attack on communists in the last issue of your parish magazine, and wonder how you who live figuratively speaking, in an ivory tower completely divorced from the millions of people who toil for their bread, have the temerity . . . where is Christianity's challenge to slums, overcrowded living conditions, and wars, each one bloodier than the last? Your reference to gamblers in the village recalls to my mind one of Dr Hewlett Johnstone's books, in which he advises people who deplore the tastes and lack of culture in working folk, to open the door to better things . . ."

That letter was both a rebuke to me and a challenge to take some action about 'The Blocks.' There was clearly a need for better dialogue between the Church and the communists, and not least between myself and one of their number. I did live in what was formerly the Mission House, and I had no doubt had a much easier life in earlier days than my communist brother who wrote the letter. Yet I and the folk of Fallin Church were also 'workers' concerned for the well being of others in the community, not least for all whose homes were in 'The Blocks', in which, it must be said now, were many very good people who kept beautiful homes, despite the needs and the difficulties of their environment.

But how to engage in politics in order to bring about some radical change in 'The Blocks'? The whole issue was raised in the Kirk Session, and a letter went from the Session Clerk to the Council, telling them of the urgent need to take remedial action about so many of 'The Blocks' houses. There came back a letter telling us that the job of a Kirk Session was to deal with spiritual matters, and that the Council had so many other matters requiring their immediate attention that they could not promise anything in regard to 'The Blocks' of Fallin. So it was clear that without a struggle little was going to be done. However another step was decided: people from the Parish Church would go round 'The Blocks' and take a note of all outstanding and very urgent repairs eg where the roof was leaking badly, or the toilet out of use, or the fire bars in the grate no longer adequate, or health-destroying damp at work, or some house hopelessly overcrowded, or some long standing deprivation unattended. When this was done, the Fallin Headmaster was a great help, and there was a meeting arranged with Council representatives. They still said that they could not help in the urgent way we wished. So finally it was only when it was pointed out that all the urgent repairs would be given to the papers, that there were sent down to 'The Blocks' from the Council some workmen to begin attending to urgent repairs.

It is also pertinent to note here that a hectic debate often went on in the housing committee as to who was to get the next available council house. The Councillor for Fallin, and the Headmaster and some of the community served on this, and as Minister of the Parish, I was also asked to become a member.

For the Council, it appeared that spiritual concerns were not material concerns. That was certainly not the soldiers view. To have a spiritual concern for the soldier included concern for his body, and for where he was housed, and for his clothes and food, and pay, and for the state of all he is given. In writing about 'The Soldiers Return' George MacLeod rightly said - "An Incarnational Faith" is "concerned with the total lives of men".[2] He also rightly said "we claim material considerations are spiritual concerns, and involvement in them the condition of our spirits growing towards perfection; if only because our spirits are incarnate".[3] If it was right to reach out to the housing issue, it was surely also right to go to the Pit, for that was where so many of the men in the Community and Church did their work. If the Fallin housing opened my eyes, so also did the difficult conditions in which men worked in their Pit. It was not hard to be taken down and shown the seams of coal where the work was being done. It was not easy, in wartime, to sit in water in a trench for some days, I thought it much worse to extract coal from a seam, only two to three feet high, in some places. Yet so often those who worked there had a great sense of humour, and though they sometimes had rows with one another, on the whole they were comrades and friends, sharing the same work and danger. It was indeed a privilege for me to be shown where they worked and how they worked.

Some of the most loyal and steadfast elders on the Kirk Session of Fallin Church were those who worked at the coal face as well as on the surface. I felt how fortunate I had been to know and be minister to such people, one or two of whom were on the Union committee, and who at times entered into a strong debate (or battle!) with equally convinced communist fellow workers! Once or twice George MacLeod came himself to speak with the miners. He said the same to them with regards to the Cross as he had said to the students long ago in the Men's Union in Edinburgh University in 1939; "You were made for a cross. Take it into the pits and give yourselves to your brothers there". That was difficult to take and it caused a big debate, for what did he mean? Did he mean; "take upon yourselves the cause of the sick who often seemed to be put on the dole when the coal dust had ruined their lungs? Did he mean; "fight for better wages?" Did he mean; "go and help another group when you find yourself finishing early?". "Would that not mean you weren't being asked to do enough work in your section?" But George wanted to discuss all these things, for this was what Christianity was about. They believed in the Resurrection, did they not? The more they gave their lives away in costly sacrificial love, the more life, abundant life, they would each have and the more they would be used to bring it to others. The risen Christ who comes to us always shows us the challenge of his Cross. Christ was for them, not against them, and he came to them not to condemn but to save. The miners gave him, I thought, a rewarding night, though they felt he had a mighty poor car, as they pushed him up the village street to get it started as he left us!

3. The Challenge of Events -

A Storm and a Tragedy and Days of Celebration

Every Parish has, sooner or later, dark days as well as joyful ones. I had not been long Minister of Fallin Church before great damage was done in the community by a powerful wind storm. The Church House was damaged as were a number of houses, but, not least, the Church itself suffered the cruel blow of losing the cross on its gable end. This was seen in one way as God's judgement upon Minister and people, yet as we looked at that cross lying on the ground in front of the entrance to the Church, it was also a call to action. So I wrote in the Church magazine: "We must take up our Cross–it will be a costly business, even lifting up this stone one. Many of you will rejoice when your chimney stacks are repaired, as I shall, but I'll also be glad to see the Church cross taken up and set in its place once more". After some months this stone cross was rebuilt and lifted up to the gable end, but what about other crosses which had to be raised and lifted high by the membership in Fallin Church? For the Cross stood for the love that reached out from Jesus to all the world. Did not Jesus Christ say: "And I, if I be lifted up will draw all men unto me". Was it not time to visit those who were not members of any church? Any Parish mission or message of friendship to a parish community cannot be done in a short time. It needs thought and prayer and planning. However this was done and eventually a visitation of the Parish, as distinct from the congregation, was carried out. Elders and some congregational members did the work, and on the whole they received a kind welcome. So towards the end of 1953 I was able to write in the Parish Magazine: "I am grateful, as are the Kirk Session, for the generous welcome we received at the homes of the people, and I have been encouraged by the large number of people who have said that they wish to become members of the Parish Church".

And yet there were critics of this reaching out to those not members of the Church: "Not everyone in your first large class often attend now the services (and some of these don't work on Sundays!)". In so far as this was due to lack of pastoral care on the part of the Minister or elder or church member, we asked forgiveness.

At any rate 54 members of the Parish attended this Communicants' Class, and an attempt was made to have more than the Minister conducting it. I wrote: "I want to acknowledge openly my debt to four elders who helped me with the conduct of the lessons . . . many of the communicants have been glad of the opportunity given in the group of asking questions, and of hearing what other members of the groups have had to say. More than one of the communicants have expressed appreciation of what the elders have said. I also wish to express my gratitude to the members of the class for their faithful attendance over the three month period".

When anyone is engaged in sowing the seed of the Word it is quickly realised that much seed is lost, but that there is a harvest–the good fruit of faith and love and hope is forth coming. New leaders were provided for Fallin Church and Church House, and I believe there were new lives lived in our communities of Fallin and Throsk.

I have only time to mention one of some tragedies that happened in the Parish when I was Minister. One of the houses in Fallin went on fire, and there came the day that the coffins of four children lay in the Church. Once more I wished I had more experience in dealing with such an appalling event, and that I could have given comfort to that home in a better way. But there was no doubt about the sympathy of the community and of many people beyond it, when an appeal was launched to help this family there was opened up a huge spring of financial generosity. And if the people of the Parish and congregation were very kind in relation to a perceived need in the community, they had shown themselves to be the same when they came to realise the needs of the Church at home and abroad. A free will offering scheme was begun in the Church and it was not long before an astonishing amount of money was flowing in to the Treasurer.

Another way in which the community expressed its generosity was in the tremendous support given to the Youth Revues. These were chiefly the work of the Club Leader–Herbert Christie, though he would have been the first to acknowledge the part played in them by so many gifted young people. The Revues were held usually in the Miners' Welfare Hall, Fallin, for most evenings in a week, and they included an opening chorus, and much excellent singing and skits and sketches. These Revues gave performances beyond Fallin, and they were in aid of the Presbytery and of the Pearce Institute, Govan. In 1954 the Youth Revue by the members of the Church House, Fallin, was in the Little Theatre in Stirling, and was again very well supported.

I am glad to remember that there were far more days of celebration in Fallin Parish Church and community than sad days. But there are different kinds of celebration–personal and family, church, and community. I cannot remember discussing this issue in all these spheres of activity, but I was very much aware that our celebrations were under judgement. To celebrate another person means to make room for them, to listen to them and to rejoice with them in some way that would affirm them.

I and others came to realise the inadequacy of some of our Church celebrations. They showed poor gratitude or thanksgiving for grace, for the undeserved goodness of God in creation and in redemption. I felt that there was usually genuine celebrations when our people came to Fallin Church for a baptism or for a marriage. They were thankful for the gifts of God, at such a time, in the birth of a child or in the wonder of their life partners to whom they had been led.

But I did not always feel that all who came to the Sunday Services were filled with joyful thanksgiving for all the gifts of God in creation and in Christ, and I particularly did not sense this, when the congregation celebrated Holy Communion or the Lord's Supper. As Minister I felt under the judgement of God for this though I tried to use the right forms suggested in the Book of Common Order 1940. I was reminded of what had been said to me at my Induction and Ordination: "having a form of godliness, but denying the power thereof; from such turn away" (AV) or, "They will maintain a facade of 'religion' but their conduct will deny its validity. You must keep clear of people like this" (Phillips). But was this really where the Minister and membership of Fallin Church belonged? A Service of Holy Communion, being at the Lord's Table, was a solemn occasion, a time for the recognition of sin and for confession and for forgiveness, a time when people were asked to see how far away their lives were from Jesus and from their Father and from one another. Certainly all that was right, but the Lord's table was meant to be a feast, a place where the returning sinner found an amazing acceptance, and was affirmed once more as the Father's son or daughter, a place too where he was trusted yet again to do the Father's will in the family and in the world. I was helped to see this joyful side of the Lord's Table when once or twice I managed to go to Iona from Fallin. The Abbey was filled with so many young people, the singing was strong and uplifting, and if those who came forward towards the Table saw the poverty of their own hearts and lives in terms of faith and hope and love, they also were lifted up to see the Risen Christ. They should indeed have clean hands and a pure heart, but Christ was there to enter them. He not only willed to enter their minds with his Word, but also their lives, by the bread and the wine, with his life. This was the way Jesus Christ had planned to renew his people, to achieve the At-one-ment with himself and the Father and all other worshippers; this was the way all who went to Communion were to be made in the words of the Liturgy "very members incorporate in the mystical body of thy Son, the blessed company of all faithful people and also heirs through hope of thy everlasting Kingdom" (BCO 1940). It could be appropriate here to say that George MacLeod had huge numbers of young people visiting Iona in the 1950s but he wasn't too busy, one time I was there, to ask me one evening about 11 pm to go to the Abbey with him in order that he might pray for my family and for all I was seeking to do in Fallin with my people for the advancement of Christ's Kingdom. This action was typical of the caring identifying concern George had for a young minister and his congregation. I have not forgotten it.

What happened in the Abbey of Iona that evening raised in my mind ministerial priorities in Fallin Church and where prayer and scripture stood among these. I was much impressed again by the fact that a Minister did not read all the lessons in the Abbey services nor say all the prayers. I had tried to grapple with the reality of prayer in the homes of the people and their words and talk had given substance to the prayers which I had offered. However I had not given opportunity for any who wished, to be at a prayer meeting, prior to the Sunday Service or on a week night. I now started such a prayer meeting, though only a few people ever came to it. I also altered the responsive Iona Morning Service so that the members of the Youth Fellowship and any older people who wished to come on Sunday might have the chance of corporate prayer, on occasions led by a young man or woman. There were also opportunities given to have the lessons read by someone other than the Minister. Many people in the congregation did not wish to see the way of worship changed; a monological order of Morning Service suited them, though they never objected to the corporate nature of the praise. All this reminded me of George MacLeod's story of a town where each denomination had its buildings in the most appropriate place: The

Salvation Army was near the fire station, the Wesleyan church near the gas works; the Anglican beside the Drapery Store–while the Presbyterian Church was correctly placed between the ice house and the bank! I was not so sure about Fallin Church being near the bank but it sometimes seemed very near the ice house–so many of us seemed frozen in our habits of prayer and scripture. It was very hard to pray together in a different way, or to open the Bible seeing it as an exciting unexplored country where great treasure was to be found. About this time I discovered William Barclay's *Daily Bible Studies* and sought to encourage members of the congregation to use these as aids to understanding the Bible.

I must pass on to say a brief word about community celebrations. Certain events had been enjoyed long before I became Minister and were being continued. The men of the village on Saturdays used to go to watch the Fallin Church Football Team, or Stirling Albion or the Glasgow Rangers. There was also, in the summer, cricket in Throsk in which I was very happy to share. There were the usual community dances, sales of work, but most evenings in Church House there was the celebration of some group of young people from Fallin and Throsk.

The spirituality of a congregation can so easily be misunderstood; it does not mean that those who belong to it, or come into it, have to cut themselves off from community life. On the contrary, commitment to Christ within the congregational fellowship means so very often for many of its people the celebration of and making time and room for, the young of the community. "Men erroneously imagine that 'to go mystical' is to turn away from the affairs of this world. They read that they "must be born again", and imagine it means goodbye to the interests of this world's family".[4] At any rate in Fallin Church and community there were many who were willing to work together and to give time to cherishing and leading the young people.

At one time a Church House Football Team was picked, and it played in the Senior League of the Stirlingshire Union of Boys' Clubs. It was said that they learned about the meaning of the Atonement on the football field, being tripped up but not tripping others in return!

Because we believed that the life Christ came to give, was conveyed not only by words but by the common life, the togetherness both of the Church Bible Class and Sunday School, and of some of the clubs in Church House was strengthened by these groups having their own summer camps–tents and groundsheets etc being made available by a grant from the Church House Trust. These camps operated well in the last year of my Ministry in Fallin, and I have clear memories of three camps near Balquidder–of a weekend Bible Class Camp where the Session Clerk and some other elders gave invaluable help; also of a Club Camp for a week which was also much enjoyed; and yet again of a Sunday School Camp later on in August where the Sunday School Superintendent and some of the teachers did a magnificent job and were hosts with the children to a Parents' Day, when 60-70 of them visited the camp.

Too little perhaps has been said about Fallin Church. It was often admired by visitors, though it was a mission Church from the Parish Church of Bannockburn, planted in Fallin early in the 20th Century. The pews were of pitch pine and the roof had beautiful beams. In addition there were three powerful symbols below the central pulpit–a very lovely carved cross, a Communion Table, and an open Bible. The Cross was empty and spoke of the Christ who had conquered there and continued his saving reconciling work in the members of the Church and in the world. The Communion Table spoke of the family in heaven and on earth who came to be present there, and who were fed by the bread and the wine, Christ's body and blood, which were taken into the lives of that family circle, teaching and empowering them to be one with Christ and each other, and enabling them to go out, sanctified and renewed, to serve others in Christ's name in the world. And the Bible reminded all who came to the Church that Christ could also encounter them in his read or spoken Word as well as in grace materialised in the bread and wine, and in the corporate life of all who had become men and women 'in Christ' or within his Kingdom.

During the last years as Minister of Fallin it had been felt that it was time to increase the beauty and to improve the lighting of the Church, and to open up the space around the Communion Table. This renovation of the Church cost about £620, and covered the painting of the vestibule and of the Church itself, the re-wiring of it and the installation of new lanterns, the removal of the choir rail and the laying of a carpet at the front. A Morning Service on the 30th September, 1956 marked the re-opening of the Church for public worship. The preacher was the Revd Chalmers Grant of Dunblane Cathedral. He dedicated three new pulpit falls at the start of the service, and took as his text 1 Timothy 3 v15 where are these words: "the Church of the living God, the pillar and ground of the truth". Mr Grant said that it was through the Church that God's truth came into the world. This truth included the vision of the true life as found in the service of others, the knowledge of man or woman as the child of God, whose true character could be shaped here on earth, and the knowledge of God, through Jesus Christ, incarnate crucified and risen, as the Father over all in joy and in sorrow, in prosperity and in suffering. The Church as congregation could have a powerful effect for good on the life of a community, but it also had real significance for the life of each individual. It was very hard to maintain the Christian life apart from the fellowship of the Church. Further, despite her faults, the Church of God is an anvil that has worn out many hammers, and will outlast all her critics. She will have an enduring significance for the world as for the individual for she is not man's creation, but the Church of the living God, the place of his abiding in Christ, and has been and is and will be the pillar and ground of his truth.

4. A New Sphere of Ministry

In the early spring or early summer of 1956 I received a letter asking me to become one of the Secretaries of the Student Christian Movement in Scotland, and to be the organiser, under instructions from the S.C.M. headquarters in London, of the Quadrennial Conference, or Congress, planned for 1958 in Edinburgh. Apart from one other invitation to consider going as a missionary teacher to West Africa, I had no other suggestion of a new job, while Minister in Fallin. This S.C.M. post seemed initially an unsuitable one. By this time I had two children, Elizabeth and Alison, under school age, and I had envisaged them going to Fallin School. Margot, my wife, also had helped a Stirling doctor in a medical practice there, as well as taking the First Aid class for miners from Fallin. She had also a regular meeting with the ladies of the Women's group in the Church, and had got to know well some of the younger girls, and had gone with them one year to Iona. Further I had accepted, and enjoyed the work of being Padre to the local T A Battalion of the 7th Argyll and Sutherland Highlanders, which meant two weeks at an Army Camp each year as well as other things. Yet again it seemed unwise to move out of the Parish Ministry to work solely with students, and perhaps with some of their teachers. Would there be a way back again into the Ministry in the parish in the Church of Scotland? And what about housing, for there would be no manse provided? When I was trying to decide what to do, another letter came, this time from John Baillie asking me to accept this new work. This made me consider the possible change of job in a more serious way. I came to see that in the local S.C.M. branches and in S.C.M. Conferences very interesting ecumenical and international doors could be opened which would mean entering into a new world of thought and relationships. One other positive point came to me that my future work would be done, to a considerable extent, with small groups, and I remembered how much, in the time prior to Army call up, I had benefited from being a listener in these, both to words said, and to the prayers offered. And so eventually we felt it was right to accept the offered post and leave the Ministry of the Parish Church in Fallin and Throsk, and move to a house which would be forthcoming somewhere in Edinburgh. We were reminded of the biblical character who "went out not knowing whither he went".

Every Minister knows the difficulty of leaving his first Parish, especially if the people of that congregation and community have been good to him, which was very much the way it had been in my case. I was leaving men and women, many of whom had become happy companions–with some of them I still keep in touch, for example with my Session Clerk–a greatly appreciated elder and valued friend. These elders and members of Fallin Church had helped me grow in Christian faith and in relationships. So many of them had been very generous to my immaturity and had encouraged me to be better at leading worship and in loving the people, and I can see now that in future parishes I made some progress in these regards. For example, I was later to read Professor John McIntyre's most rewarding book *On The Love of God*, and came to recognise that love must be at the heart of every Christian ministry, and indeed must be at the heart of every Christian life, for the love of God is at the centre of the Gospel. John McIntyre wrote "First of all, we have to affirm what no Christian Church dare ever forget that the love of God as made known to man in the life, death and resurrection of Jesus Christ is the whole content, sum and substance of the Gospel. This love must be made manifest, whenever the Gospel is preached or the Sacraments of that same Gospel celebrated. The love of God is what the Gospel is about. It is, then, the whole content of our faith, as it is its whole object. It is the entire basis of our hope in the life that lies beyond this life into which that same Christ is already entered as our forerunner. It is our consolation for that same reason when this life becomes emptied by the departure of our dear ones to be with Christ in glory. This love is the context, then, within which our life is daily led in this world. In love were we created, by love were we redeemed; through love will we be ultimately sanctified".[5]

Margot and I and the children had received much of this love of God in Fallin Church and Community, and we had tried to share it with them. It was into the hands of this love that we gave those we were leaving; it was also in this same love of God–forgiving, prevenient, and providing–that we were trusting, as we set out for whatever was in store for us in the Student Christian Movement in Edinburgh and Glasgow and beyond.

Notes

1.   W Manson - 'The Gospel of Luke' - Hodder and Stoughton - London - pp89-90.
2.   G F MacLeod - 'We Shall Rebuild' - The Iona Community - Glasgow - p72.
3.   Ibid - p73.
4.   Ibid - p53.
5.   J McIntyre - 'On The Love of God' - Collins - London - pp11-12.

Chapter VI

The Student Christian Movement Years

1. Grappling with the SCM Staff Secretary's Task

Had I known the shock that awaited myself and my family in Edinburgh after I had left the Parish Ministry in Fallin Church, I might well have stayed where I was! It took much longer than I had thought to find a house in the University area; eventually, when one was made available with the help of the University authorities, it needed much work there before a family could occupy it. So the only way, at that time, we could quickly find an Edinburgh home was to ask if we could return to my parents' house in the suburb of Colinton, and stay there with our two children–Elizabeth, now over three, and Alison not yet one. My parents were very understanding and kind and took us in, until the necessary work in 28 Buccleuch Place, Edinburgh, our future home, was finished.

I remember being very unhappy at this stage, and much concerned about when Margot and the family would be given entrance to the house, and about how they could survive in it. The Manse in Fallin had certainly been no palace, despite the communist parishioner's description of it, but it had proved a suitable family home, and we soon saw we had good friends around us. I have to admit also that I was anxious about the new job, for what exactly was it, and would I really be able to do it? It would certainly mean a great deal more than the usual SCM Staff Secretary's work, for I would be acting also under the instructions of the General Secretary in Annandale, London, the SCM headquarters of Great Britain and Ireland. I was further aware that the Student Congress for about 2,000 students and staff from the British SCM and from overseas, had been planned for April, 1958, and my appointment in Edinburgh, the location of The Congress, had to do with arrangements for this. Anyhow Niebuhr's phrase from USA days came back to me: "anxiety is the pre-condition of sin" and I remember thinking I was projecting myself into the future, and becoming anxious about my place in it, as well as the family's; whether I also recalled then the necessity for "holding fast to faith and a good conscience" I cannot be sure.

To return to 28 Buccleuch Place, I remember the General Secretary of the SCM (London based), Philip Lee-Woolf–a very gracious colleague–saying to me: "Don't make the flat too Ritzian!" But this certainly wasn't done as the black zinc bath in the ancient bathroom was not replaced, and the large new copper boiler was set in the kitchen, unlagged, and in full view of all! In January, '57 we at last managed to enter the house, and Margot set about cleaning it up. I recall her down on her knees scrubbing the floors they were so dirty. I should have given her much more help then, but, a poor excuse–I was overwhelmed by the demands of the new job, there were so many people to see, and so many places to visit in Edinburgh and Glasgow Universities, SCM branches there, as well as smaller ones in the Commercial and Art Colleges. In addition the Scottish Council as well as the General Council London meetings had to be thought about, and attended from time to time.

One of my first tasks was to get to know who were the student leaders in the University branches. I soon met them, and realised how fortunate I was in having so many friendly and reliable young people in the leadership in both branches–later on I found out that some of them had very radical views, not least about the Church and its ways of worship! These men and women had shouldered responsibility in their committees–as Presidents, Secretaries, Study Secretaries, Treasurers as well as Prayer, Overseas, and Magazine Secretaries. The Spring and Summer Term programmes of 1957 had already been planned, and I was soon taught what meetings lay ahead and what study groups were continuing or were probable; these were concerned with contemporary issues, worldly or ecclesiastical. My predecessor, as Scottish Secretary, was the Revd Andrew Morton, and because of his thoughtful and very conscientious work, the University branches were in good heart, not least the Glasgow University branch. If in this Spring Term I was discovering friends in the SCM branches, it is appropriate to mention briefly here that my wife also had found support and friendship. In the summers of 1957-59 Margot was able to take the children into George Square Gardens, and there she could relax with wives and mothers who were at a similar married stage; she found the philosophising of some of the garden wives very stimulating!

Although I had been a member of SCM in 1939-41 and in 1946-49, I had to remind myself in the late 1950s of the SCM Constitution. A few years before I began as a Staff Secretary of the SCM this 'aim and basis' had been adopted: "The Student Christian Movement is a fellowship of students which seeks to acknowledge, or to lead others to acknowledge, God through Jesus Christ in the power of the Holy Spirit. It works for the understanding and acceptance, in the thought and life of college and university, of the lordship of Christ over the whole life of mankind. It seeks the extension, unity, and renewal of the Church throughout the world, and calls students to bear witness as responsible members of a particular church, in personal commitment to Jesus Christ as their Saviour and Lord" (from an SCM document adopted in 1950). Because SCM is a searching group for the truth about God, all seekers are welcome, both Christians and non Christians.

What methodology could be used to support such a constitutional purpose of the SCM? In the parish I had had the visitation of the homes of the people as one of my priorities, but so many Edinburgh and Glasgow students did not even stay within their cities. However it came home to me that an SCM Staff Secretary could have even more help than elders gave a minister, for in making and keeping contact with the members of a university, or college, he could have the huge assistance of the students themselves, who not only frequently worked or played games together, but so often lived with one another in University residences or in private accommodation. I discovered again what I'd forgotten that many students were very good, even enthusiastic about inviting others to come to the SCM activities; they also were sometimes better at bringing along their friends to branch meetings or study groups or conferences. On this issue of mission, the SCM Staff Secretary could in some places have a low profile, though he could always be the encourager of the students to do this vital work.

And if the methodology of contacting and reaching out to students was student led, it was study directed. I had myself benefited from being addressed by fellow students in a SCM study group in 1939–41, and this same method had worked even in the Revd Robert Mackie's day in the early 1930s, when he was General Secretary of the British SCM.

As Nansie Blackie has written in her excellent portrait of him called *In Love and In Laughter*: . . . "Robert remained firmly convinced that the appropriate methodology for a student movement was the study group, as a valid expression of its primary vocation". She then quoted Robert Mackie's own words: "Right action springs from true thinking, and it is one of our principal concerns to reset study in the centre of our work as the primary organised means whereby our evangelistic task is carried out".[1] Again and again the study group was the place where God spoke through persons, and where new insights and understandings were given. Especially was this so when discussion was based on a printed or duplicated study outline of a Bible book or Epistle or of a contemporary issue, such as 'Politics' or 'What is a Good Student?' or 'The Christian in the University'. "The SCM study group", the Editor of the SCM Press wrote, "is thus, to many, the focus which brings out the true meaning of all student life".[2] At any rate these groups were so often the places where students got time to discover the Christian faith or life among themselves through many blunt questions and sharp answers. This was Robert Mackie's discovery also when he wrote in *One man's experience of the SCM*: "In the ordinary world the Church - in some form or other - did religion . . . but here in the student world some of us found that we had to do religion for ourselves and find our way into a developing faith with the help of our friends . . . we knew that nothing human was foreign to the Gospel".[3]

Another very important field of work and witness for the Staff Secretary was that of Christian worship and prayer. Here again there was a big difference from that of the Parish Church, for the leadership was provided by the students. Not only was there a student Prayer Secretary within each SCM branch but prayers there were student led, and were often superbly surprising as well as orthodox with different words! The nature of these deeply meaningful and moving prayers remained with me as a powerful impetus to attempt to change the normal monological Sunday worship of the Church of Scotland in the Parish Church, to which I was eventually called after the SCM years were over. It was really from this spring of refreshing water that there came a motion put by me in Edinburgh Presbytery in relation to the Doctrine of Reformed Worship. This led, contrary to the desires of some senior ministers, to the formation of a Special Committee of the Presbytery, and out of this came a major General Assembly consideration, of "The Doctrine and Practice of Public Worship in The Reformed Church". At a later time, in the 1980s, a different kind of Sunday Morning worship was introduced in St Magnus Cathedral. But more of this later.

It should not be thought that students were flung into the leadership of Christian worship without any training. Apart from help given by senior students, or by the Prayer Secretary, or by the SCM Staff Secretary, or from the student's own experience within a particular denomination, there was available the small book called *Student Prayer*, a reprint of which came out in 1957, and which contained many valuable suggestions as to how the Bible could be used in worship, and which gave selections of prayers for different needs and occasions. In addition to this, there was a pamphlet from Annandale, London, called *The Leadership of Corporate Prayer,* which was also a good resource for leading branch prayers. The more I was able to listen to what the students were saying about the Church or the Faith or the World, the more I was able, at least on occasion, to help them achieve what they often had the capacity to do in terms of leadership of corporate worship, and so to become more open to the New Humanity of Jesus Christ, to his life of prayer as of truth and love.

One further field of the SCM Secretary's work is noteworthy: helping students to reach out to where good teaching is being given. The good shepherd leads the sheep to where they are able to feed themselves on good grass. Such teaching is given through the written word as well as the spoken. The Revd David L Edwards, the Associate Secretary in my time, and later an Editor of SCM Press wrote: "The SCM staff has come to be a body of teachers, very frequently addressing or advising the branches".[4] But such teaching as I've said often took written form, in study outlines (biblical and of other kinds) or conference booklets, but also in *The Student Movement*, and in *The Student World*, magazine of The World Student Christian Federation and not least in the many stimulating books of the SCM Press. However it was particularly in *The Student Movement* the magazine of the SCM of Great Britain and Ireland that good teaching was given to the students on a wide variety of subjects, in relation both to the Church and world.

Before passing on to the specific work of preparing for the Congress of 1958, something must be said of how each SCM Staff Secretary had to direct the thought of a Branch, with the help of its main office bearers, to what was going on beyond its own borders. One of the best ways of doing this was to draw attention to the work of the World Student Christian Federation. The SCM structure helped here for there was recommended a Universal Day of Prayer to all branches in the Northern hemisphere of the WSCF; this was on behalf of all students of the world, and for the work of the Federation. Also in the Spring Term branches were encouraged to hold a Federation Week, when by means of speakers or bookstalls or films, information and education could be given about the Federation's work. Opportunities could also be given for financial giving by students–in their branch or college or university. Further, one of the best ways to learn about the WSCF was to listen to an overseas chaplain, or to hear from their staff from Geneva, or in the *Federation* copy of the Student Movement, or in their magazine *The Student World*, but not least opportunity was there to listen to what was said about the Federation at a Council or Conference or Congress. And this brings us to the preparations for, and the programme of the Congress of 1958.

2. The Edinburgh Congress, 1958 - Theme: 'Life For The World'

In the 1958 Congress Handbook there is written this question: "What makes a large conference <u>Christian?</u> One thing only–prayer. We must lift up every part of this Congress in prayer. We must see to it that prayer is right at the centre of the Edinburgh programme". I believe that this was to a large extent done, both in the detailed prayers in preparation for all the speakers and for the leaders and members of the Commissions and Area Groups, and through the 'Prayer For The Congress' which ran like this: "O God our Father, who hast given thy Son, our Saviour Jesus Christ, that the world through him might have abundant life, we ask for thy blessing on our Congress. Guide with thy Holy Spirit all who shall speak, lead or administer. Grant that all whom thou dost bid to come may hear thy command, and coming may surely know thy purpose for their lives. Show us thy Church, and rebuke our complacency; show us thy world, and shame our narrowness. Show us our neighbours, and show us thy Son, who died and rose for all; who now liveth and reigneth with thee and the Holy Spirit, one God, for ever. Amen". Besides what has been mentioned, there were important detailed prayers for all who administered the Congress, and not least that "The risen Christ may be known in the worship and fellowship of the Congress".

Further preparation for this Congress was made in certain written documents, particularly in the Introduction to the Congress Handbook, where it was pointed out that the character of the Congress was both interdenominational and international, and that many leaders from the World Student Christian Federation would be present, as well as students from different countries, not forgetting a good number of those studying in British universities and colleges. *Hard Facts*, the Congress Study Book by John Lawrence, was another way to help Congress participants prepare for the event, for it sought to open all eyes to the tough world in which student lives were set. As the Congress Handbook puts it: "one of our chief aims in this Congress is to see how a revolution is irresistibly sweeping the world . . . a revolution offering a new abundance of life to the hitherto underprivileged countries and the hitherto nameless masses. . . In the name of the Christ who was a carpenter and healer, we say 'Yes' to it. At the same time there are new stresses and fears involved in existence in the twentieth century, and it is perhaps the vocation of Europe to be aware of them; for what does abundance of life mean for most people in a modern industrial city–in a continent with a great mushroom cloud hovering over it?" But not least significant in the written preparation for this 1958 Congress was what was written in the Editorials and Articles of *The Student Movement* the magazine of the Student Christian Movement. Here is an example of what was written in one Editorial just prior to the start of the Congress in an attempt to clarify what was its object. The writer said that the foundation of the SCM and the WSCF were to be found in "the affirmations and in the promises of God". He did not mention these in complete detail, but he wrote: "There is no point in holding a Christian Congress unless it makes an affirmation. Life for the World is such an affirmation, and the title makes it plain that the affirmation refers not only to the Church, nor yet to 'little Britain', but to the world . . . both the tradition of the British SCM and the present concern of the WSCF with 'The life and mission of the Church' recall us to our foundations; and these are none other but the affirmations and promises of God".[5] Then the Editor continued: "St Paul says of Jesus Christ in II Cor 1 v 20 that 'however many are the promises of God, in him is Yes'–the affirmation incarnate; and St John's conclusion is that 'These things are written that you may believe that Jesus Christ is the Son of God, and that believing you may have life in his name': To take such affirmations out of the realm of easy speeches and pulpit rhetoric–to appropriate them as realities for ourselves in the midst of the modern world: that, roughly speaking, is the object of the Edinburgh Congress, and it is not a modest object. We have no hope whatever of attaining it unless the Holy Spirit himself goes before us". The writer of these words was Pat Rodger, the SCM Study Secretary and the Editor of the *Student Movement* in those days; he later became the Bishop of Oxford. One further quote from what he wrote is worth making again in relation to the Holy Spirit and to a reaction to it: "He is the Spirit of Christ–his area of love is no less (ie he is concerned with the redemption of the world), and he gives life as Christ gives it and not otherwise".[6] Yet Pat recognised that such courage is very hard for so many people to accept: "But the last thing that they would think is that this life comes from Jesus Christ or that his Church is here to mediate it to them. On the contrary, their view is that Christianity is one of the world's greatest restrictive practices, to be classed with other religions–by definition 'things which bind' - by Marxists or by our so called humanists".[6] The Editorial went on to speak of the Christian countries challenge which asks the question 'what is man?', and raised the further question whether students and others "have paused long enough to think about it". Had they thought about Augustine's words? "Thou, O Lord, hast made us for thyself, and our heart can find no rest until it rest in Thee".

Preparation for the 1958 Congress were made in many other ways through the setting up, under direction from the SCM London headquarters of certain hard working committees, especially the financial committee (Chairman–Mr Eric Ivory; Hon Treasurer–Mr W F G Lord and the hospitality committee (Conveners–Her Grace The Duchess of Hamilton: Lady Clyde, and Lady Philip). In addition, arrangements had to be made for where groups of participants (some of them) were to be accommodated, where Congress members could have meals, for the Congress

Dramatic Presentations in the Adam House Theatre–two short plays by Charles Williams–'The House by The Stable', and 'Grab and Grace' - and for the Exhibitions in Adam House: "Science Serves Society" (First Floor); Inter Church Aid and Refugee Service (Second floor); and an Art Exhibition which included work by Scotland's four Art Colleges.

It is now time briefly to indicate the Congress Programme following the opening meeting on the evening of 8 April, when the Chairman was the Lord Provost of Edinburgh, and the opening service conducted by the Rt Revd Dr George MacLeod, then Moderator of the General Assembly of the Church of Scotland. There were main talks given each morning, after morning Prayers, also in the McEwan Hall. These were given by Drs D T Niles, W A Visser't Hooft and the Rt Revd Dr George MacLeod.

In addition to being present at these, Congress participants were invited to be present at the Commissions and Area Groups which met in the late morning or afternoon. There it was hoped students would be given the opportunity to learn the difficulties as well as the opportunities before particular professions or areas. Further, in the evenings, besides Evening Prayers, there was a chance as the Handbook put it, "to learn realism from the talks to the Congress by a scientist, an economist, a parish priest from a new housing estate, and by the General Secretary of the WSCF".

It might appear from this brief summary of the Congress Programme that it was a very solemn and serious one, but the Congress was meant to be penetrated by merriment:- "we go to Edinburgh for fun and why not? But we go in Easter week, also to meet him, who is the first and the last and the living one, and who holds in his hands the keys of death and hell".

3. - After the Congress

It is always difficult to assess what a large international Congress has achieved, for about 2,000 students and senior people had attended Edinburgh 1958, but here is part of one reaction, written by a member of the Swedish delegation–Gunnar Hallingberg,[7] after he had heard the Bible studies and the Main Talks, and after he had shared in the Commission and Area Groups. He recorded his gratitude for the hospitality of the British SCM and of the city of Edinburgh, but he also told of how he would never forget the coldness of that spring in the mornings and in the evenings: "Certainly it is somewhat of an adventure to visit Great Britain when the spring is late, and a considerable lot of sportsmanship is required to dress in the mornings . . . The nice fellowship around the fire in late night hours with a cold back and a grilled face is for me a real part of the week at Edinburgh". Gunnar went on to say that Edinburgh '58 had been "extremely well prepared in advance" through *Hard Facts*, the study book, "an ambitious attempt to draw up a real background for the Conference". He also said he thought the study material for the Area Groups and Commissions provided "a comprehensive view of the Christian responsibilities in our world". Yet again he told of how he had been aware of a challenge - "perhaps for many of us a vocation". He had found in the Revd Dr D T Niles talk "an eastern immediacy" connected with "intellectual honesty". He would always remember Niles' words: "Christ is risen and we have come to meet Him in Edinburgh because He can be met, because He is alive on earth". In relation to Dr Visser't Hooft's address on "Life Through The Church", Gunnar thought he had made a "humble defence of the Church", where on a world scale, he told the students that still in their "generation they could see the Holy Spirit powerfully at work". There was no denigration of Christ's Church by one of its committed leaders! In relation to Dr G F MacLeod's words on a 'A Dying And Rising Life' "he had heard the call to recognise the reign of God over evil, now and in the midst of the modern world and to participate in this".

Gunnar saw in the closing worship in St Giles Cathedral, and no doubt at other times–a vocation to Christian unity: 2,000 delegates had been united there in the prayer:- "The bluntness and prejudice of denominational pride which dims the realisation of our Oneness in Thee, forgive us, O Lord".

Gunnar also was present at the evening talks:- 'Christians and Economic Progress', "The Kingdom of God in a Housing Estate, and "Where is Science Taking Us". A foreigner recognised in those, "familiar problems analysed from a British point of view: for instance, that of economic progress and the failure to relieve community life in our cities and places of work". Gunnar further recorded his joyful appreciation of the exhibitions, dramatic performances and of the concert in the McEwan Hall which "reminded us that Edinburgh also is par excellence a festival city".

It could be thought that after the excitement of the Congress the fire of the British SCM would burn low. Many people would disagree for they would recognise that the fire of God's presence broke out afresh in different places, not only in new thoughts and inspirations in the branches but in the SCM conferences in Swanwick, Derbyshire. Here in July, 1958 there was held the SCM Summer Conference when the main speaker was the Revd Robin Barbour, then Lecturer at New College, Edinburgh. The theme of this Conference was "The School of Christ" and many of those who participated in this found Robin Barbour's talks profoundly stimulating and helpful for understanding and living out the Christian Faith in the Church and in the world. Something of what had been said by Robin on 'Baptism' and 'Holy Communion' was published in *The Student Movement* magazines in December, '58 and in January, '59. They are still well worth reading and pondering.

I would like to pay tribute to so many wonderful friends, both staff, colleagues and students, by whom I was upheld. Those on the London staff included The General Secretary, Philip Lee-Woolf; The Study˙Secretary, Patrick Rodger and The Associate Secretary of SCM, David L Edwards. Not least in Scotland, the Staff Secretary, Miss Mona Ryrie, who was concerned chiefly with SCM branches in Aberdeen and St Andrews–she and the Students in the University branches there are also remembered with gratitude. Jim Wilkie at Council, Hugh Wylie, Douglas

Lamb, Ronald Lawson in the Glasgow SCM and Ian Mackenzie, Abraham Kurien, Tess Tindal, Margaret McDonald and so many others in the Edinburgh SCM come quickly to mind. It was very good to have some contact with most of these, long after SCM days were past. My debt also to those Ministers who were directly involved with the students of Edinburgh University is not forgotten. The Chaplain to the University, then the Revd James Blackie, and the Overseas Chaplain, The Revd Ross Flockhart were constant helpers and wise friends, and they did everything they could to support the work of SCM at the Congress, and in the University.

Entering the SCM from the Parish Church seemed at the time a dangerous and foolish thing for a minister with a young family to do, and initially I felt this, but I learned again that the Risen Lord can go before his people corporately and individually, as well as being beside them in an upholding fellowship. Dr D T Niles whose books I was stimulated to read after the Congress of 1958 called this, "The Previousness of Jesus".[8] He went before Saul and met him on a strange unexpected road when he was travelling to persecute the Christians in Damascus; he went before so many student believers and agnostics and doubters and met them in the strange place called the McEwan Hall in Edinburgh; he spoke there through laymen and ministers to many students and the result was that, for some, Edinburgh '58 was an Easter Congress in which the Congress prayer became real for them, and they were among those who came to know God's purpose for their lives in a new way, and they understood better what it meant to pray "show us thy Church, and rebuke our complacency; show us thy world and shame our narrowness; show us our neighbours, and show us thy Son, who died and rose for all; who now liveth and reigneth with Thee and the Holy Spirit, one God for even. Amen".

I believe that there would be some students moved to a decision about their position re the Church and they would be willing to become learners in it, some indeed active members of it in different denominations. I believe too that other students would decide about work at home or overseas in some of the professions or areas at which they had been looking. I further was delighted to learn before leaving SCM that there were students who felt the call to The Ministry of the Church of Scotland–some kindly asked me to write a reference for them–and I know that since these far off student days, they have given splendid witness to their Lord as Parish Ministers, Lecturers, Missionaries and Teachers and Servants of their people.

Before leaving behind my time with the SCM, it is right to say that so many thought-provoking experiences and encounters have been unmentioned. It was good for me as for many other students and Staff Secretaries, in and after the '58 Congress, to encounter men and women from other Christian Denominations. The ecumenical experience was never far away from the SCM group or branch meeting. Particularly was this so in the Edinburgh University Branch when we were joined by many Anglican Students, and when the Anglican Chaplain to the University, the Revd Bill Nicholls, had much to say to us about Apostolic Succession and the need for episcopal structure and regular Holy Communion in the Church of Jesus Christ.

Many of us then had not heard about the constant need for the negative capability of Keats in relation to our Anglican brothers! However dialogue with the Anglicans and the Romans was a kind of mission which drove Church of Scotland students as well as others back to their ecclesiastical roots and foundation beliefs. Other areas of encounters in the SCM opened doors into the modern novels of the day and into a new world of art and music, as well as into stimulating theological books, often written by those who had no connection with the Protestant Church. It also raised what was to many a difficult issue, how far was Christ present in the lecture rooms of the University, if indeed he was present at the Congress talks in the McEwan Hall? Are the University teachers also priests revealing truth of different kinds?

The SCM also opened the door for some of its members into the hard problem of what a University was seeking to do for those within it. An introduction to this subject was given in Sir Walter Moberley's book *The Crisis in the University*. This book is discussed in a helpful way in Professor J Davis McCaughey's writings in "Christian Obedience in the University"–a study of the life of the SCM of Great Britain and Ireland 1930-1950.

But now my period of work with students and SCM Staff was over in the autumn of 1959 and it was time for me to return to the Parish Ministry with the Church of Scotland.

Notes

1.   N Blackie - 'In Love and in Laughter' - St Andrew Press, Edinburgh - p53.
2.   David L Edwards - 'Movements into Tomorrow' - SCM Press (1960) - p45.
3.   N Blackie Ibid - p15.
4.   D L Edwards - Ibid - p38.
5.   P Rodger - Editorial - 'The Student Movement' - March, 1958 - p2.
6.   P Rodger - Ibid - p3.
7.   Gunnar Hallingberg - Editorial Secretary of the Free SCM of Sweden - 'Edinburgh 1958: An Impression' - 'The Student Movement' - May - 1958.
8.   D T Niles - 'Upon The Earth' - Lutterworth Press, London - p46.

Chapter VII

Ministry in St Thomas' Church, Leith

1. The Manse in Ferry Road

When I left the SCM work in August, '59 I did not think it would be the middle
of 1960 before I had a new ministry in a Parish Church. But I had a good lesson to
learn; a ministerial call can take a long time to come! I tried for several charges in
late '59 and in the early months of 1960 but no call came to me from any
congregation. However I was able to take services in Edinburgh and the surrounding
rural area. I well remember going to such a charge in Berwickshire. It was icy cold
in the vestry and when I mentioned this to the Church Officer, he told me to go and
sit inside the church; the members would soon be coming in two or three cars. He
further said what I'd heard elsewhere: "Remember this Kirk is heated from the
pulpit!". Another help, at least to me, in those uncertain months, was when I was
asked to give extra mural university lectures on the New Testament for some months:
preparing these gave me stimulus and constant interest. Eventually in the early
months of 1960 my name was submitted for St Thomas' Church, Leith–I think the
Revd Denis Duncan, whose father had been an excellent former minister of it, had a
hand in this. I remember taking a service in a Penicuik Church, when the vacancy
committee were present. Thereafter I was asked to be sole nominee, and conducted
services, morning and evening, in St Thomas' Church, and in due course I was
elected to be it's Minister.

I was not entirely thrilled either by the Church as a building nor by the manse
in Ferry Road, but I liked the people of St Thomas' Vacancy Committee and
congregation, in so far as I had got to know them. I was further very grateful for this
call, and to have a new job once more within the Church of Scotland. The Session
Clerk of St Thomas' Church was the church historian in my time as minister, and it
is fitting that he speak about it when I come to deal with the Stewardship Campaign.
I can only say that, without knowing its history, I was not enthusiastic about it's
surface appearance on the inside. No doubt this building had served well large
congregations in the 19th and early 20th century, but it was really a Victorian
preaching station, and seemed ill suited to house the much smaller attending
congregation of the 1960s, even though the membership roll in 1960 was thought to

be over 1300. The interior of the building was in much need of redecoration and of change in terms of the front of the Church, where the organ pipes seemed to dominate the whole space.

A word should be said here about the Manse. This was situated at 148 Ferry Road, and it was to this large house, on three floors, that we moved in May, 1960, my father coming with us. Our son Andrew was born in January, 1960. The Revd Professor W S Tindal whom I had got to know as a friend and teacher at New College and afterwards, came to be the preacher at the first service, and baptised Andrew that day. Elizabeth had been baptised in Fallin Church by the Revd Dr Anderson Nicol of the West Church of St Nicholas, Aberdeen, while Alison was also baptised there by the Revd Robin Richmond, a great friend though a blind minister, but an excellent one, both in his charges in Portpatrick and Stonehaven, with a delightful wife, Elspeth.

I have already mentioned what the Revd Dr D T Niles has called 'The Previousness of Jesus', and we were once more, I believe, to be recipients of this ministry in our move to 148 Ferry Road, Leith. It turned out that the house had a retired minister on one side and a Leith doctor on the other, who had a daughter, and a much younger son about the same age as Alison, our younger daughter. When I met Dr McNair I knew him, but could not remember where, whether in the Army or at University. He reminded me that I had known him at school in Edinburgh. Anyhow the McNairs were very good neighbours, and it was not long before he asked Margot, having discovered she was also a doctor, to join him in his practice. I felt that he was very fortunate to get her, though she had to undergo more training. Life in the manse became more and more hectic as the parish duties increased, and as Margot had to cope with the family in the house as well as cope with the demands on her in this medical practice. Especially was this so when the manse family was extended in different ways: Margot's brother came to stay in our basement while doing a PhD at Edinburgh University, and then we had different people coming to stay with us for short or longer periods. This however was beneficial for us and I trust also for them. Representatives of Africa and India came to be with us. I remember well an African lady with whom we all got on splendidly, to whom, after so many years long ago in Kenya, I tried to speak some Swahili. It was further a great benefit for us to have others in the house, for longer periods. A welcome visitor was Abraham Kurien from South India. He came to recover from bronchitis. He was a distinguished medical student at Edinburgh University and was President, one year, of the University Student Christian Movement. Abraham eventually went to the USA and we still keep in touch and we were delighted when he came to visit us some years ago in Orkney, and it was so good to see him and hear him at a recent gathering of former SCM people in Edinburgh. We had also with us in the house sometimes, people from the Telephone Samaritans–the Chaplain to the University the Revd James Blackie had encouraged me to become a Deputy leader there. I recall one man who stayed with us for a week or less who gave us a fascinating description, at an evening meal, of life in Dartmoor prison. We discovered he had done ten years for robbery with violence and I am ashamed to say that when I gave him his bedroom in our basement, I locked the downstairs door and remembered there were bars on the basement windows!

In addition to all this we had many groups in our manse–Communicant classes, Sunday School teachers, Church District gatherings, as well as a special gathering of Church Leaders to meet the then Moderator of the General Assembly after he had preached at a Communion Service in St Thomas' Church, following its alteration and redecoration in 1965.

2. Deeper Experience of Christian Fellowship Encountered in St Thomas' Church

A new minister coming to a congregation means very often not only new experiences for the congregational members, but new experience of faith and fellowship for the incoming minister. This was what happened to me in my coming to St Thomas' Church. I have to confess that I went to the congregation with a certain anxiety about being able to cope with such a large congregation of over 1300 people, who, as in the West Church of St Nicholas in Aberdeen, were scattered over the town, and in some cases, beyond it. Life in the SCM and elsewhere had taught me that the way God operated, the way the Risen Christ often worked, was again and again in small groups when his truth and love reached out from one person to another. I very much wondered if this could happen in such a large congregation as that of St Thomas' Church. I had a conviction that large numbers were not inevitable partners with grace and fellowship and Christian strength; only when Gideon's army was radically cut down in numbers was it ready to fight God's battle (cf Judges 7). However within the congregation and leadership groups of St Thomas' Church I was in for some creative surprises. Within this congregation of so many members there were indeed places of Christian fellowship and deep caring of one person for another.

After a few Sundays I realised that the Kirk Session–so often despised these days–was one such place. Sunday by Sunday I found myself locked into a fellowship of Christian leaders deeper than I had experienced before. Of course they were not all people completely filled with the risenness of Christ, or able to articulate well the Gospel, but there were many who to some extent, did know and understand God, and who prayed to him as Father, through Christ, their crucified and risen Lord. They also knew that they were recipients of the Holy Spirit, whom they were struggling to obey, in the love and service of other congregational members, and in the world. This Kirk Session always gathered together, before a Service, in the Session Room, prior to going together into the Church at 11 am, or in the evening. At such a time the talk was often about the world, about football matches on the Saturday, whether at Boys' Brigade or professional level; it was also about members of the congregation who had fallen ill, and were in hospital or at home, or about some bereaved family. Then too, prayers were said with Kirk Session and Choir before the start of the Church Service. I soon discovered that there were some Senior Elders, especially, who knew a great deal about the Christian Faith, and whose lives were very committed to the fellowship and mission of the Church: a good number of them gave themselves in splendid time-consuming service to young people, not least in the Boys' Brigade Companies of the Leith Battalion. I can still see them–so many of them, after more than 35 years, men who gave me a new vision of what it meant for the lay person to give his life over to the risen Christ in the Church and in the world: for example George Houston MBE, Session Clerk and BB Captain; Hugh McKenzie, Church Treasurer and BB Officer; James Aitken, a Senior Elder and also a BB Captain; and his brother Tom; John Inglis (FWO Treasurer); William Greig, Clerk to the Congregational Board and at the same time an Elder; Jack McGregor, magazine editor, Elder and BB Officer; Duncan McLachlan MBE, Stewardship Convener and Elder (formerly a Session Clerk in another Leith Congregation). All these, and many more, gave a fruitful example in worship, and a challenging Christian witness and service to the Community.

I am tempted to go on to the Sunday School, describing some of the saintly devoted inspirational figures there, such as Miss Shaw and Miss Aitken and many others, and to the excellent leaders of the Boys' Brigade attached to the Church–for example these officers:- Jack McGregor, Bert Alexander, John Orr, Wilson Black and Jim Houston, but I will confine myself to the BB Bible Class which met on a Sunday morning prior to the Church Service, and to the BB Camps and shows.

The Sunday morning Bible Class was conducted and spoken to by the officers, and I was asked sometimes to go and share in this. The camps were held in different places in the summer, and sometimes I was able to visit these. Also the BB Shows were excellent, held sometimes in the Leith Town Hall, and these gave opportunities to many young boys to make a start in drama. I am quite sure I did not appreciate how fortunate St Thomas' Church was in its youth leaders, both within and without the Boys' Brigade. For there were very good leaders in the very large youth group which met on Saturday evenings in the Church Hall–200-300 young people from Leith community.

Meantime I was attempting to go round the congregation of about 1,200-1,300 but this was an enormous task, scattered as were these members over such a wide area. It became clear to me that there was a genuine need to draw all members together, so that they might see one another in one place, and hear there the Gospel proclaimed to them afresh and give thought particularly to their response to it. The mind and spirit of a minister, not least a new minister, is meant to be open to the working of the Spirit, which again and again calls for an Abrahamic faith, for adventure, for moving out to what is new and exciting and to what can be fruitful both for a community of people and for the individual. But was there any contemporary movement of the Spirit which was present then in the World Church, and which should be noticed and thought about, and acted upon within a congregation? It was here that my old teacher, whose teaching at New College I have already mentioned,–Professor John Baillie–drew our attention to Christian Stewardship. This was a movement of the Spirit which could be called seismic, and it had already, prior to the 1960s, shaken Churches overseas, not least in the USA, and it had begun to make inroads into the Church of Scotland. Why should it not be allowed to make an impact on the congregation of St Thomas' Church?

3.   The Christian Stewardship Campaign - 1961

The Campaign began when the Stewardship idea was introduced into the Kirk Session at a retreat. Thereafter, with the Session's agreement, the Revd Campbell Ferenbach, of Liberton Parish Church, Edinburgh, who had experience of one of the first Campaigns in Edinburgh Presbytery, spoke to us, and it was agreed to launch our own.

One of the first things done was to issue to members of the congregation a Prayer Card, asking them to share in preparation for the St Thomas' Church Stewardship Campaign. Each day of the week had a Scriptural passage, and prayer subjects were suggested: for example, prayers were invited for the speakers on the Stewardship Campaign evening–17 May, 1961–in the Eldorado Ballroom, (often used as a wrestling stadium!) when a Buffet Supper would be provided, for hopefully, over 1,000 people from the congregation. These speakers were the Revd Dr R Leonard Small, St Cuthbert's Church, Edinburgh, the Revd Denis M Duncan BD, Editor of the *British Weekly*, five Elders of St Thomas' Church, and the Minister (Epilogue). Further, on another day, prayers were asked for the Convener and for Sub Conveners of the Campaign, those who dealt with clerical work or gave out invitations to the meal or were hostesses at it, or undertook visiting in the follow up work, or acted as Stewards in relation to the entry to the hall and to seating at the tables. Training was also given to congregational visitors when the Revd Dr J G Matheson, Secretary then of the General Assembly's Stewardship Committee, was present.

In due course, hostesses called more than once on all the members of the congregation, inviting them to attend the Buffet Supper in the Eldorado as their guests. When the great day arrived, over 1,000 congregational members were seated, and the best audio equipment was made available, as well as good decorations for the hall ballroom. The evening was recorded as well worth all the organisation and care which was required to make it possible. The nature of Christian Stewardship, which is essentially a response to the Gospel in terms of offering the three Ts–time, talents, and treasury, to be used to God's glory and in the service of humanity, was well covered by the Speakers. After the Session Clerk, Mr George Houston, spoke about "St Thomas' Parish Church–Its History and Heritage" and a solo by Mrs John Inglis, Dr Small gave an address on "The Gift of the Gospel" which was followed by Mr James Aitken, speaking on "Christian Stewardship–Its Meaning and Practice". Then 'Reminiscences', 'Opportunities of Giving', and 'The Church–It's Needs and Service', were each dealt with by Mr Robert Alexander, an Elder, by Mr Hugh Mackenzie the Treasurer, and by the Revd Denis Duncan. In closing the Minister conducted the Epilogue, followed by the closing Praise and the Benediction. A Service of Thanksgiving and Dedication was held on 4 June, 1961, when the Preacher was the Revd Professor John McIntyre DD, Edinburgh University.

As in many other Stewardship Campaigns of the 1960s, many benefits came to the congregation, each member being given a commitment card asking what they were prepared to do. Every organisation in the Church was helped in terms of membership, a series of district Socials was begun once a month in the manse, and the financial position of St Thomas' was much increased. Current practices in worship and service were judged and improved: some individuals acknowledged that they had been moved forward in their Christian life. When thinking about what we had felt moved to do in St Thomas' Church, I made the discovery in my desk of records which brought home to me all that had been said or sung on that evening in May more than 35 years ago. Listening to what was said to us then made me realise that on that occasion we were indeed surrounded by a great cloud of witnesses past and living. For these recordings, St Thomas' Church is much indebted to Willie Greig, an Elder of St Thomas' but later Session Clerk of the present United Church in Leith, called St Thomas'–Junction Road. I would like to say something of what our then Session Clerk, Mr George Houston, told the company that evening not least about Stewardship and about "St Thomas' Church–It's History and Heritage".

Mr Houston began by reminding our people that St Thomas' Church had no long history yet it had a significant one of 120 years: he told us that a suitable text or focus for what he had to say could be found in Genesis Chapter 28 Verse 22: "And this stone, which I have set for a pillar shall be God's house: and of all that thou shalt give me I will surely give the tenth to thee". In these words we were reminded of how Jacob made a covenant with God who had amazingly blessed him, promising to create a place of worship and to give to God of his prosperity. This was surely one of the "first recorded accounts of an appreciation of stewardship, and it was with a similar sense of appreciation and gratitude to God that we are gathered here tonight". Mr Houston then went on to speak of the origins of St Thomas' Church. "In lands now occupied by Sheriff Brae and Mill Lane, a man called James Logan, later Sir James Logan, built a Mansion House where St Thomas' Church now stands. This was later acquired by the family of Gladstone who demolished the house and in its place in 1840 built the Church, the adjoining manse, the school and the asylum". This was erected by Sir John Gladstone of Fasque who built it as a memorial to his father Thomas Gladstone, and "as a manifestation of his attachment to his place of birth". He set up stones as a place of worship and set aside part of what he had to maintain the buildings. Hence "The idea of Stewardship is nothing new at all; at no time could we have been called a wealthy Church, but because of the deep sense of stewardship of many no longer with us, yet of many who are still with us, we can say that, in all truth, we never owed a penny to anyone: rather these 'many' have contributed to the house and service of God through their sense of gratitude". Mr Houston then spoke briefly of certain past ministers of St Thomas' Church: of the Revd Fleming, and of the Revd C Keith McWilliam, not least of the Revd R Duncan a distinguished minister for 15 years including the 1939-45 War, who wrote regularly to every member of the forces in the Church, and who sent wireless sets to many servicemen in lonely stations in that time. He was kind enough also to say: "Once again we have a minister with us now who will certainly lead us to make an impact, not only on the Christian life of our own congregation, but also on our community: Leith will receive such a shake up as it has never known before". In conclusion Mr Houston said that it might appear that far too much had been said about the ministers but he pointed out to everyone that none of these ministers would ever have claimed that the life and witness of the Church was their work. That was a united effort and sprang from the response of so many men and women within the congregation. "This is the heritage which we have and it is because this spirit of service is still with us that a fuller sense of stewardship will produce results in Leith. We are here to consider this matter and to consider how we can honour our responsibilities to the Church of Jesus Christ".

I have only time to mention that following Mr Houston's talk and a Solo by Mrs Inglis "Arise O Sun", Dr Small spoke on "The Gift of Christ" when he made it very clear that Christian Stewardship is just our chance of saying how grateful we are for all that God in Christ has done for us. "The Gift of Christ is always behind our Stewardship of time, talents, and possessions, and anything we give in return is only our response".

It might be thought that the evening in the Eldorado was too heavy with history and theology. In the view of so many that night, this was not so. The food and the fellowship was much enjoyed and "The Reminiscences of St Thomas' Church provided by one of the Elders, Bert Alexander, were much appreciated by the old as by the young. He dressed up as the ancient Hughie McShuggle. Hughie got the date of the evening wrong and came down the evening before to the Eldorado to find himself in the ring with 'the Monster'. He well remembered his wedding day–Hibs got beat 2-0–the Minister said to him "Will you take this woman to be your wedded wife?" He said to the Minister, "Would you?". The Minister said "No" So Hughie said to him: "Then why are you trying to palm her off on to me?" Hughie took his nephew with him to the Church one day. He didn't feel well. Hughie told him to go out and get some fresh air. When he came back, Hughie asked if he was feeling better; "Yes for I found a box outside saying 'For the Sick', so I filled it! His relation from far away was staying with him and required some things washed. He was told to go into the bathroom, and he could use the washing machine. Hughie's relation came back soon saying "your washing machine in there doesn't work: I put my shirt into it, and pulled the chain and it's no there any more!".

Once the Eldorado evening was past, it was resolved by the Kirk Session that the Stewardship of St Thomas' Church should be pursued in certain directions–in prayer and worship, in unity and in mission. To focus such themes a congregational gathering was held in Leith Town Hall on the 17 May, 1962 with the subject of "Our Continuing Stewardship" when the guest speakers were the Revd Dr J G Matheson, the Revd J L Cowie of Rosyth Parish Church, and the Revd Dr Murdo Macdonald of St Georges West Church, Edinburgh. Those who attended were asked to indicate if they wished to be interested, and prepared to come to meetings about the Prayer Fellowship of the Church, and its worship, or about meetings with other Denominations, or about doing some preparatory thinking and bible study with a view to a Mission in one or two years time in the Parish of St Thomas' Church.

St Thomas' Stewardship Campaign was meant to make the people of St Thomas' Church look at themselves, and their witness to Jesus Christ in the Church and in the world in a new way, and to encourage them constantly to take radical action in terms of their offering of time, talents, and treasury in Christ's service. We were all being asked to die and rise again in ways that were no doubt difficult but that penetrated to the radix or root of our individual and corporate lives. How far this really happened is known only to God, and would be empowered by His Holy Spirit. There was evidence that at least in the lives of some of our members this took place.

4. *Changes Called for in St Thomas' Church Building and in the Presbytery of Edinburgh*

But radical action, change that went down to the roots and origins was being called for in other directions, both within the inner structure of St Thomas' Church building, for example, and in a sphere largely outwith its congregation, within the Presbytery of Edinburgh.

Both the Minister and the Kirk session felt that the condition and layout of St Thomas' sanctuary had, for many decades, been neglected. It was time not only for repainting the whole, but also for renewal or rearrangement, especially of what lay in the area of the organ, pulpit, choir stalls, and communion table. All this was not finally complete until 1965, but thought and planning took place some years before.

Interest in this internal reshaping of St Thomas' Church will be limited, so it will be best to give a brief description of what the result of the renewal work was, together with reference to the Communion and Dedication Service–27 June, 1965–when the Moderator of the General Assembly of the Church of Scotland, the Rt Revd Archibald Watt preached the sermon and when the MP for Leith, Mr James Hoy was also present. The local paper wrote–"The visit of Archibald Watt is thought to be the first to St Thomas' by a reigning Moderator for at least 100 years".

The internal reconstruction of St Thomas' Church saw the removal of the pulpit from the centre to the side, and the erection of a large cross where the organ pipes had stood. Hence the central feature of the Church was this Cross, mounted on a yellow background, surrounded by red drapes, and standing on the back wall behind the communion table. It was an empty Cross that now dominated the interior of St Thomas' instead of organ pipes. A photograph, taken not long after the completion of the work, shows well the internal transformation made. The new organ was positioned in the front rows of pews facing the communion table. Of the Dedication Sunday a journalist wrote: "The Church was packed . . . the mixed feelings of joy and excitement felt by the congregation were well illustrated by the gusto with which all sang the opening praise–Psalm 43 v 3-5 which begins "O send Thy light forth and Thy truth; let them be guides to me". After the Minister read the Old Testament Lesson, I Kings 8 v 22-30, and the New Testament Lesson, St John 15 v 1-17, the Moderator preached from I Thessalonians 1 v 2 and 3: "We give thanks to God always for you all, making mention of you in our prayers; remembering without ceasing your work of faith, and labour of love, and patience of hope in our Lord Jesus Christ in the sight of God, and our Father". "Faith when real", the Moderator said, always produces results and it was the lack of this quality that gave rise to so many problems . . . every major step we take in life requires faith . . . lose faith and you lose the capacity to produce anything worthwhile . . . Faith built this Church". The Moderator went on to speak of the 'labour of love' and 'the patience of hope'. "Perseverance is what matters. Any number of people are good at starting things but not many are good at continuing with them. It's easy to fall in love, but not so easy to stay in love: it's easy to join the Church but not so easy to stay a full partaking member . . . Through the trials of life we must carry the bright light of an unquenchable hope in Christ as St Paul did".

Little has been said in these chapters about Presbytery work but opportunity had been given to me when in Fallin Church to have a part in Stirling Presbytery, and now in the 1960s I was again offered an opportunity to deal with youth work, being asked to become Youth Convener of Edinburgh Presbytery. In addition to this, it was not long before I looked for a chance to raise there the whole issue of the theology and practice of public worship.

In the Presbytery Minutes of 7 May, 1963 the following motion was moved by myself and was seconded: "That the Presbytery acknowledging the widespread desire for change and renewal within the church at large appoint a Special Committee to deal with the following:

(a) to consider the grounds for radical change urgently needed in the present pattern of congregational worship and fellowship
(b) to bring forward any special suggestion about the form such alteration might take, having in regard such changes as had already taken place within the bounds of the Presbytery".

This committee was appointed and met regularly and made reports to the Presbytery–1963-1966. It dealt with the Administration of the Sacraments, amongst other things, and certain resolutions were agreed to by Presbytery and were sent down to Kirk Sessions along with the Report. After this, there could well have been an end to this whole discussion about public worship. Indeed there were some members of the special committee who took this view. But ultimately the Presbytery of Edinburgh "agreed to appoint The Revd D R Easton and The Revd Dr W C Bigwood to promote an Overture before the Synod of Lothian and Tweedale and the General Assembly. So it was moved and seconded that the following be transmitted on Public Worship from the Edinburgh Presbytery:
. . . It is humbly overtured by the Presbytery of Edinburgh to the Venerable the General Assembly to instruct the committee on Public Worship and Aids to Devotion to examine, in the light of contemporary scholarship, the nature, sources, and function of public worship in the Reformed Churches in order to:

(1) make clear the purpose and principles of public worship;
(2) provide a source of teaching material about the meaning and practice of public worship; and
(3) suggest ways in which the form of public worship in the Church of Scotland can be developed, so as to become a more adequate means of grace to the people of this generation".

This Overture was accepted by the General Assembly of 1967. Thereafter a Working Party was set up in the Public Worship Committee, which had the help of Edinburgh Presbytery, the Panel on Doctrine, and from the Divinity Faculties. Eventually a full report was made in 1970 to the General Assembly and was included in the Reports to the Assembly of that year. It was called "Worship in the Reformed Church: The Purpose and Principles of Public Worship".

The final report of the Working Party on the Doctrine and Practice of Worship in the Reformed churches was made, again through the Committee of Public Worship and Aids to Devotion, to the General Assembly in 1973 and in that report took into account what had been said by Presbyteries.

But above all, in relation to the Presbytery replies, the Working Party "wish to single out as of supreme importance one basic point, viz, the use of the Lord's Supper". The Doctrine of the Lord's Supper required to be studied–for it is central in Christian worship–and it needs to be <u>celebrated</u> more regularly. It was noted that, after the Reformation, "for the first time in the history of the church, Christians started to observe the Lord's Day without the Lord's Supper". . . "we suggest that the Church of Scotland, in common with other Churches of the Reformation, should move as quickly as possible to the restoration of the weekly Lord's Supper".

In relation to Section (2) of its remit the Working Party told the Assembly that it was publishing a booklet entitled *Weekly Communion in the Church of Scotland* and another intended for group study, entitled *Learning Together about Christian Worship*. These were commended to the Church. The first booklet was written for the Committee on Public Worship and Aids to Devotion by the Revd A Stewart Todd and the second by myself.

The General Assembly received the final Report of the Working Party on the Doctrine and Practice of Public Worship in the Reformed Churches and sent that Section of it on the form of Public worship (dealing with the Lord's Supper) for study and action to Presbyteries asking them to report their findings to the Secretary of the Public Worship and Aids to Devotion Committee.

5. The Leith Council of Churches: St Thomas' Youth Club

Interest in other Christian denominations in their life and public worship, had been stimulated for me by my time in the SCM, but also by my membership for a good number of years in the Public Worship and Aids to Devotion Committee, and by the Working Party which had given many Reports through the above to the General Assembly. Another impetus in Leith was given to us by the thought and work of the late Revd Dr Rudolf Elrich, the Minister of Junction Road Church. He was engaged in writing a book about the Reformed-Roman Catholic Dialogue and regularly met with the Roman Catholic Teachers in Drygrange, near Melrose. I was asked to join the Church of Scotland ministers who visited there and also to give a paper on 'Worship in the Church of Scotland'. I derived great benefit from discussions with the Roman Catholic Teachers there, and in particular from the spiritual director of their Seminary, Father John Dalrymple, who was later to become a distinguished author and Edinburgh Parish Priest.

These talks and experiences led me to look at the ecumenical scene in Leith. There was very clearly room for greater togetherness with our ministerial friends Episcopalians, Methodists, United Free Church etc. So it seemed best first of all to consult The Revd Dr T D Stewart Brown, Minister of the Parish Church of South Leith. Mr Brown was not too fit at this time, but he agreed to give the thought of a Leith Council his backing, if the other denominations thought the idea acceptable and worth pursuing. Eventually, the Council was set up with T D Stewart Brown as the first Chairman, and myself as the Secretary. Experience of what the Leith Council of Churches did was a good training ground for what was to be done later in the already started Kirkwall Council of Churches, and it also led me to think if there would be ecumenical support for a community youth club to be set up in the excellent halls of St Thomas' Church.

St Thomas' Youth Club

However there was little help given from any other denomination in Leith for this club, when it eventually began, but it had good support provided by certain St Thomas' Elders: it ran for a good number of years on a Saturday evening 7.30–11 pm. These Elders' wives were not very happy about their husbands being committed to a Saturday evening slot, so I had to be careful! There was usually a large group of teenagers, many of them in drape suits, waiting to get in at the hall door, near 7.30 pm. There was at this time in the early 60s no other large club for this group in Leith. The St Thomas' Deaconess,–a splendid person–Maureen Mathieson, was of enormous help at this event and in so many other ways. The Club was basically a dance, to a five piece Rock Band. The noise was ear splitting, though there were spells when refreshment was made available. At a later stage, these refreshments were made open to a smaller number in an upstairs hall when there was a better chance of speaking with certain individuals. This was the time of a two year call up to the Forces, and many young people were given a copy of the Scriptures and our good wishes when they left us. The Club also led to attempts to get jobs for one or two members, and also to represent someone in court. I–and I suspect a good number of those Elders who helped us, like Willie Cathcart and Ian Hutchison–wondered how much good we were often doing. For sometimes we were not back to our homes till after midnight, some young people having flooded the toilets or had a fight, requiring removal to the casualty ward of Leith Hospital, directly opposite our hall doors. The Club was a hard struggle but it was a genuine attempt to reach out to the youth of Leith Town, to speak with them, and to try and learn something of their thinking and pressures and problems–the vast majority of them, having no connection whatever with any Church. So many of those who came regularly on a Saturday evening had, we felt, their own culture and genuine friendships, but most of us in the Church were strangers to it. At any rate I will always be grateful to all those from St Thomas' Church who made a real and costly effort to meet, and sometimes to be of some use to these club members. I believe that there were those in the Leith community who appreciated its being open on a Saturday evening. I was sometimes stopped by mothers in the Leith street and asked when the club was opening in September: They had their concern for their sons and daughters of 15-20.

6. The Call to St Magnus Cathedral

The call to St Magnus Cathedral came to me in an unexpected way. I was at a course at Carberry Tower when Jim Davidson a Minister of a rural charge in Orkney whom I'd known as a fellow student at New College, spoke to me about the vacancy in the Cathedral in Kirkwall. The Cathedral had been vacant for more than a year, and still had no one for the charge. I had now been eight years in St Thomas' Church and the family was settled in Leith, with the children in schools in Edinburgh, and with my wife for a considerable time a partner in a Medical practice. I did not want particularly to go to Orkney. However some time later I received a letter asking me to go up and take a service in Finstown, outside Kirkwall, and have a meeting with the Vacancy Committee of the Cathedral. No commitment was expected from myself or from the Cathedral. No doubt several factors made me accept the invitation, not least that I hadn't been too fit and was down to $9\frac{1}{2}$ stone. Perhaps a move could give me a new start and better health! Two other Leith Ministers had just died, and one was in hospital! In the end I visited Orkney and did what I was asked, and received an invitation to be sole nominee for the Cathedral. That meant a difficult decision for both Margot and myself, taking into account also what it would mean for our children having to make a fresh beginning in a new place and at new schools, and at the same time remembering how generous the Kirk Session and people of St Thomas' Church had been to us over the years. We decided, after much debate to go to Orkney, and this time Margot came with me to see Kirkwall and its Cathedral and the manse. In due course, after the services in the Cathedral, I was elected Minister and we were faced with leaving St Thomas' Church and the Medical Practice and the Schools and our many friends and relatives. Leaving was especially hard for Margot and the children, and I wondered what I was doing, for some people were very much against our going from Edinburgh. And yet I felt I had been given a call and I ought to go–"holding fast to faith and a good conscience"–to a place, where as one Minister told me, they had a primitive life style and regularly lit their oil lamps! I had little appreciation at this time of the magnificent historic Cathedral to which I had been called or to the thoughtful and generous people to whom I would minister.

Chapter VIII

Early Years in St Magnus Cathedral

1. A Warm Welcome to the Cathedral: Yet a 'Tough Job' for the New Minister

My leaving St Thomas' Church was made not so difficult as I had thought by the generosity of the eldership and the people. So many in the congregation expressed to us their good wishes for the next stage in our pilgrimage, and the Kirk Session gave us a happy dinner, when kind speeches were made, and songs sung, and when we were presented with beautiful table glasses. I hope I was able to say a fitting 'Thank You' for all that we had received and learnt in St Thomas' Church.

Our arrival in Kirkwall was not less generous, both in regard to our new Manse, and in relation to the Induction. Alterations were made in our home, and I was told that the decision had already been made that another Manse would be purchased in the future. I was welcomed at the Induction Social by the Convener of the Vacancy Committee, Alec Doloughan, an excellent Elder of the Cathedral, who had at one time been the teacher, and lay preacher on Fair Isle, and then became a senior official in the Education Department in Kirkwall. For many years he was to me a wise counsellor in Cathedral matters. He told the new minister that "there was inevitably a tough job ahead of him" but I was assured of the "whole hearted support of the Session, Board, and the various organisations of the Church", and he appealed to the members "to rally round the minister to encourage him in his task". Mr Doloughan also warmly welcomed my wife and the children. Part of the reason why the new minister was faced with "a tough job" was that the vacancy had lasted almost two years, and there had been a considerable loss of commitment and enthusiasm amongst some members. Further welcome was offered by Provost Scott on behalf of the City and Royal Burgh of Kirkwall, by Mrs Stephen, the President of the Woman's Guild, who presented my wife with Orkney jewellery, while I was given robes by one of the oldest Cathedral members, Mrs Leask. In a brief reply, I included that I looked forward to coming to know the congregation, to meeting the Kirk Session and leaders, and to learning about the Parish, and about the history and tradition of the magnificent rose-coloured Cathedral of St Magnus, to which I had the honour to be called as Minister. In conclusion, I quoted some words from the late John Oman, an Orcadian from Stenness in Orkney and former Principal, Westminster College, Cambridge: "Reconciliation sounds a large theological term, but it means simply coming to ourselves and arising and going to our Father. As the essential significance is that it is to God 'of whom are all things', restoration to friendship with Him makes all things new. . . It is not a sentimental relation to a remote spirit in the heavens, but a practical dealing with all things here and now. . . For ourselves, it is, in particular, reconciliation to our discipline and duty, and being enabled in everything to give thanks, which is the only real fulfilment of the First Commandment to have no other gods before God".[1]

After tea, addresses were given by Mr George Houston, the Session Clerk of St Thomas' Church, by the Revd G. L. Parkinson, extending a welcome on behalf of other ministers in Kirkwall and of the Kirkwall Council of Churches. There was time for more speeches, but the most humorous one was by an old college friend, Robin Richmond, of the South Church in Stonehaven. He told how his father had at one time been minister of Shapinsay, the nearest of the North Isles to Kirkwall. He had been good to many young people, and some used to come to the Manse door. All in the Manse at this time were looking forward to the birth of a baby. The great event took place on a Saturday evening, when the minister was in his study, struggling with his sermon for the next day. The maid could not contain her joy, so she rushed to the study door and said, "its a boy, Sir". To which the minister replied in a somewhat irritated way; "Well, for goodness sake, go and ask him what he wants".

It is appropriate to say here that the move from Leith to Kirkwall deeply affected my family and my wife. The children all went to Kirkwall Grammar School—Andrew to the Primary, and Alison and Elizabeth to the Secondary—from Edinburgh Schools, Andrew from the Edinburgh Academy, and Alison and Elizabeth from Mary Erskine. Elizabeth especially found it hard. She had had a different maths course at her single sex previous school, and though her teacher was very understanding and helpful, the change of school was not easy for her. She knew no one in her class, and felt that those, in the old Grammar School, who sat in the front seats were warm near the fire, while those at the back were freezing! However, those problems, with the shift to the new Grammar School, were eventually sorted out. Meanwhile Margot had been a busy partner in a Leith Medical practice, and suddenly this had finished, and she had to come to terms with being a home maker, in a new home, in a new place. She managed wonderfully well, as so many others in similar situations have done and was very well befriended, both by good neighbours, and in the Cathedral.

Part of the difficulty of the job in the Cathedral Ministry was that the minister had to take account of the wishes of more than one authoritative body or person. Besides the Kirk Session, he soon found that the Town Council of Kirkwall represented the people of Kirkwall as owners of the Cathedral, and its Provost,

Baillies, and members had to be consulted about both certain services, and about any change in the building itself. Then there was the Friends of St Magnus Cathedral, and their views also had to be considered. Further the carefully thought out opinions of the Cathedral architect were also often important. Once the Town Council of Kirkwall was merged into the Orkney Islands Council in local Government re-organisation, their views, often after consulting with experts in a particular field, were regularly heard on different matters, such as Cathedral repairs, new heating for the Cathedral, the historic bells dating from the sixteenth century, the clock, the sound system, and not least, the Cathedral Organ, a Willis organ of 1925. A Sub Committee of the Orkney Islands Council, where these matters were considered, was chaired by the Orkney Islands Council Convener, and consisted of certain Councillors. The Architect frequently spoke at these meetings, in which the Lord Lieutenant of Orkney and the Minister of the Cathedral were allowed a place.

2. *The Lifeboat Service*

Although the Cathedral minister was often written to, and called 'Dean' or 'Provost' (even 'Bishop!'), he was a Church of Scotland minister within the Presbytery of Orkney, and St Magnus Cathedral was a charge within its bounds. However major Orkney Services were almost always held within the Cathedral. These took place on Council or Community or Anniversary or Celebratory or Tragic or Royal occasions. From time to time in Orkney, or off Orcadian shores, there took place a tragic event which deeply affected the whole community in the Islands. One such was the loss, the total loss, of one of Orkney's lifeboats only some months after the new Minister's arrival. The Provost 'phoned the Manse and told the minister that Orkney felt there should be a Memorial Service in its Cathedral for the Coxswain and Crew of the *T.G.B.* Lifeboat so sadly lost at sea recently. This was one part of the 'tough job', pulpit-wise, required of the Cathedral minister, at an early stage.

The Cathedral for this Memorial Service was overflowing; Orcadians came from the Mainland, and from the North and South Isles. There were also many distinguished visitors from the South including senior representatives of lifeboat management. I felt I should set down here what I'd been given to say in the sermon, for it was not only a tribute to the Coxswain and Crew of the lost boat, but also an illustration of the admirable spirit of the men who have again and again served the Royal National Lifeboat Institution so magnificently, very often with such neglect of themselves and of their lives in the hour of danger. The text chosen was from 2 Samuel 1, part of verse 23: "Saul and Jonathan were lovely and pleasant in their lives, and in their death they were not divided". The Sermon was called, "In Memoriam: The Coxswain and Crew of the Longhope Lifeboat".

"We are met here to remember with humble thanksgiving before Almighty God the Coxswain and the Crew of the Longhope Lifeboat who were drowned at sea on the night of Monday-Tuesday, 17th/18th March, 1969. It was then that their 47ft lifeboat, the *T.G.B.*, capsized and was lost with all hands in the Pentland Firth, while on a rescue mission to a Liberian cargo ship, in difficulties off South Ronaldsay. My friends, human words are utterly inadequate to express the genuine and deep sympathy which all Orcadians and others now present surely feel for their loved ones and dependants. However, it was thought by many people in Kirkwall, Stromness, and elsewhere in Orkney, that it would be right to hold a service in this ancient Cathedral in memory of the lost Coxswain Kirkpatrick, and his Crew. And so it is fitting that we should now remember them, and their sacrificial actions, with gratitude, before God.

To some in this large congregation this morning, these men were known as relations, or as friends and companions; to others, perhaps to most of us, they are only known by hearsay. But whether we have known them at first hand, or have only a slight and indirect knowledge of them, certain things emerge about their lives and characters. And if we can learn from the way they lived and died, and be strengthened by them for the good life, then this service cannot be dismissed as official religion or merely formal memorial tribute.

Initially I would remind you briefly of the men who have been so tragically taken from their families and friends, and from the Lifeboat Service, to which they gave themselves so unstintingly. First, there was Daniel Kirkpatrick, one of the most experienced, able and courageous coxswains in the Lifeboat Service, and his two sons, Ray and Jack. They worked with their father at the Lyness Royal Naval Oil Fuel Depot. Then there was Robert Johnston, the senior engineer of the boat, the one permanent paid man, and his two sons, Jim and Robbie. They were fishermen, and with their father, were highly respected in the small community of Brims and Longhope, as were all the other members of the crew. Next there was James Swanson, the assistant mechanic, who worked as a member of the boat, the *Hoy Head*, well-known to many Orcadians, and was by all accounts one of the most obliging and considerate of men. Last there was Eric McFadyen, a merchant seaman, a man with strong family connections with the Longhope lifeboat, who generously volunteered to go at the last minute, though not a regular member of the crew.

So much for a short statement about the men whose memory we seek to hallow this morning. Death has a way of bringing into sharp focus a man's life, so that certain distinguishing marks stand out. And so it is that in the lives of these men of the Longhope lifeboat, are to be seen certain clear characteristics.

Volunteers For Danger, With The Courage To Stick To It

Though none of these men would have drawn attention to the fact, it is nevertheless true that they were volunteers for the dangerous life, and had the courage to stick to it.

While from an early age some of the recent crew used to assist in the launching of the boat, and in the berthing of her safely after being out (permission having been given for them to get off school for this purpose), and while they were taken out on the boat on exercise runs, long before they were of age to be crew members, these men nevertheless did not have to join the Lifeboat Service. Yet they chose deliberately this life of difficulty and real hazard, and they knew that the possibility of death and disaster was before them every time the boat was launched into stormy seas, whipped up by force nine or ten gales. These men were content that their own lives, and their family life, should be subjected to what can be called the discipline of dislodgement, whenever, near their lifeboat station, there were those in peril on the sea, and the call came to go out.

All this means, surely, that in the men of the Longhope boat there was the kind of courage, which isn't simply called forth by a hazardous situation, but which deliberately places a man into such a situation. It was the kind of deliberate courage of Captain Scott, who, along with his comrades, volunteered for the expedition into the dangerous wastes of the Antarctic; it breathes through this letter of Scott's, written in the tent where he and his men died, and quoted by the late Sir James Barrie, in his Rectorial Address to the students of St Andrew's University: "We are pegging out in a very comfortless spot . . . we are in a desperate state–feet frozen, etc, no fuel, and a long way from food, but it would do your heart good to be in our tent, and hear our songs and cheery conversation . . ."

Comrades In A Great Rescue Team

The men we remember today were volunteers for danger, and possessed of a deliberate courage; they were also those who knew the meaning of real brotherhood and teamwork. In many a situation of hazard and stress, they had learned to rely on one another, and trust one another. No one was spare, each had his job to do. One can see clearly this working comradeship in the account given of one of the Longhope lifeboat's rescues, the rescue of the nine men from the Aberdeen trawler, the *Ben Barvis*, on the night of 3/4 January, 1964. "The maroons were fired at 10.16 pm, ten minutes later the lifeboat was launched, and reached the wrecked trawler about 11.30 pm. It took some time to secure the lifeboat in a suitable position for the rescue work to begin, but by 12.15 am the coxswain and his crew were ready for the operation to start by breeches buoy". The account further says: "The whole lifeboat crew was fully employed, bowman Ray Kirkpatrick and his brother Jack manned the outhaul forward. The second coxswain and Robbie Johnston manned the inhaul amidships. James Swanson tended the nylon warp, while assistant mechanic Robert R Johnston attended to the engines and radio. The coxswain (throughout) continued to keep firm control of the situation. As each survivor crossed in the breeches buoy, the tide swept him away astern, and it was difficult and exhausting work heaving them into the lifeboat. After the second man had reached the lifeboat, the trawler's oil fuel tanks were fractured, and the ropes and deck of the lifeboat were covered with diesel oil . . . The deck became very slippery and the work of rescue even harder. The scrambling net was rigged amidships, and as each man came across, he was hauled aboard by the coxswain and by Ray Kirkpatrick, the bowman . . . The rescue was completed about 1.20 am, and the survivors landed at St Margaret's Hope by 4.30 am. For this action a second silver service clasp was awarded to the coxswain, and the thanks of the Institution, inscribed on vellum, were awarded to the crew". This rescue, like so many others by the Longhope boat, was a team effort; they trusted one another each to do his job and they combined together not to destroy life but to save it. They combined to snatch human lives from tempestuous seas and to bring them to safety. And in this hard task each was glad to have comrades standing by him, and working with him.

Volunteers for the dangerous life with the courage to stick to it, men experienced in brotherhood and teamwork, and, one further characteristic, men who were prepared to sacrifice their lives in seeking to save others.

Men Who Put Their Own Safety Last

It has been told of one of the greatest British sailors, Lord Horatio Nelson, that when he was a young boy, he was one day on the way back to school, with his brother William, after the Christmas holidays. William especially did not like the idea of going back, and he suggested that they should go home, and say that the snow, which was lying on the ground, was too deep for them to get through. Horace, as Horatio was called at home, agreed. So both boys were soon back at the country parsonage and told their story to their father. Their father listened to them, and said: "Make another trial, and I will leave it to your honour. If the road is dangerous come back but remember I leave it to your honour". Once again the boys set out, and this time they came to a place where the snow was somewhat deep. William thought there was a good excuse to go back, but nothing would make Horace do this. "We must go on", he kept saying, "remember he left it to our honour". And go on they did until they got safely to school.

The last journey of the Longhope lifeboatmen is like that story, without the happy ending; their last voyage is the tale of brave men who set out on incredible stormy seas and who did not turn back, for they surely felt it had been left to their honour, as members of a great service, to go on, in an attempt to rescue lives in danger. "It was an act of 'singular courage' for the boat to have put out in such conditions as those of Monday night" said Mr William Rodgers, Minister of State at the Board of Trade. And the MP for Banffshire said in the House of Commons that "The incredible behaviour and self-sacrifice of lifeboat crews were exemplified by the Longhope vessel putting out on a mission of mercy in such appalling weather conditions as last night". Most people in Orkney waited anxiously for news of the Longhope boat when there was no word of her coming in on Tuesday morning. But the waiting must surely have been longer and more harrowing for the loved ones of the men. Then as we all know, about 2 pm on Tuesday came the sad news that the *T.G.B.* had been found upturned, four miles west of Tor Ness, Hoy.

The Courage and Brotherhood and Sacrifice of our Lord

By a strange coincidence this is the Sunday the Church Universal knows as Passion Sunday, the time Christians remember the commitment of their Lord to the dangerous road to Jerusalem, the road to His Cross and Passion. Jesus Christ did not need to go there, but he too, in the profoundest of all ways, was a volunteer for danger, and with deliberate courage he set his face to go to the Holy City, where he knew that great storms of human hatred awaited him. For he felt that this was his Father's will for him. "The Son of man must suffer many things, and be rejected of the elders, and of the chief priests, and scribes, and be killed and after three days rise again".

And our Lord, too, may I remind you, was one who chose in his grace, to have men for his brothers, and who rejoiced in having around him a team or band of disciples. He called them to believe in him and to trust their lives to him, and in his mysterious humility was pleased to have them with him, pleased to have their comradeship, pleased to call upon them to go up to Jerusalem with him, pleased to have them as his disciples, for they would find their lives, if they lost them in his service, and in the service of others.

Above all, Jesus Christ our Lord was the One who gave his life in seeking to rescue or save others. "For God sent not his Son into the world, to condemn the world, but that the world through him might be saved". The men we remember with thanksgiving today put their lives at the disposal of others in need of rescue on the high seas. Jesus Christ, the Father's Son, put his life at the disposal of the whole world in need, a world in need of rescue from the high seas of unbelief, greed and pride, which was engulfing it, and which can still engulf it.

Inspiration and a Great Hope

And yet is this all we can say? For all their fortitude is the loss of the Longhope lifeboat crew an unmitigated disaster? We must tread carefully here, for to their bereaved families just now, it must seem so. Yet already the gallant self-sacrifice of this Coxswain and his Crew has been an inspiration to many people. It has opened our eyes to the kind of humble, self-effacing, sacrificial life which those men lived; constantly ready, constantly available for the service of others, at the risk of their own lives. In comparison with such men we must surely feel our littleness, all the poverty of our petty complaints, and sometimes of our self-seeking; our need of our Saviour's loving rescue and renewal for his way of life.

And in closing, we must remember that, as Tennyson said, "Somehow good will be the final goal of ill . . . that not one life shall be destroyed, or cast as rubbish to the void, when God hath made the pile complete". The men of the Longhope lifeboat were, like Saul and Jonathan of old, lovely and pleasant in their lives, for they were volunteers for the hazardous way and full of splendid courage; they were men who rejoiced in the brotherhood of the sea and in working together, and they were those who generously gave their lives in a rescue mission. In their death they were not divided, and it is our faith and our strong hope that they are together still, that he who brought life and immortality to light, our Saviour Jesus Christ, has not suffered them to lose him or one another, but has brought them to his Eternal Haven, where they, even now, know that fullness of peace and joy, which is ever the heritage of the Redeemed.

How bright those glorious spirits shine!"

[The Lord bless to us this preaching from his Word, and to his Name be praise and glory–Amen.]

3. The 'Save the Cathedral' Appeal

It was difficult to be faced by a tragedy which affected the whole Orcadian community, but it was as hard, soon afterwards, to be informed that the whole structure of the Cathedral nave was threatened by severe cracks, and that unless immediate action was taken could be in danger of collapse. This disturbing news was given to the Annual General Meeting of the Society of the Friends of St Magnus in September, 1970, by the then Cathedral architect, Mr Alexander Heward, of Miller and Black of Glasgow, who had been invited by Kirkwall Town Council some years ago to report to them on the state of the building. While he would be giving his report in greater detail to the Council, Mr Heward gave the Friends of St Magnus a clear view of the problems involved. He felt that the condition of the vaulted roof, covering the Cathedral nave "is serious but could be remedied by prompt action". It would be necessary first of all "to tie the building together" with reinforced concrete beams along the wall heads and clerestory and with a series of steel rods across the building above the roof vaulting. Mr Heward made the interesting suggestion that the earth tremor experienced in Orkney in January, 1927, could have caused some movement to take place in the Cathedral, which in its turn, and over a period of years, caused cracking in the masonry and vaulting.

At any rate it was clear that this would mean major repairs in the nave, making worship there impossible. It was also obvious that such restoration would be very expensive, and would mean a special appeal or campaign for funding, for the Town Council of Kirkwall did not, at that time, have money to meet the repair bills, a large amount having been promised for the ongoing renovation of the Cathedral organ. I remember thinking at this time, that the Town would require assistance raising the money required for the Cathedral reconstruction, so I went to see Colonel Macrae, Orkney's Lord Lieutenant, and asked him if he would help us. This he was very willing, after consideration, to do.

With vision and with great energy, he set about this very important task. He told the Kirkwall Town Council in 1971 that "a world wide campaign was to be launched next month, (January, 1972) to save St Magnus Cathedral". He explained the reason for this appeal. "Briefly the trouble is that the West Gable is being pushed outwards at the top. There is cracking in the vaulting and cracks in the walls adjacent to the west gable. This means that the fine support of the roof has been disturbed. The Cathedral is now in a dangerous state, movement is still taking place, and, if allowed to continue, the roof would undoubtedly collapse. To put things right will cost about £50,000 (in the end it cost very much more!), and the Society of the Friends of St Magnus, of which many of you will be members, have been asked to try and raise the money". Colonel Macrae went on to speak about the launching of the 'Save the Cathedral Appeal': "It is starting with a Press Conference here in Kirkwall on Thursday, 18 January, 1972, when we hope for broad representation from the National and Scottish newspapers, as well as BBC and Independent Television coverage . . . more than anything we hope for a good response from Orcadians both at home and overseas". These following words were also in Colonel Macrae's talk to the Council on the crisis in the Cathedral: "It is over 800 years old, and still a place of worship, and at this point in our history it is in our keeping. It is clearly our duty to see that we hand it down to posterity in good order". Help was further forthcoming from the Orkney County Council itself, for the then Convener, Mr J Donald Brown, recommended to Council members that they should underwrite the difference between the cost of initial repairs and the funds which would accrue from various sources. This suggestion was boldly made for, as Col. Macrae had previously pointed out, "The Town Council of Kirkwall, to whom the Cathedral belongs, recently used up all its available money on the renovation of the Cathedral organ, unaware that a major catastrophe was facing them in the structure of the Cathedral itself. . ."

The 'Save the Cathedral' Appeal turned out to be a great success, and was wonderfully well supported at home, and by generous people in different parts of the world, not least in America and Norway. It is noteworthy that the *New York Times* gave the "Save the St Magnus Cathedral" Appeal important coverage. It is worth remembering too that the day the Appeal was launched coincided with a great wind storm, which meant that the specially chartered Press plane had to be force landed on its return from Orkney. It is said that the Press representatives had to be encouraged to fly back, having remembered their rough ride to Orkney, with liberal quantities of Highland Park whisky!

Meanwhile, when repairs were being carried out in 1972–the nave covered in scaffolding from the floor to the roof–public worship was switched to the choir, and to St Rognvald Chapel at the east end of the Cathedral, and this was made known in *The Orcadian* paper, but the organ was available for use at all services, being on the east side of the screen which was erected from floor to roof just before the choir stalls. This meant that there was no access from the choir to the transepts, or to the tower or to the west part of the building from then on. It was made clear too to all members of the congregation that they could only enter the Cathedral for worship through the Priest's door, in the south east end of the building–another door on the north side could be used in an emergency.

However repairs to the Cathedral took much longer than had been thought–there was major rebuilding of certain roof vaulting at the west end of the nave, as well as grouting of all the nave pillars–and it was not until 1974 that it was thought right to have a Service of Thanksgiving for the Cathedral reconstruction achieved. This service took place on Wednesday, 7 August, 1974, at 3.30 pm and the Orkney Islands Council, and the Orcadian people, and the Cathedral congregation, were honoured to have Her Majesty Queen Elizabeth, the Queen Mother, attend it.

The seventh of August was seen as a Day of Thanksgiving in and beyond St Magnus Cathedral. The service was a happy occasion. The hymns were sung with joyful enthusiasm, the choir was in excellent voice, and there was a brief sermon as well as readings and prayers. All who were in the Cathedral that day were glad to offer thanks to Almighty God "for the successful completion in the Cathedral nave of reconstruction and restoration work, which has been the means of saving the

Cathedral from collapse". People remembered with gratitude how quickly, after the damage to the Cathedral was discovered, the "Save the St Magnus Cathedral" Appeal Committee was formed, how the Cathedral looked on the day the Appeal was launched, and how soon thereafter money flowed in. The text for the sermon was from I Chronicles 29 v 13: "And now we give thee thanks, our God, and praise thy glorious name", and the Sermon was entitled: "A Day of Thanksgiving".[2] This included 'Thanks for Restoration', 'Thanks for Co-operation' and 'Thanks for this Opportunity of Christian Celebration.' Before the end it had this quotation from George Mackay Brown. In that delightful book, *An Orkney Tapestry*, there is a vivid picture drawn of Earl Rognvald, founder of this building, and of his crusaders, home from their travels in the East, and standing in the nave of their Cathedral, still then being built. They may well have seen in vision at that time that the ship of "this church must carry the people of Orkney across many centuries–seas of tranquillity and rage and apathy–the years flashing and falling from her bow like cloven waves, towards the City of God".[3]

This was followed by these words of the Minister: "Can we in our day share this vision? Can we see the ship of this Cathedral sailing on through centuries yet to come because we are determined that she shall not founder now through lack of care and maintenance? Let us have a purpose in this matter sufficiently ribbed and edged with steel to overcome the difficulties ahead. Let us build above our deep intent the deed of full restoration and endowment, so that generations yet unborn may here worship and praise and magnify the Lord, The Father, and Son, and Holy Spirit, one God, blessed for ever, to whom be glory throughout all ages".

4. New Elders

As the shepherd gets to know and care for the members of his flock, so the minister, with others, has to know and care for his congregation and parish people, in joy and in sorrow, in good days and in bad. In most churches, the minister very much requires help in this caring duty, and he has been given this in the Church of Scotland for a long time, especially through the eldership, but also through teachers and members.

I was very glad that there were still in St Magnus those who were the eyes and the ears of a minister, who could inform him about the people of their district, where they stayed, who was in the family, and sometimes they had some idea of how deep was their faith (or indifference!), and of how much they were already doing within the membership and for the parish. While all this was true, it became clear that there was a great need for the strengthening of the eldership, through the coming in of new members into the Kirk Session. There are different ways of appointing elders, but in accordance with congregational tradition in St Magnus, I gave the Session time to think about suitable people before I asked elders for names and addresses (no female names at this stage!). Subsequently I began to go round and invite these members to take on this calling. Many of them were uncertain whether they could do this as they did not feel worthy of the eldership, though they so often saw it as something very well worth doing. They saw that the eldership would give them entry into homes, the opportunity of coming to know a family over many years, and of having the privilege of inviting members to come again, and receive the Lord's Supper or Holy Communion at certain times of the year. They knew also that district eldership could well mean seeing their people if they were ill or bereaved, and the remembering of them before God in prayer. They were further aware that it would often be their duty to tell the minister about these. There were other important points to be considered, such as the obvious Sunday attendance at Church, and at Kirk Session Meetings, and at the Prayer Meetings on certain Sundays.

I have to record that I was much encouraged by the ultimate response, when on Sunday, 26 January, 1969, ten men were ordained to the eldership, and one admitted to that office. I see that I wrote in the *Cathedral Magazine* "I have no doubt at all that these men will be warmly welcomed by the present members of the Cathedral Kirk Session, and by the Cathedral members, and I am confident that they will also find different ways of making a real contribution to the encouragement of our people in worship and in service". It could well be interesting for Orcadians to know who these men were:

George Donaldson	38 Quoybanks Crescent	Butcher
John Donaldson	30 Quoybanks Crescent	Oil Staff
Denis Eunson	Glenarde, Quoybanks Drive	Library
David Kemp	Eastmount, East Road	C.A.
Charles Millar	7 Broadsands Road	Council Foreman
Alan Munro	British Linen Bank	Manager
James Norquay	9 King Haakon Street	Airport Engineer
Arnold Rendall	75 Quoybanks Crescent	Joiner
John Smith	12 Old Scapa Road	Banker
James Wylie	10 Garrioch Street	Butcher
John Robb	Bank House, East Road	Manager

Some of the above are no longer with us, but some of them are, and I still think of them all with much affection and gratitude.

Many more elders were ordained or admitted into the Session in the next 20 years of my ministry, including eventually ladies. Without all these, the work and witness of St Magnus, both in the Cathedral and in the community, would have been greatly impaired, and in some cases drastically reduced. It is true that some elders did not feel that they saw much response to all their district work, but the vast majority still persisted in what they had to do, and many of their visits, unknown often to the elders, were greatly appreciated.

The Kirk Session, as is well known to its members, is responsible for the young of a congregation as well as for its communicant members.

5. The Training and Nurture of Young People and The Parish Development Programme

When I was interviewed by the Vacancy Committee of the Cathedral, prior to my being made sole nominee, I said to them that I did not feel I could conduct two Cathedral services each Sunday. I offered, instead of the Evening Sunday Service, to initiate two Youth Groups–a Bible Class for 12-15 year old boys and girls, and a Youth Fellowship for the 15-18 years. These groups in those days were often called together by intimation from the pulpit or in the magazine, but they were also brought together when elders or parents encouraged the young people to attend. Perhaps the best recruiting agent was the young people themselves, provided they felt they had a good peer group into which their friends could be invited. The Bible Class went along well with the help of the pianist, Miss Leslie. Later on the Cathedral Assistant or an elder or member did the very significant job of leader. The Youth Fellowship took shape in 1969. It met initially in the Cathedral Manse but it soon grew in numbers, organising its own programme with a President, Secretary, and Committee. The Fellowship came to have one or two weekend meetings in a year often in Hoy Hostel, which the Minister attended. It is good to realise that some of these Bible Class and Youth Fellowship young people have now moved on to Communicant Church membership and to the eldership.

I see that as early as September, 1969 I wrote in the *Cathedral Magazine* about the Cathedral Christian Education Programme. What I wrote then reminded me that any congregational Education Scheme had to cover earlier age groups; it had to cope with the different groups in a Sunday School–Beginners, Primary etc. What John Knox had written about "the necessity of schools" was indicated to congregational members: "Seeing that God hath determined that His Church here on earth shall be taught not by angels but by men, it is necessary . . . to be most careful for the virtuous education and Godly upbringing of the youth of this realm, if ye now thirst unfeignedly for the advancement of Christ's glory or desire the continuance of the benefits to the generation following" (*Book of Discipline*). Knox's methods are in many ways dated, but he was surely right to emphasise that Christian Education, both instruction and nurture in the Faith are essential to the building up in Christ of "the generation following". The Cathedral Kirk Session was to some extent aware that this education had a place in both the Primary and Grammar Day Schools. In the primary school the Headmaster often did this, or at a later stage, a teacher prepared the school service with her class of children, for the Friday Service. This service was occasionally taken in the term by the Cathedral Minister. In the Grammar School Religious Education–rather than Christian Education only–was given in certain classes–from a certain time an RE teacher was in charge. But the Rector–a Cathedral elder early in my ministry, took a service once a fortnight for certain age groups, to which he sometimes invited the Cathedral minister.

The Cathedral Session, however, knew that it had responsibility for its Sunday School Department, in addition to older Youth Groups. It is worth noting that the Cathedral Session did not just have a visiting interest, but, through some of its members, participated in teaching in the Junior or Senior Departments. I shall always be grateful, as well as to others, to George Donaldson who gave five years to this work and to Bobby Windwick, who gave ten years. The latter always had a trout fly-tying class for his class in the winter, taking them out on many Saturdays on the Orkney lochs in the summer (100% attendance of the class on the Sunday almost!). Also in the Junior and Senior Departments, Mrs Violet Grieve and her staff–many were ladies–gave wonderful years of dedicated service to our children.

As far as the Beginners and Primary Sunday Schools were concerned, new teachers were found, and the whole congregation was much indebted to Mrs Margaret Kelday–and later to Mrs Shona Linklater–who gave so many splendid years of patient and creative thought and prayer to our younger people of Nursery and Primary age.

Leadership in the Cathedral in the years of the late 1960s and in the 70s had certainly to do with the strengthening of the Kirk Session and of the Christian Education groups, but it also took the form of adult education, of new opportunities for learning and service for congregational members. What helped the Presbytery of Orkney and many congregations within its bounds in this regard, was the National Church Programme called PDP–Parish Development Programme.

In St Magnus Cathedral this programme certainly stimulated our effort in adult Christian education. A PDP was one in which congregational members were asked to make every endeavour to come to six Sunday Morning Services. In these the Gospel was proclaimed afresh, and all who heard were asked to consider once more their response in terms of worship and service in the Church and the world. I notice that in the *Cathedral Magazine* in June, 1970 I introduced the PDP with these words:

> "He either fears his fate too much
> Or his deserts are small,
> Who fears to put it to the touch
> To win or lose it all"

"So wrote the great Montrose, and his words apply in the sphere of congregational life and witness. In the live congregation there should always be something going on, some new development taking place, some renewal beginning once more, some adventure being embarked upon. Of course it may be said that God works in a hidden way, so you never know what is really happening in the secret places of people's hearts and lives. Indeed that is true for the living God is pleased to do his saving work, and plant the seeds of his Spirit often in unseen ways, and he makes these seeds grow quietly under the influence of his Word and Sacrament, or in the teaching and loving fellowship of the congregation. And yet, from time to time, it is proper for the leadership of the congregation to present themselves, and their fellow members and adherents with opportunities for renewed understanding of the Christian Gospel, and for response to it. This is the basic purpose of the PDP within a congregation for it brings the Gospel into sharp focus and it clarifies the individual's response to it, sometimes the congregational response.

This PDP was twice discussed in the Kirk Session, and each Elder was given a PDP Manual and leaflet in order that he could read about it, and come back to the next meeting able to make an informed decision. Ultimately the Minister was authorised to gather a committee to progress the Cathedral PDP, the committee Secretary being Mr J R Shearer. The first committee meeting took place on the evening of Pentecost Sunday and many trusted that that could be a good omen.

3 steps were outlined in the Cathedral PDP:-
1. The personal invitation to each member. 2. The hearing of the message of the Six Services. 3. A visit to every home by an Elder. Under the last point every member was given an opportunity of responding to the message given in a way they chose. Commitment cards were also provided to help members make their response. In this way a congregational member had a chance of indicating some service they felt they could do for the Church or for the community, or of stating a group they would wish to join. The other card handed out was the normal Freewill Offering Card. The Minister and the Kirk Session were aware that there would be resistance in the congregation to such a new adventure as a PDP, but, as I wrote in our magazine: "It has been well said that every new vision of Jesus means a more real response to him in life, and a worthier giving of ourselves in this service whether in Church or beyond it". The results of this PDP were considered in late 1970 and in 1971. Looking back now I believe that Minister and Kirk Session could have done a much more vigorous follow up to the responses made by our members.

However, there were refreshing and encouraging results in new people coming into more active membership in different ways both within and without the Cathedral. The Session Clerk at this time was Mr Alexander Stephen, who succeeded an excellent Clerk (1944-1970), Mr Eric Flett. Alec Stephen was Deputy Rector of Kirkwall Grammar School, and in this PDP, as in so many other ways he was a tremendous help to Minister, Session and Congregation. Alec summarised all the members' responses and made them available to the Kirk Session

It would take far too long to describe what was done to make use of the very encouraging response to this PDP, however these few points can be made:

The elders helped greatly in the follow up, along with certain members. Sometimes an elder or a sub committee were required to see what could be done in relation, for example, to 'the Visiting Group' or to 'The Cathedral Lecturers' - eg 'The Cathedral woodwork', 'windows', 'architecture', aspects of the Cathedral History etc. In relation to communicants I decided that, on the next occasion, I would have two classes, for younger and older people.

Eventually in 1971 35 people were accepted by profession of faith, and 15 by certificate of Transference. Little has been said about the Cathedral Prayer Meeting, and it has to be noticed that, despite the PDP, there were never large numbers attending it. Yet those who came were always able to be of much assistance to the Minister each week, at 10.45 am (later on it was 6 pm) in the St Rognvald Chapel. They often gave him names of sick, or bereaved, or of those in trouble in other ways, who could be prayed for and visited. This Prayer Meeting was certainly the place where the Minister and those with him could pray for the new communicants.

The years 1968-1973 were, I believe, renewing and rebuilding years, not only for the cracked building of the Cathedral, but for its people, not forgetting inside it, the renovation of the organ, and outside, the provision of the promised new manse, and the availability of better accommodation in the Cathedral hall, where new rooms and toilets were added. In relation to the new manse what our Session Clerk wrote in the December, 1972 magazine is relevant: "The manse committee recommended that 'Norlands' should be purchased from Mr James Brass . . . no visitor to the manse can have failed to notice the inconvenience which Mr and Mrs Cant have cheerfully borne, not least being the intermittent conversion of the Minister's study into a dining room. Unfortunately, they still face a period of change, but we hope to see them soon settled in a comfortable and commodious manse. . .

The Session Clerk also noted with pleasure Mr Cant's appointment as a Chaplain to Her Majesty in Scotland".

6. The Restoration of the Cathedral Organ, Its Re-dedication and Future Use

More must now be said here about the Cathedral organist appointed in 1969. He was Mr Norman J B Mitchell LTCL LTCL(CMT). Mr Mitchell came to Orkney to be the Principal Teacher of Music in Kirkwall Grammar School, but also proved to be an excellent Cathedral choirmaster and organist, and was with us for ten years. He made a very creative contribution to the music in the Cathedral and at one point took the choir on tour to Leith, Paisley Abbey, and St Giles. It was also in relation to the renewal of the organ itself that Norman benefited both Cathedral and Town. The Kirkwall Town Council agreed to pay for this renewal and Mr Mitchell wrote for the magazine in 1971: "At the beginning of April the Cathedral organist visited the Liverpool workshop of Messrs Henry Willis and Sons, Organ Builders. The organ console, which was one of the main points of deterioration in the instrument, has now been completely stripped of all old equipment and is in course of being rebuilt. A brand new system of transistorised solid state circuitry, which is more efficient than the previous equipment is to be used for the electrical mechanism of the organ. With the advent of such units wear and tear is reduced to nil, as there are no moving parts to pit and corrode. This new system has been devised by Mr Henry Willis in conjunction with Solid State Logic of Suffolk and the Cathedral instrument will be the first "Willis" organ to have it incorporated".

The organ rebuild took longer than had been thought but the following was reported in *The Orcadian* newspaper for Thursday, 23 December, 1971: "Sunday was an important day in St Magnus Cathedral, for its magnificent Henry Willis organ, out of action for a whole year, while it was being rebuilt and extensively modified in England, was re-dedicated at the Morning Service. Members of Kirkwall Town Council, led by Provost Leitch, were present, along with a large congregation. The Town Council–who, on behalf of the people of Kirkwall, own the Cathedral and its furnishings–financed the work on the organ at a cost of originally £12,000. Its representatives were able to hear, in the lovely music which made the service so memorable, how splendidly the restoration and modernisation of the instrument has been done. The organ is now, for its size, one of the finest in the country". "The message was considerably heightened by the Minister's remarks on the part music can play in the praise of God, and in the joyful proclamation of the Gospel . . . not only will the organ be heard Sunday by Sunday in the Cathedral but through a number of broadcast services shortly to be made for the BBC–one of them for the BBC's World Service, its sound will penetrate to many corners of the earth". . . "The Service began in silence–the Choir and Minister entering without any organ music . . . The short order of dedication from the Book of Common Order was read . . . 'In the faith of our Lord Jesus Christ, we do solemnly dedicate this organ and declare it to be for ever set apart from all common and unhallowed uses, and consecrated to the praise and worship of Almighty God, in the name of the Father, and the Son, and the Holy Spirit'." "The dedication spoken, the Cathedral was almost immediately filled with music: The organ, congregation and choir, with the help of six trumpeters–three from the Salvation Army and three from Kirkwall Grammar School–joining in Vaughan Williams' noble arrangement in the 'Old Hundredth' 'All people that on earth do dwell'. Very apposite to the message of the sermon, and the joyful mood of the Christmas service was the anthem, 'The Magnificat', by Stanford. The special organ music chosen by Mr Mitchell included Bach's 'Wachet auf'. . . A quotation from Mary's song of joy and praise, 'The Magnificat', which in a modern translation reads "Tell out my soul the greatness of the Lord" was the theme of Mr Cant's address". . . This included these words: "It is not only in preaching and prayer, it is not only in words, that the Gospel is proclaimed. God has been pleased to use music, the singing of psalms, paraphrase and hymns to magnify his name, to lift up before his people his grace and sovereign power which is mighty to save". "One purpose of this organ", "is no doubt to bring joy and great satisfaction to the musically educated, some of them in this congregation, but its primary purpose is to raise up God's people–all who come to this place of prayer: people of this town and from the Orkney Mainland and the Islands; visitors from all over the world; wise and ignorant, rich and poor, believers and unbelievers–into God's presence. It is to help them sing of God's glory, of his grace and power, so that Mary's Song, and others like it, shall come to possess their hearts. So that they shall go away into the world with the praise of God's majesty and greatness, and the praises of their Saviour throbbing in their minds and hearts".

One use of the organ which at this early stage few people had ever imagined, was its part in the St Magnus Festival. The inspiration for this was, in part, Mr Mitchell's and that of his friend, Mr Maxwell Davies, now Sir Maxwell Davies. Over the years of this Festival distinguished organists have played the Cathedral organ, but also it has been used not only in the St Magnus Festival Service, but for special musical pieces, one of the earliest and best known of these was Maxwell Davies' own moving work - "The Martyrdom of St Magnus". This St Magnus Festival still takes place in 1999, and draws a large number of distinguished musicians and poets and dramatists to Orkney, and not least to Kirkwall. For a good number of years the initial concert of the Festival was always held in the Cathedral and was the work of the Cathedral choir and their organist.

Notes

1.   John Oman - 'Concerning The Ministry' - SCM Press (1936) - pp48-49.
2.   'Songs of Renewal in Congregational Life' - Cant - Kirkwall Press - p53.
3.   G M Brown - 'The Orkney Tapestry' - Quartet Books London - p123.

Chapter IX

Preaching: Membership in the Committee of Forty: Ten Years in St Magnus

1. The Role of Preaching

When I came to St Magnus Cathedral, the congregation–by far the greatest of them–felt that I had come not only to be their pastor, especially remembering them and seeing them in hours of need, but also their Minister of Word and Sacrament, the one called to lead their worship, and to proclaim the Gospel to them from Scripture and at the Lord's Supper. Holy Communion was celebrated three or four times in the year, but Sunday Morning worship, with praise and prayer and the reading and preaching of the Word went on week by week. The people felt the conduct of Sunday worship, and not least the preaching of the Word, was the Minister's business. They did not expect normally to say prayers; occasionally someone might be asked to read from Scripture.

If the music, choral and congregational were seen as vital in the Cathedral worship, so was the central place of the Word of God read and preached, though it was recognised that it could also be sung, or acted, or carved, or displayed in the windows, or prayed, or made fellowship. The Revd Dr Neville Davidson, of Glasgow Cathedral who came to Orkney on one occasion to be the preacher at our Holy Week Services, wrote: 'Give us God' (words spoken to George Borrow) "That is the deepest need of man; the cry spoken or unspoken in the soul of every man. The whole vocation of the Christian Minister consists really in this one supreme task: to give men God; to make the reality of God clear to them; to make his majesty and love known to them. That is the impelling commanding motive of all he does: his preaching, his pastoral visiting, his prayers, his ministration of the Sacraments".[1] And one of the ways ministers of the Church of Scotland have tried to do this, through many generations or centuries, is by telling the story, the wonderful story of what God has done through his Son. He came to this earth and indwelt our humanity in Jesus of Nazareth, and was crucified, raised from the dead, and is at God's right hand, set free in the world to pour forth his life and Spirit upon his Church, and inform and save all who turn to him. So we find Dr Davidson going on to write: "In the Church of Scotland, for many centuries, great stress has been laid upon the proclamation of 'the Word'. Indeed we have sometimes been accused of giving exaggerated prominence to the sermon. There is however ample biblical authority for this. St Paul puts in the very foreground of the minister's calling the task of preaching. And he leaves us in no doubt as to what he believes should be the central note in preaching: 'Unto me is this grace given that I should preach the unsearchable riches of Christ'. The Christian preacher is to point men to Christ. . ." [2] To do this in St Magnus is as difficult a calling as it is to do it in one of Orkney's small country Churches. But there are at least two great encouragements to dare to do this in the Cathedral: One is the magnificent East window, which dominates the Cathedral, and draws the eye of many a member or visitor, on entering it. Our Lord is depicted on these lights as crucified, and ascended, surrounded by his men, eager to communicate with his people; encouragement comes too from looking up in the pulpit, for there, cut into the sounding board's roof, is a dove reminding the minister that he does not speak in his pulpit, only with human wisdom, but in the power and Spirit of Christ himself.

Because in my first year as Cathedral Minister, I was not often in Edinburgh at a Church meeting in 121 George Street, (the Church Headquarters), I gave much time to prepare the Cathedral Services Sunday by Sunday, in all their parts, not least their order, and the preaching and the prayers, and the nature of the praise. Many Sundays I felt that I had been helped to preach by the prayers of others, and by the consciousness often, when I came to do it, of the Dove, or the Holy Spirit not only above me, but within me. And yet there were, I thought, bad days, when I tried to get the right word to say, but felt I had failed miserably. Some words of The Revd Dr Whitley come to mind: "Again and again through the years doubts came: the dark night of the soul is no mystic's delusion, but the recurring nightmare of every preacher who seeks to be obedient to the Word of God".[3]

However my congregation were kind. Perhaps they sensed my awareness of failure in the Service sometimes; at any rate they were good enough to say that they would like to read something of what had been preached. This gave me the thought that I could publish some sermons in a small book. I did this, while enjoying Harry Whitley's story of how the same man in his first charge, came many time to express appreciation of his sermon. This was mentioned to the Session Clerk who, from the Minister's description, identified the man: "Oh, I know whom you mean. That must be Sandy Connel–he's ninety four, and stone deaf!"[4]

This little book was called *Preaching in a Scottish Parish Church–St Magnus and Other Sermons*. I got encouragement to go ahead with this from Professor John McIntyre from his books, and from his coming to St Thomas' Church, Leith, as the preacher–and from the late A M Hunter, Professor of New Testament in Aberdeen who read the book at an early stage. Lord Birsay kindly found time to write the Foreword. What was written is out of print now, but it was divided into four sections:

'Special Occasions; Significant Events in the Life of Jesus Christ; The Christian Life, Corporate and Individual; and Doctrinal.' In the Introduction, amongst other things, this was said: "Two things have moulded these sermons: one has been the Word of God as it has been studied and pondered week by week–sometimes, I trust, under the illumination of the Spirit; the other has been the thought and the life and culture of the people of the Cathedral congregation and parish".

I felt it was right to be involved with this publication, despite the fact that there was a big question being asked at the time about preaching–it is still being asked! "The title of *Preaching in a Scottish Parish Church* might seem irrelevant in a number of ways. First it may be objected that today the radical question is being asked not 'How shall we preach?' but 'Is there still any place at all for preaching? . . .'" But my contention was: "there is still a place for preaching in the local Church provided there is a genuine knowledge of, service to, and communication with the people of the parish, and their problems and needs".[5] In relation to this point, about preaching, the late Lord Birsay kindly said in his Foreword: "All who are privileged to read this book will surely give unqualified assent"

What is done in the world again and again has consequences. This happened in relation to this small book. It seems likely, for it was sold in the South as well as in Orkney, that one or more people, who had to do with the appointment of the preacher at the General Assembly, must have seen or read it, and so I was asked to preach the Sermon at the General Assembly Service in May, 1971, in St Giles Cathedral.

It was Ascension Sunday so that gave me great help in choosing the text, and in writing what was to be preached. I viewed this invitation with considerable concern, yet I saw it was a door opening into many representatives of Church and State, and I gave it much thought and prayer, as I tried to do for the Cathedral services. The text "I will put my words in thy mouth" came to me, and I trusted that there would be a positive response to the whole service as to the sermon. I received a warm welcome in St Giles–not least from the Minister who conducted fruitful prayers that day–the Revd H M Jamieson, and afterwards in Holyrood Palace where The Rt Hon Lord Clydesmuir was the High Commissioner that year. The Sermon was called: "Christ's Blessing on His Church" and the text was:

"The Lord their God is with them, acclaimed among them as king" (Numbers 23, part of Verse 21). (NEB)

"I have received command to bless; I will bless and I cannot gainsay it". In these words Balaam told Balak, King of Moab, that it was impossible for him to curse Israel; he could only bless her. Why? Because Balaam saw the living God present in the midst of his people. Hence he cried out, "the Lord their God is with them, acclaimed among them as king".   Our Gospel Reading this morning was also a story of blessing in which we heard how Jesus blessed his disciples, telling them of the promise of the Father to come. Of the disciple band also it could be said, "The Lord their God is with them".

Yet what are we to say of the Church today? What are we to say, in particular, of what in the eyes of some people, is the ass of the Church of Scotland which they feel called to beat? Can we say of its congregations, "the Lord their God is with them acclaimed among them as king?" Despite their weaknesses, despite so much contemporary denunciation of our Parish Churches, this can indeed be said. The reason for so saying lies in the grace of our ascended Lord who draws near to his people and gives them his presence through the Spirit. As a German writer has put it: "When Jesus walked on earth, He was close only to a few—only the little group of disciples. His presence was limited by space and time. Then only a few heard His word; today it spans the world. Then only a handful of his friends could plead, 'Stay with us for it is toward evening;' today millions of hands fold in prayer, and where two or three are gathered . . . He will be with them". But if truly our Lord is present in his Church, what is he there to do? Christ is in his Church not to scold or denounce, but, first of all, to bless—so the subject of this sermon is "Christ's Blessing upon His Church". Our Lord wills to bless his people with his gifts. These are varied, but one gift is for us all, for the nations indeed as well as for the Church, it is the gift of the Gospel.

Christ Blesses us with the Gift of the Gospel

But we need light, do we not, upon this gift? For, like a diamond, the Gospel has many facets, and we need constantly to be turning towards it. There is an interesting passage in George Mackay Brown's book, *An Orkney Tapestry*, in which he tells of the visit of Jock, the tinker, to the tomb of St Magnus in Birsay. Jock has come to ask for the blessing of light for his blind wife, Mary. After lighting his candle, and setting it up, Jock speaks like this: "Light for light, Magnus. Ask the Lord to put·a glimmer back in her skull". One of the greatest needs of all of us is to have glimmers of the life-saving Gospel of Christ, constantly put back in our skulls, for none of us is omniscient; we cannot forget that in the school of Christ, and his gospel, there is no leaving day. Ministers need to pray more for their people at this point, and people for their ministers. It has to be admitted that we ministers have often hard and resistant hearts, and we only hope that our elders and people, after interceding for us, will not be driven to say of us, the kind of thing Jock the tinker said of his blind wife Mary: "There was too much badness in you, the saint couldn't do a thing.

Each of us, then needs light upon the Gospel, we need to have done for us what Jesus did for his disciples, namely to have our minds and hearts opened to himself. This is the work of the Spirit who takes of the things of

Christ and reveals them to us. We need him to lead us into the great Cathedral
of the Gospel and show us more clearly what this Gospel is. We need to be
taken often into the nave of our Lord's incarnation and earthly life, where we
can see him as both Son of God, and as the gracious friend, who was faithful
through all his people's unfaithfulness; we need to be brought repeatedly into
the fascinating transepts of his teaching and preaching; we require to be
moved on to the high altar of his saving work and passion, the mystery of his
death for our sins, and so also, to the equally mysterious and power-giving
great East window of his resurrection and ascension. And let us remember
this, lest we appear to be forgetting that Christianity is a way of worship, and
a way of life as well as a way of thought, each time we glimpse something of
the meaning of our Lord's life and death and resurrection and saving acts, he
grasps us afresh, and brings us into a new friendship with himself, and into the
joyful relationship of being sons and daughters of God, our Father, from
whom comes peace and guidance and strength. He leads us, too, into his
community, into all the intimacy and freedom of his family of faith and hope
and love.

We have been given a wonderful Gospel in which to believe, though
we are only too aware of the poverty of our formulations of it. It overflows and
breaks through all our little words. It is the land where sometimes the mists lie,
but also where the rivers rise.

Christ Blesses us by Way of Judgement

Christ is in his Church to bless us with the gift of the Gospel, but also
to judge us, for sometimes this is the only way his blessing can come.

If you go into St Magnus Cathedral, in Kirkwall, on a summer evening,
when the rays of the setting sun pour through the West window, you will
discover that these rays not only light up the various colours of the pillars, so
that you see the reds, and the golds, and the yellows, and the pinks of the
stones, but you will find that the many cracks in the masonry are also revealed.
The light of Christ shows us his own glory, but in that light we see too the
cracks, the deficiencies in our congregations and in ourselves. Our Lord is
showing us at present the inadequacy of much of our congregational life, for
example, the massive irreverence of many members who stay away from the
sanctuary, and the great ignorance of many others concerning Christ and his
truth. For certainly behind the crisis in worship, there hides the crisis of faith.

It is good that judgement should begin at the House of God, but
Christ's judgement upon our congregational life and witness, is not, let us be
clear, for its ruin, but for its renewal, it is there in order that vigorous renewing

action may be taken whereby Christ may prune his church, with a view to the busting forth of new life.

Our Lord's judgement is also over our individual lives, so that we need forgiveness of sin, for we recognise in how many ways pride can stain our souls, and how our self-interest can come first. But we also require renewal of faith for both in the Church and in society these days, we can be very lonely and despairing. This can arise in the Church, overseas and at home, from having too few leaders and active members; in the world it can arise from having too many people around. As Pope Paul said in his recent Apostolic letter, "Man is experiencing a new loneliness. It springs from the anonymous crowd which surrounds man, and in which he finds himself a stranger. He is so often a victim of urbanisation, undoubtedly an irreversible stage in the development of human societies".

So we require renewal of our faith, not just a surface faith that trusts in God, when things go well, but out Lord's own deep faith, according to which he still went on worshipping and obeying God, the Father, although in his loneliness of purpose and despair no answer came to his cry for help, 'let this cup pass from me,' and no divine deliverance was granted and he died alone on the Cross yet saying, 'Father, into thy hands I commit my spirit'.

Christ blesses his Church with his Gospel, showing us himself, and with his judgement, showing us our congregations and ourselves. One last thought—He blesses us with his reign. "The Lord their God is with them," our text said, "acclaimed among them is king".

Christ Blesses us by Reigning over us

Christ's reign over his people means, in part, both his commanding them, and his empowering them.

What Christ commands his Church is to go out into the world, encountering it in its darkness and its light, in its weakness and its strength, to go out into the world—and here I quote from the Special Report on Priorities of Mission, "with courage and openness, taking risks, not clutching at its own security". This may not be very pleasant for us sometimes, so we require to be strengthened by the weakness and worldliness of Jesus. We often strive to move away from the dark and dangerous and uncomfortable places to the light and safe and comfortable ones. Jesus, as a Swedish writer recently put it, moved <u>downwards</u>, identifying himself ever more closely with the needy and the suffering. "The picture of Christ crucified" this author wrote, "alone and abandoned by the pious, but surrounded (at the place of execution) by the lowest level of society, is electrifying in the present world—the effect is social, it sends those who truly believe in him out into the world to be his servants".

The more the Church, at home and in other lands, has the courage and faith to put this servant role at the centre of her life and witness in the parishes, the more I believe will she be able to become better convinced about the reality of her living Lord, and so be able to deal with the crisis of faith–for he who does God's will shall know of the doctrine; the more, too, will the Church be able to break out from her structural fundamentalism, and be able to re-think her ministry, and re-shape her worship. 'Seek ye first the kingdom of God', Jesus said, and that means, not least, the reign over his people now of the humble, serving, suffering love revealed in our Saviour, and in that holy love, let us remember, there is all the dynamic saving power of the Eternal God himself. The Cross incarnate in the lives of God's servants, means, sooner or later, the pulling down of the citadels of evil.

And if all this seems too demanding, we must recall that the Christ who commands, is the Christ who strengthens us in different ways: by interceding for us, and inspiring others to do so, by raising up helpers for us, often people both political and prayerful, by sending his Spirit to invade our hearts and lives, by encouraging us to be explorers in the great continent of his saving power, for frequently we only stand timidly on the edge of it. So let us ask, with the people of Scotland particularly in mind, that God, who is Father, Son, and Holy Spirit, may put forth in increasing measure, his strengthening and uplifting power.

And in Chesterton's words, we can surely pray:-

> Bind all our lives together,
> Smite us and save us all;
> In ire and exultation,
> Aflame with faith, and free,
> Lift up a living nation,
> A single sword to thee.

The Lord bless to us this preaching from his Holy Word and to his Name be the praise and the glory".

No minister can ever know what is the full result of his conduct of worship and delivery of sermons. And yet we believe that when the seed of the Word is sown, though much is lost, there can be a harvest of penitence and forgiveness, or of new faith, or of comfort and assurance, or of judgement and mercy, or of new initiative in the service of the needs of people in the world.

These words of Neville Davidson have encouraged me, and no doubt others in the role of preaching and of conducting public worship: "Only one thing is of fundamental importance in the proclamation of the Christian Gospel–namely that men and women shall listen and understand and believe and obey. Only one thing is of primary importance in public worship–namely that those taking part are enabled genuinely to pray, to hold converse with God".[6] Such 'converse with God', when flowing from the heart and mind, and inspired by the spirit of Christ, again and again leads to confession and increase of faith, and to thanksgiving, and to intercession, and to patient, creative, even suffering service in the world. I went out from Orkney to Edinburgh to the General Assembly, and to this Assembly Service in St Giles with the faith that Christ would go before me. These words of The Revd Professor Robin Barbour seem now strangely appropriate to what happened: "You go out into the world with the power of Christ in your heart, not knowing in the least where you are going (that is to say, knowing quite well that you are going to such-and-such a place to do such and such a thing, but not knowing in the least what will happen to you there); and something comes about which shows you afresh that Christ is there, working secretly. Suddenly you realise, rather to your surprise, that you had a hand in it, through something you said or did or managed to avoid saying or doing; and that is mission. But it is precisely also receiving the promise of God".[7]

I pass over quickly some further speaking and preaching opportunities given to me in the 1970 years in different spheres, and sometimes to a larger number. I was asked to give the Lee Memorial Lecture in Greyfriars Church in Edinburgh and I called it - "Christian Worship: It's Crisis and Renewal". I see that at the start of the Lecture I wrote: "I want to speak later on, I hope positively, about one aspect of worship–its renewal–but I want first to make reference, as the Trust Deed of the Lectureship suggests, to a feature of the present times, namely to what has often been called the Crisis of Worship. I begin by reminding you of some of the causes of this crises . . ." I also was invited to preach in Crathie Church, and in the King's College Chapel, Aberdeen, and to engage in certain Radio Broadcasts. I remember very well these different occasions (and how on edge I was in at least one of them!). I especially recall the Recorded Radio Broadcasts in February, 1972: one was an Overseas Broadcast for St Magnus Day (April, 16th); another was Sunday Half Hour Service of Praise (Radio 2), while the Cathedral Morning Service was to be broadcast on the Home Service of the BBC (Radio 4). This was the first of four services, at that time, from certain Cathedrals of Scotland; the other services came from Dornoch, Glasgow, and Dunblane Cathedrals. Why I remember these Broadcast Services clearly was not simply that they were recorded on one Sunday, but because they had to be carried through in the East end of the Cathedral. The Nave was filled with scaffolding, and the congregation and choir were crushed together into a small space (which may have helped the singing, if not the seating of the people!).

2.   The Committee of Forty

Another very important event for the Cathedral and myself in the 1970s was my nomination at the General Assembly for the Committee of Forty. This was set up "as a kind of think tank to do some forward planning for the Church. It has reported fully to each year's General Assembly, and is giving its final report in 1978".[8] This was the Committee's task: "to interpret for the Church the purpose towards which God is calling his people in Scotland, to investigate and assess the resources of the Church in persons and property, and to make recommendations for the reshaping of the life and structure of the Church". There was published, after the C of F had endeavoured to carry out its remit, "A Summary of The Reports and Recommendations of the Committee of Forty 1972–1978". This was called "People With A Purpose" - "The 40 File". In the preface to the 40 File we read: "We don't claim to have done justice to such a huge task. But we have tried to discern something of what God is calling his people to do, and we have made a number of relevant recommendations. We are convinced that God's purpose includes all his people. And so we commend this booklet to the whole Church".

Parish ministers can often take on too much work in Assembly Committees, but I accepted nomination to the C of F (Committee of Forty) not only because I felt it had an exciting remit, and could teach me much, and be for the benefit of St Magnus Cathedral congregation, but also because I was fulfilling an ordination promise when I said "Yes" to this question - "Do you promise to be subject to the Lord in this Presbytery, and to the superior courts of the Church, and to take your due part in the administration of its affairs"? Had I known for how many years this C of F was going to last, and how long each meeting was to take–usually a whole weekend–I might well have hesitated in joining it!

It has been said that "The minister will always be subject to the temptation to view things the wrong way round: to forget that it is the duty of the Church to be interested in the welfare of the world, and to think of the world as existing to minister to the welfare of the Church".[9] The C of F must have helped many ministers to deal with this temptation, for one of the very valuable things it did was to make its members (not all ministers) look afresh at the quickly changing and needy world, at the secularised world which God had made, and in which he was working despite the views of so many people, and where he was calling his people to be his fellow labourers. So it is not surprising to find that the 40 File, after looking at the interpretation of God's purpose (to be done with the Church rather than for the Church) immediately passed to the chapter headed "God's World". This can be a suitable point to say that the Convener of the C of F was the Revd Professor R S Barbour MC, BD, who had clear convictions about the world and the Church, convictions which were no doubt strengthened, may be an occasion initiated by the members of his committee. These were expressed in the very valuable and fruitful reports which were given to the General Assembly, and so many of these are summarised in the Forty File. The huge global, and in Europe, secular, and often secularised world in which we now live, is a new world into which God has brought us, and in which we have a fresh challenge - "The challenge to overcome corporate selfishness, if the rising expectations of the whole human race are to be met in any way at all, is something with which men and women have never been confronted before. To love your neighbour is now to love all humanity and nothing less; and to care for the created world in a new way is an imperative of life - 'this do and you shall live'.[10] But this "present situation", Professor Barbour also wrote, "is not a disaster for the Church, but a God-given opportunity to discard the non-essentials, and concentrate on the vital things by which alone any Church really lives: the power of the Risen Christ bringing life out of Death and, in material terms, the water, the bread, the wine and the book, which cost us little and give us everything we need".[11]

In regard to the meeting of the C of F, the Convener wisely at most of these made provision for the celebration of Holy Communion. The last meeting by his generosity being a sacramental one in his home at Fincastle House, near Pitlochry. Such celebrations bound members together, and enabled us better to make our contribution as committee members.

This sacramental decision enabled for us an act of corporate obedience to our Risen Lord, and it was seen as an essential way of Christ being remembered in our midst and of his renewing in us faith in the Church despite its many failures and in view of our need to communicate the Gospel in fresh terms to its people. This making room for our Lord's presence in the world and in the sacrament of the Church was crucial to the C of F not least because it was engaged in so much necessary criticism of its working.

It is right to remember one of the early outstanding speakers to the committee–the Very Revd Dr Archie Craig. He had some hard things to say about the Church of Scotland in the 1970s. He felt that the C of F required to hear a big sound, a word of divine revelation to awaken us so that we might have something to say to the Church, which so often seemed to be stuck in barren soil. Elizabeth Templeton wrote in 1991 a stimulating book about Dr Craig, called *God's February*, and she recalled his trust in the Church. For however much he saw into its poverty and weakness and betrayal of Christ, "he would not have crumpled into despair" - rather he would have said, "You know, there are remarkable things happening, really remarkable things. And he would have produced some small encounter he had had, or a conversation, or the news of eastern Europe, and would remind one of the molecular forces of growth in apparently barren February soil".[12]

But to return to the outside world, the Forty File, said: "God wants us to face up to what is happening in the world".[13] He wants us to face up to so many good things by way of scientific discoveries, but also to bad things, like the pollution of the earth and air and water, and to the hunger of peoples, and to their sin and suffering and often violent deaths. So the C of F says: "Through events He is calling us to show a new kind of love for our neighbours, and a new awareness of being one human family . . . God means us to do something about these concerns". The point of the C of F was to stimulate discussion and action in the Church of Scotland and elsewhere, not only in the matters of Church structure and Ministry and Worship and Christian education, but <u>also</u> in the sphere of serving the world, and of seeing God's works there.

All this was raised in another Chapter in the Forty File, "What the Church is for". So while "<u>the job of the Church is just to be the Church:</u> to be the place where Christ, his love and Resurrection are always at the centre" . . . "in another sense, <u>the job of the Church is to take the Gospel to other people</u>–in word and action to make known God's saving love. We have lost sight of this main aim. Many of our congregations seem more concerned just to keep going, . . . or to care for their own members, rather than to reach out to others near and far in Christ's name . . . <u>A generation is now growing up in Scotland many of whose members know nothing at all about Christianity</u>. If we are going to get back on course and be guided by the main aim of taking the Gospel to <u>people where they are</u>, then certain things follow. . . Now we shall need new parishes and groupings, new forms of ministry, new uses of the resources of the Church; a new flexibility and readiness to experiment in order to take the Gospel to others in a rapidly changing world. <u>It is not our job to keep the Church of Scotland the way it has always been</u>".[14]

So the Forty File went on to deal with "A new shape of Church"; here is the relevant summary of the C of F's vision of this: "We have tried to sketch the main features of this new shape of Church in the next few pages.

Broadly, what we foresee is a Church with a greater variety of groupings–many congregational units remaining but much less self-contained; working together in larger units called <u>community parishes</u> and containing also many smaller and more personal groups.

We foresee a Church more obviously concerned with the community and with witnessing to the Gospel in areas of work and everyday life.

We foresee a Church less dependent on the professional ministry, developing new forms of ministry and involving members to a much greater degree. We foresee a trimmer more efficient General Assembly structure, with a greater role for Presbyteries, which would be more responsible for planning the outreach of the Church.

Above all, we foresee a people sustained for their purpose and renewed for Christian living by a deeper spirit of prayer and worship".[15]

It is surely encouraging to learn that in 1997 in the Presbytery of Orkney, something of the vision of the C of F has become reality. There is the emergence of a community parish in the East mainland, and one is planned for the West Mainland. Ministry also is different now in the late 1990s; Church services are often less monological, with elders and members participating more in them. Public worship too has changed. It has become, at one service in one parish, essentially participating and dialogical and sometimes prepared for, in a far greater way than was the case in the 1970s. Again Sacraments of Holy Communion have been increased in a number of parishes, following the view of the C of F that "The Church of Scotland must now depart from its long infidelity to its own origins and restore a more frequent Sacrament".[16] Training for elders and members has developed more and more, and has functioned through the emergence of groups run by a congregation and Presbytery with the help of Training in Leadership and Service with its base in Edinburgh.

Presbytery now thinks in a wider and deeper way of social needs like housing, jobs, care of the elderly and the disabled, and of the problems of the NHS and Social Work, not least in relation to alcoholism and drugs. The Church of Orkney cannot forget what was written by the C of F in one section of its early reports to the Assembly called 'Scotland in the World': "The challenge to the Christian Church is to engender the development of revolutionary consciousness that works outward in time of the pursuit of new social goals coupled with a God-given assurance about the future of man".

In regard to the Presbytery's own pastoral care, it is right to say that the care of ministers has become better, but the central issues for Presbyteries suggested by the C of F have not, to my mind, been truly grasped, at least by the Presbytery of Orkney eg "the planning and support of the missionary strategy of the Church in the Presbytery area should be the primary concern of the Presbytery itself.[17] To say that does not mean that there have not been missions in different parishes, or encouragement of non believers to become members of the Church, but there has been little radical drive to help the congregations change their allegiance from Churchianity to a Kingdom Christianity—The reign of God means not least the reign of God over all in the world. The danger for those who become Christians is that often nothing is asked of them beyond Church witness and reading the Word and prayer: "But for those who want to put themselves at the service of the Kingdom, it is a different story. A disciple is someone who binds himself to his master . . . And invariably the pull of discipleship for the Kingdom is, in terms of social probability, downwards . . . The purging and cleansing of the Church happens when this process of moving downwards takes place en masse. History is enabled by such people".[18]

More needs to be said about mission but the C of F did say "The task of mission is now on our doorstep". Yet mission is more than "a message of friendship" to a parish, and it is more than co-operation with a student team coming to a town, visiting schools there, and sharing in worship and meetings in a Church or hostel, or hall, or home. Mission teams did come to Kirkwall, and of one team in 1976 this was written by the leader in the *Cathedral Magazine*: "We were happy to share in the work which the Revd Robin Ross (the then Cathedral Assistant) had been doing with the young folk, building up the relationships which he had established with them".

This last point leads on to something being said about the excellent work done in Kirkwall by Robin and Annie Ross from 1975 to 1977. Robin was Assistant

Minister at different times in the East Church and the Cathedral and in the minds of many, he made a significant contribution to the Church and community of Orkney.

This was particularly true of his work with our young people. He was their companion to Iona and in the camps there, but it could be said that his outstanding work was done in the sphere of the Youth Hostel in Kirkwall. Robin's job there was pioneering, for this new school hostel had just been built, and he was the first minister of religion to have made his home among the staff and pupils, with his charming and gracious wife, Annie. In ways that cannot be truly described but were realised by many of the pupils, and by some parents, Robin and Annie became trusted by the Hostel young people, and some were later willing to share in the Hostel prayers or to come with Robin to public worship, or to follow him in other creative ways in the community.

What Robin Ross and his wife were doing in the new school hostel was, the initiation of Abrahamic mission, going into a new place to receive together God's promise of his presence with them and with some young people gathered around them. This going out corporately into new places in the community, or into difficult places in the community, was no easy task but once more it was in line with what the C of F meant when it foresaw "A Church more obviously concerned with the community and with witnessing to the Gospel in areas of work and everyday life:" And it was not only in the School Hostel that an attempt was made to make a witness to the Gospel in the community. The Kirk Session of the Cathedral decided to make a corporate effort to assist in re-opening the local cinema when it had to be closed through vandalistic behaviour of no doubt a small minority. Elders volunteered to be present on a certain evening for many months. Politically too the Church shares in community life: Elders and members of the different Churches becoming Office Bearers and Council members of Kirkwall Town Council, or of the later Orkney Islands Council. The Minister of the Cathedral had, and still has the privilege of being Chaplain to the Council.

3. After Ten Years as Minister of St Magnus Cathedral

I realised in 1978 that I had been ten years Minister of St Magnus, and I preached a sermon then which gives some indication of the changes in the congregation and community at that time, but also of God's undeviating saving purpose for his people.

Text - "The grass withers, the flowers fade but the word of our God endures forever". - Isaiah 40.8.

The Background of The Text

I remind you of the background of the text. In the middle of the 6th century BC the Jews were captive in Babylon. "By 550 BC, that is after 38 years of exile, nearly all the strong men of Israel's days of independence must have been taken away. Death had been busy with the exiles for more than a generation. There was no longer any human representation of Jehovah to rally the people's trust, the monarchy–the priesthood and the prophethood–whose great personalities so often took the place of Jehovah's official leaders had all alike disappeared".[19] Small wonder the Jews allowed themselves to fall into the pit of depression, feeling that their God had forsaken them, saying "My plight is hidden from the Lord and my cause has passed out of God's notice".

However, despite all the changes through which they had passed and despite their depression and unbelief, the prophet was told to preach that God had not forgotten His people. God's Word, that is His plan and purpose for them was sure and abiding:

"The grass withers, the flowers fade, but the word of our God endures for ever more". The subject of the sermon this morning is therefore 'The Changing World and Our Unchanging God.'

The Last Decade

"I began my ministry here on the first Sunday of September, 1968. It has been a great privilege to have been minister through those years and to have had your support and encouragement and kindness through them all. Looking back I am aware, as you must be, of great changes in the spheres of community, church and home. Community-wise there have been major changes in local government, educational opportunity and economic life. We have lost the old Town Council of the City and Royal Burgh of Kirkwall and we are now controlled by the Orkney Islands Council, who have a difficult job to do and we must seek to believe the best concerning them all and wish them well, permanent officials and elected councillors alike. In the educational sphere we have lost the old Grammar School but gained new buildings, affording better facilities in Papdale. In the economy there is, on the whole, greater prosperity in Orkney now in 1978, than in 1968. This is not unconnected with what has happened in Flotta. There, in certain parts of that island in Scapa Flow the grass has literally withered and the flowers faded, and in their place there now stand the great oil tanks that house the North Sea oil. As far as the Church goes there has been a considerable loss of members over the whole Presbytery, and a fall too in the number of ministers, though it must be pointed out that the giving of the church in Orkney has never been higher. In terms of this Cathedral we have witnessed traumatic events; cracks in the ceiling at one stage necessitated our moving out of the nave and our worshipping in the East end. But then there came the huge renovation to stop the movement of this building westwards, and we trust that this has been successful and that stability has now been restored to our Cathedral. Stability and continuity too, in terms of our congregational life has been secured by an in-flow of younger leaders into most organisations. As far as the Kirk Session is concerned about forty new–and mostly young–elders have been ordained and/or inducted in the last decade. And yet there have been disquieting factors also both in the community and in the Church. You and I have seen a considerable increase in alcoholism, and a drift away from the church of the 10-20 age group. In relation to the domestic scene some very precious people have passed from our daily presence in the last ten years. Some of us have seen our children growing up, reaching the teenage years, leaving school or going to work or getting married and having children of their own. We ourselves have grown older, less able to do some things, but I trust more mature mentally and spiritually if not physically. You and I have known what it means to say "the grass withers, the flowers fade," but do we also know what it means when the prophet says "the Word of our God endures for evermore"? The Sermon concluded with short statements about 'the Word of God's Assurance and Forgiveness', the Word of God's Power, and the Word of God's Shepherding Love.

Notes

1.   N Davidson - 'Reflections of a Scottish Churchman' - Hodder and Stoughton - p13.
2.   Ibid - p13.
3.   H C Whitley - 'Laughter in Heaven' - Hutchison & Co Ltd - p25.
4.   Ibid - p30.
5.   H W M Cant - 'Preaching in a Scottish Parish Church' - W R Mackintosh - The Kirkwall Press - Introduction.
6.   N Davidson - Ibid - p15.
7.   R S Barbour - 'What Is The Church For?' - Department of New Testament Exegesis, King's College, Old Aberdeen - pp48-49.
8.   'People With A Purpose' - Preface - p3.
9.   L Hodgson - 'Christian Faith and Practice' - Epworth Press - London - p90.
10.   'Reports To The General Assembly' - C of F Report - May, 1978 - p494.
11.   'People With A Purpose' Ibid - Preface - p3.
12.   A C Craig - 'God's February' - BCC/CCBI Inter Church House, 35-41 Lower Marsh - London - p169.
13.   'People With A Purpose' (also called 'The Forty File') - p7.
14.   Ibid - p8.
15.   Ibid - p10.
16.   Ibid - p12.
17.   Ibid - p23.
18.   D Reeves - 'For God's Sake' - pp34, 37-38.
19.   G A Smith - The Book of Isaiah (Vol II) - Hodder and Stoughton - London - p82.

Chapter X

An Interlude - Family Life

Even a short review of the places where I have stayed and of the parishes in which I have served, would reveal how very fortunate I have been. Again and again I have been surrounded by so many gracious and gifted people. I see now how slow I often was to recognise this; it has been so not least in the Parish where I spent my longest time as Minister, that of St Magnus Cathedral. It is so easy for a Minister to have his mind on all the things that he has to do, and which will be expected of him, that he can be blind to the context of the people in which he must do his work. It took quite a time for me to waken up to the people of the congregation and parish where I was called to serve, but my wife and my family helped greatly in this awakening when the time came for our arrival in Kirkwall, Orkney.

We had a few weeks to settle in to the Manse in Kirkwall, prior to the school's opening after the summer holidays. So we had time to see something of the Orkney mainland and beyond. We had a very good introduction to Orkney, weather wise–three glorious weeks of sunshine when we could visit together some of the beaches and lochs and historic buildings, while learning at the same time about Orcadian ornithology and wild flowers. My wife was very much more aware of the children's needs than I was, and more so after Ministry in the Cathedral began. However I was soon able to get a small rowing boat with an outboard engine, and go out on the lochs, sometimes taking the family with me. I now take grand children on the golf course, but I was very poor about finding time to go with the children. In 1968 the annual charge was £9 for adult membership; in 1969 I was told, with apology, that the fee has gone up to £11!

It did not take too long before each of the children discovered friends among the Orcadians, who shared with them their often exciting and happy interests. After the initial change, Elizabeth was befriended by excellent young people in the Grammar School; this helped her to have entrance into many stimulating activities, into continuing Girl Guiding and camping, and nature learning, and swimming and squash. Alison also took enormous pleasure in outdoor pursuits, especially in riding ponies. Eventually I was able to get her her own one, Emma, who brought her delight with her foal, Danke, for many years. Andrew discovered his ability to cope with musical instruments, and quickly began to play his recorder, and then his violin, and last but not least, the bagpipes (taught by a splendid teacher in the Kirkwall Boys' Brigade).

Long before 1978 Margot was an Assistant in a Kirkwall Medical Practice, and by that year all the children had left school, and had gone to further education–Elizabeth at the Western Infirmary School of Physiotherapy in Glasgow; Alison and Andrew to Edinburgh University.

I had been told that a new Manse would be bought when I came in 1968 but after a few years there was no sign of its coming, and I raised the matter one day with one of the senior Orcadian elders. He said to me in his kindly way: "Don't worry, Minister, you'll surely get your hoose!' How strangely right he was, for soon after this, another senior elder, also an Orcadian, spoke to the man living in a large house, opposite our own. It turned out he didn't like owning it; he was now alone, and it was far too big. "Who wants it anyway?" he asked. "The Cathedral would like to buy it for a Manse" was the reply. Not long after this, an arrangement was made with a Kirkwall lawyer that the house and the garden and a small field nearby, would be sold to the Cathedral, and after some months of restoration work, our whole family moved into it. This was a healing move for each one of us, more accommodation for the children (and for friends and visitors from the South!), and for groups from the congregation and the parish. We gradually (too slowly I now think) discovered healing people as well as places. Many of these were from within the Cathedral congregation, and some lived on our side in Berstane Road, like Alex and Chris Stephen, but there were others across the road like Francis and Ethel Cusiter who were very good to us also. Not least, we were given as neighbours, Sidney and Elsa Robertson who were wonderfully generous to so many Orcadians; they were particularly kind to us, who lived initially at the end of their drive, and later just on the other side of the road. We have many memories of their generosity at family parties and other humorous occasions. Once our Andrew's goat escaped, and it was said to have butted the rear of Elsa (Mrs Robertson) as she was attending to some roses or bushes! Sometime later Alison's rabbit went across the road, and was eaten by one of the Robertson's terriers! I hope we were a hospitable family in return for all the kindness we received, for a perceptive family peer group can be such a creative force for good. Yet it is very easy to romanticise it, and see it only as a wonderful web of forgiving and fruitful relationships. But how often it is that parents can fail to see members of their own family in depth, and in their hidden needs.

George Mackay Brown in his very honest and revealing autobiography *For the Islands I Sing*, tells how he was once asked by a lady, Norah Smallwood, a Director in a publicity firm, to write a novel. George initially did not think he could do this, but he tells how he had imagined an island in Orkney with a small village at one end. Then he came to imagine who the villagers might be, and who the island farmers and their families, and he saw the school playing field full of children. Then he writes: "Most of the characters remained 'flat' . . . it was impossible to look deeply into them all. . . The creators of great characters–Shakespeare, Tolstoy, Mann, Forster, Molière–are more than puppet masters: they have seen that every individual–even 'the living shadows' passing on the street, seemingly empty and without meaning–are "diamond, immortal diamond".[1] It should be added here that G M Brown did not just see one of his imaginary characters in this light, but he occasionally saw a member of his own family in this way. More than once he saw his father, not as 'flat', doing his usual job of tailor and postman, but in depth and in his complexity . . . "once or twice, as a child, I listened outside the door of his bedroom where he paced back and fore, uttering aloud his doubts and his worries. These soliloquys put a kind of wonder and disquiet on me. Perhaps I was beginning to realise that human beings are much more complex than they seem to be".[2]

I slowly came to see that I was often pre-occupied with the affairs of the Cathedral congregation, and with town matters, so that the children were not often seen in depth. It seemed for long to be enough if they were discovering the usual good things and interests and people at school, and in the community, yet what about "diamond, immortal diamond"? What about the wonderfully unique and precious things each ordinary child or youth really is, their essential goodness not yet obliterated or damaged by their practice of doing wrong? One of George MacLeod's stories comes to mind. It concerned his own small daughter. It was a splendid morning for her; she just wanted to see her dad before she set off for her first day at school. George was busy in his study writing letters: "I was self important . . . she came into my room, in her first school uniform. I said, "Your tie is not quite straight". Then I looked at her eyes. She wasn't crying. She was unutterably disappointed. She hadn't come for a tie inspection. She had come to show that she was going to school for the first time. A terrific day, and I had let her down . . . I ran downstairs. I said all the right things. I crossed the road with her. I went to school with her.

I had missed the moment, missed the point. I will always see those eyes. Sometimes when I am very busy; sometimes when I am writing letters, I am forgiven, but I won't forget. If we want to show our forgiveness, we must unfailingly believe that we are forgiven . . . when we do, we cannot be other than forgiving".[3]

I have also thought, like some other parents, that I have "missed the moment, missed the point" with my children, not least when they went off south from Orkney, failing to encourage and support them in their initial attempts to reach out to others in relationships and friendship. For example I remember very well going to the Veterinary College in Edinburgh to see how Andrew was getting on. I went to a board where I thought results could have been indicated, but all I saw was on another board, a competition for beer drinking in the High Street; then I read in an order of merit–"1–A Cant". I asked a janitor where Andrew and his friends might be. I was directed to a certain pub. I saw him there . . . in a corner of that building playing his fiddle with some friends. I should have seen that all this was an event in which students were enjoying their music and companionship together. I thought of it as destroying a student career, and future hopes of a job–I had seen a number of people in the Army, and to a lesser extent in Orkney, badly hurt by their drinking capabilities. I ought to have recognised that I had seen one way in which Andrew and some of his friends were finding enjoyment and relaxation in a peer group. But I had "missed the moment, missed the point", failing on that occasion to wait patiently, and then to have had the opportunity of listening to Andrew and his fellow students and of talking with them.

The girls in their own way have sought to relate to others–Elizabeth in Edinburgh, Aberdeen, and Glasgow and later with her husband and family in Orkney; Alison in Africa and since then in New College, West Pilton, Canada, and later in Iona, Edinburgh, and Portsmouth. Both the girls, like their brother have, I believe, the ability to see good things in another person of whatever position in life. This may in part have been an Orcadian gift to them from their school days in Kirkwall. It may have been from their Baptism; and it could have been, for Andrew, from the splendid prayer offered for him before he left, with his mother, from the Salvation Army Home where he was born, near Leith.

Orkney has a strange power to call its people back to itself often after much travelling in many places. So all our children came back to be married in Orkney. Elizabeth and Alison in St Magnus Cathedral, and Andrew in the East Church, Kirkwall. We are very fortunate to have Elizabeth and her husband, Micky Austin, and their three children with us in Kirkwall–Ingrid, David and Jennifer, as also Andrew and his charming wife Alice, with their little girls, Becky and Thora. Alison and her husband, Philip Newell, now stay in Portsmouth with their four children–Rowan, Brendan, Kirsten, and Cameron, but they still manage, some years, to come and see us in Orkney, if we don't visit them.

As I have said all members of our family have been baptised, and they see the need for the service orientated life. They all know the story of St Magnus, Orkney's supreme Saint, but one wonders sometimes if they see that story as remote and irrelevant to modern life. St Magnus saw his life as given him by God, and ultimately he gave it away in Christian worship, not despising the Mass, and in the suffering service of his followers and in forgiving love to his enemies. But do our young people and many of Kirkwall's youth, who know the St Magnus story, think it is imprisoned in the distant past and not relevant to their present lives? That is the way George Mackay Brown saw it being understood. "Re-telling the story of Magnus and Hakon is well enough, but quite suddenly one morning, as I was thinking of ways to tell the actual martyrdom in Egilsay in 1117, it occurred to me that the whole story would strike a modern reader as remote and unconnected with our situation in the twentieth century. The truth must be that such incidents are not isolated casual happenings in time, but are repetitions of some archetypal pattern; an image or an event stamped on the spirit of man at the very beginning of man's time on earth, that will go on repeating itself over and over in every life . . . . The life and death of Magnus must therefore be shown to be contemporary, and to have a resonance in the twentieth century. I did not have far to go to find a parallel: a concentration camp in central Europe in the spring of 1944 -

Magnus appears as Pastor Bonhoeffer".[4]

Yet it takes a long time often for something like the dying and rising life of Jesus Christ to be recapitulated in the humanity of Magnus or Bonhoeffer or in that of the baptised that we know well and love. Members of the Church are only too aware of this as they contemplate their own baptism.

Certain Scriptural texts often remain with people; one that has often lodged in my mind and which is suitable for a family is this: ". . . The darkness is passing away and the true light is already shining". (I John2 v 8). It is applicable to communities and congregations and groups. It is too, relevant to the family in which the darkness or uncertainty of separation from God and from other people is often passing away, and the true light of love is shining out from one person to another. Hatred destroys this light - "He who says he is in the light and hates his brother is in the darkness still". (I John 2v9) Further the Celtic way of seeing should always have a place in the minds of parents in relation to their children. For one characteristic of this is to see everyone as penetrated by the Spirit of God. "How many of us were taught actually to look for God within creation, and to recognise the world as the place of revelation, and the whole of life as sacramental? Were we not for the most part led to think spirituality is about looking away from life, so that the Church is distanced from the world and spirit is almost entirely divorced from the matter of our bodies, our lives and the world?"[5] So God is not at the heart of all people, not least at the heart of our children's life?

But if there are many young people who have not yet grasped the meaning and the power of the dying and rising again of Christ in St Magnus, they may often have someone closer to them in the family circle, who not only has this grace, but who for years has shown it to them. There may not always have been a response; this witness could have been met only with a strange blindness or deafness. But we must remember that a positive response is sometimes given.

At any rate the one in a family who frequently has this grace and glory is the mother. I used to be asked at one time in my years in Kirkwall, 'What on earth do you do up there?' 'Is there not little culture around you, with some people still struggling to read by the light of oil lamps?' I regarded this as a joke and I used to reply: 'I feel my duty is to 'renew the saints' or encourage others to do this'. Literally this had to be done, for regularly some of the stained glass windows, depicting the saints, male or female, were removed from the Cathedral, sent south where they were repaired and eventually they came back to us. Then we felt we had a new saint to put back into our Cathedral. Yet this removal could be seen in a different way, for all people and Christians are "called to be saints" so in a Cathedral or Church a mutual renewing is going on: the people renewing their minister and leaders, and hopefully often the other way round!

But also in the family, awake to encounters with the Spirit, there is a mutual renewing taking place. This is the inevitable result of sensitive love and prayer, which is constantly perceptive of need in another in the family circle. This is not imprisoned in the immediate members, but soon finds its way out into the wider family and neighbourhood and community, as suggested by demand or succour. Many of us have seen something of this love and compassion at work in Christian, and not openly Christian families, and have given thanks for it. I have had the good fortune to have seen it working in my own family. It keeps renewing us there, and has its principal source in my wife. It flows from the endless reservoir which is Christ's prayer and steadfast goodness, and is constantly renewed by the Spirit, and from participation in the Word and Sacrament, and in the fellowship of people who are often being made new themselves. This grace penetrated into Margot's medical and Church life, and into all the rewarding interests she had in different community activities. Not least it is to be found in the constant love she gave and gives to the children and the grand children.

I now realise that in writing about the different members of the family with the help of George Mackay Brown, I have written too little of Margot. Like myself she had been brought up in Edinburgh, her father being in the executive branch of St Andrew's House. When she was eighteen, her parents moved from Cramond to Colinton, to some extent to accommodate her ageing grandparents.

Groups of students travelled from and to Colinton, and I met her in this way one morning, when she was a 3rd year Medical Student. She sometimes has said that I picked her up on the bus! As time passed we enjoyed each other's company and discovered that so much of our approach to life was in accord.

Margot continued to be much involved in Cramond church, in a very active Youth Fellowship and in the Girls' Association, in the Ministry of the Revd Leonard Small. She also found great stimulus in the meetings of the Christian Union at University. Sometimes, when I was at New College, I attended these C.U. meetings–not always to hear the speaker!

When I left Edinburgh to go to Union Theological Seminary in New York in 1949–I had been engaged before, and I felt badly about this, but I was very pleased to hear that the gracious lady concerned was married to an able and good person when I was in America. When I went to this Seminary I kept in touch, with Margot, and on my return to Scotland, neither of us was in doubt about the next step. We were married on 3 September, 1951 in Cramond Kirk by the Revd Dr Leonard Small. Marriage brought me into the knowledge of a happy family, for Margot had four brothers. Further, I could not have had, I believe, more accepting parents-in-law, both when we visited them, or when they came to see us in the Manse in Fallin.

Above all, Margot has helped me to understand what being 'led by the Spirit' means. She always remembers the text, often repeated by the Head Mistress of Mary Erskine School, to her pupils. "What doth the Lord require of thee, but to do justly, and to love mercy, and walk humbly with thy God?" She was also fortified in early days by the Crusader's Class, and by the fellowship of her friends in the Church at Cramond.

'Led by the spirit' herself, she was able to keep up the life of prayer to the Father, and to direct her relationships in the family and beyond it, in care for patients and in so much of her work in the Woman's Guild and in the Young Women's Group in the Church. Today she is often busy in 'Save the Children' and in the local Marriage Counselling Group where she still is the Chair Person and in providing an ever open door for all the children and grand children.

Manse families often see the dark side of the Church, but Margot seems to me to see wonderfully steadfastly the members of the congregation as the forgiven family, and treats each one in that forgiving spirit, being always open herself to the Word and the Sacraments. Her witness, I have no doubt, is founded upon the crucified and risen Christ, and each day she endeavours to live out this faith. This flows from the heart of our Christian belief that our sins have been forgiven, and that Christ wills to live in us. As it has been written: "The glory that was in Jesus when he gave himself even to death is now, in virtue of Jesus being risen and living, reproduced in those who receive and possess his Spirit. Christ's self-giving, Christ's death <u>in you</u>, Christ's glory therefore <u>in you</u>. Is that hard to grasp? It is the very meaning of Christian life".[6]

So Christ wills not only to be with us, and for us, but amazingly within us, and this is God's activity also, as another theologian, a more famous one in Europe, if not elsewhere puts it, so that we can become aware that he is doing our work: "God puts himself in our place, like a teacher who sits at the desk of a school boy and then tells him: 'Until now you've been drawing all by yourself; I want now to make your drawing for you' . . . My friend, here I am in your place . . .

A passage from Paul sums up what we have just said (Galatians 2v20). 'It is no longer I who live, but Christ who lives in me; and the life I now live in the flesh I live by faith in the Son of God, who loved me and gave himself for me'. If we understand this verse, we have understood everything. This is the whole of faith and of Christian life".[7]

Notes

1.   G M Brown - 'For The Islands I Sing' - John Murray - London - pp174-175.
2.   Ibid - p17.
3.   'Daily Readings With George MacLeod' - Revd R. Ferguson - Fount, Part of the Harper Collins Publishing Group - pp54-55.
4.   G M Brown - Ibid - pp178&179.
5.   Philip Newell - 'Listening for the Heartbeat of God' - A Celtic Spirituality - SPCK - p3.
6.   A M Ramsey - 'Introducing the Christian Faith' - SCM (1970) - p53.
7.   Karl Barth - 'The Faith of the Church' - Collins - p132.

Chapter XI

Changes and New Opportunities in the Cathedral: Events in the Congregation and Community

In the 1970s St Magnus Cathedral had already seen major changes in the building, in its leadership, and in its working life, but the early years of the 1980s were to bring many more. The most important of these in many ways was the coming of the Revd R S Whiteford MA to Shapinsay and the Cathedral.

1. Co-operation in Ministry with Bob Whiteford

This was written in the 1981 *Cathedral Magazine*: "It is a great pleasure for me to tell you that the Revd R S Whiteford has accepted a call to become, with the Presbytery authority, the Minister of Shapinsay Parish Church, together with an appointment as the Associate Minister of St Magnus Cathedral". He was a Naval Chaplain at the end of the Second World War, and later a Prison Chaplain. After periods in certain parishes, he became for more than a decade Minister at Ferryhill South, Aberdeen, where he gave outstanding service to his people. So it was no surprise when he came to the Cathedral here, and took the Morning Service with widespread acceptance.

It is good for a Minister to remember that his own ministry is not the only one in a Presbytery. With the coming of Bob Whiteford to be Minister in Shapinsay, and to be with us in St Magnus, we were given an insight into life on that island, and into new beginnings in the worship and the fellowship of its Church. In his first letter in the *Cathedral Magazine*, we heard about the power of the elements and the human effort on the part of Shapinsay folk to combat this . . . "sometimes it is a battle for the housewife to keep the washing on the line; children have to struggle to get to school; farmers have to seize every opportunity of fair weather, else they will be left without winter feed . . ." There were days when Bob had difficulty in getting back to his island, having come over, for example, to Kirkwall to the Presbytery. He went back one stormy day to conduct the Harvest Thanksgiving Service, when he was the only person on the Clytus, the little boat for Shapinsay: "The wind was whipping the top of the waves so that it looked like smoke. I asked the skipper what speed the wind was that day to do this. He thought it was about 60 knots or more. But everyone was waiting on the island, all the school children were there too, and we had a fine service that week day. But I thought Harvest Thanksgiving was never like that in Aberdeen. It was exhilarating, a little frightening, but underneath it all there was a deep sense of gratitude to God for harvest, shelter, safety and faith. The elements will always be there. The past too will be there. But it is faith which gives purpose and meaning to the past and present, and to all life". Bob closed his first letter about Shapinsay by speaking of one of the duties of the Ministry: "It is to deepen the faith and to strengthen the fellowship of Christian people in the Church. Faith and fellowship are for the present, and for the witness of the Church now to this generation. I trust that I will be able to have part in doing just that in Shapinsay and in St Magnus".

The work of the Church in Shapinsay went forward each year. In 1982 "The Church interior had been redecorated . . . A new road had been made round the Church with increased parking space. It was done by Elders and Board members lending their diggers, trailers, and of course, giving their labour. In three nights about twenty men accomplished this task. The Woman's Guild worked, scrubbed and polished the Church after the redecoration, and also raised £540 at their sale of work. This had been a fine effort . . .

Someone said to me recently that the Church is the cement of society, and without the Church, society tends to disintegrate. We have faith that in Shapinsay, the Church and island life are bound together, and we have enjoyed being part of it this past year. We thank God for the upbuilding of faith and the strengthening of witness within the fellowship of the Church".

Scriptural study was given a new and important place in the Shapinsay Church. In 1983 the Sermon on the Mount from St Matthew's Gospel was the subject, and members of the group–some 14 or 15 people–sought to relate the teaching there to daily faith and work. These words are written towards the end of Matthew Chapter 5: "But what I tell you is this: Love your enemies and pray for your persecutors; only so can you be children of your heavenly Father, who makes his sun rise on good and bad alike, and sends the rain on the honest and the dishonest" (vv 44 and 45). How explosive these words are, able to drive a person to confession of sin and to seek a new opportunity to reveal this kind of love. I like to think that when this group, chiefly of Shapinsay people, came to this difficult part of the Sermon on the Mount they were given new insight into Christ's love, and new courage to practice it better, even in this world. At any rate, what Bob Whiteford was doing in Shapinsay by way of dialogical study of scripture was a challenge to do more of this in the Cathedral, even at a new kind of Morning Service. But for that dream becoming true we have to wait for 1987.

Bob spoke to us also in his preaching in the Cathedral, not least at the great seasons of the Church Year. Here was a new voice speaking to us the Gospel, either from the pulpit or written. Here is a glimpse into what he wrote for Christmas 1984 in the *Cathedral Magazine*, when Bob was unable, because of weather, to come over to the Cathedral for the Christmas Eve Service. He told how he missed the joy and the thanksgiving of that occasion in St Magnus, and of the glory of the organ and the emotive carols. Then he wrote: "I missed more the quiet sea trip coming back to

Shapinsay when, on a beautiful night, I stood in the stern of Alfie Nicolson's boat, and watched the immensity of the heavens, the calmness of the sea, the awesome silence broken only by the lapping of the boat and the put-put of the engine. I missed that because I had time as I watched the stars and the encircling islands to ponder on the wonder and the mystery of all that took place in Bethlehem 2,000 years ago. I had time to marvel. How could it be? How could the Almighty God actually become one of us? Yet we dare to believe it. This is our faith. This is the miracle of Christmas that Jesus humbled himself to share our humanity in order that we might share his divinity . . . Forget for a while the busyness of the season, for that can often crowd out the reality, and let your mind be filled with the mystery of Jesus coming to share your life . . . We should be like the shepherds humble enough to see the Christ child, and kneel before the manger with wonder. Then we will go back, after the Christmas season, to the mundane world of office and home, praising God for all we have seen and heard".

One Sunday Bob was to be the preacher at a Cathedral Communion Service, but he did not appear in the Cathedral–I began the service wondering what was to be said in the sermon! However he came into the Cathedral after the opening hymn, and preached the sermon. Only after the service was the story told of what had happened. Bob had arrived at the Shapinsay boat, and hurriedly jumped on board, but slipped on the deck, and found himself in the water. Eventually, after swimming around, he was helped out and went back to the manse, changed, and set off once more in the boat for Kirkwall and the Cathedral, despite a cut on his leg which had to be stitched at the hospital after the service. This true episode became a joke, for it was told that the minister's wife had left him, and he'd taken too much of the spirit, and that Sunday morning had plunged off the boat into the sea!

Before his ministry closed Bob Whiteford became Moderator of the Presbytery and made a splendid contribution to the Church in Orkney, after doing much committee work and a long Interim Moderatorship. His able and delightful wife became President of the Presbyterial Guild Council, and members were welcomed on one occasion to Shapinsay "It was a memorable time for the island. It did us all good to see the Kirk completely full, with chairs even in the aisles and to know that we are part of a much greater fellowship of people who love the Lord Jesus Christ". Yet it would be quite wrong to think that all Bob's energies were imprisoned in the Church, for in Shapinsay and in other places he took part in so many community affairs, in Harvest Homes and in horticultural shows. He made a restoration of the Manse garden: "I have entered vegetables for the horticultural shows and managed to take a prize or two because the Manse garden has good soil, is well sheltered and set up to the sun".

When Bob and Joan Whiteford left Orkney in 1986, they were greatly missed in Shapinsay and in the Cathedral for all their very fruitful work and witness. With their departure I lost two very good friends, and a dedicated fellow labourer in the ministry, not only in Shapinsay but in St Magnus Cathedral.

2.   A New Role for the Cathedral - TV Broadcasting

In 1977 an Easter Day "Word for Living" had been broadcast 'live' by Radio from St Magnus, but the 1980s saw the beginning of TV broadcasts. These took the form of a Morning Service in June, but also later in November came a 'Songs of Praise'. At every Sunday Service there is given to the Choir and the Minister, not least, an enormous trust by God to worship him through Jesus Christ, and to have a renewed vision of his glory and presence. This is even more so in a televised service, for there is a much greater congregation and the service can penetrate into the homes of a vast number.

The Revd Dr Archie Craig, when an Assistant Minister, never forgot his visit to the home of Mrs Smith in the "ineptly-named" Pleasance in Edinburgh. There he received an insight into what sustained her in one of the worst slums at that time in the district. Archie, on entering the house, commented on how hard it must be to live in such a setting. But he was taken to the back of the house, and pointed to the view of Salisburgh Crags from her back window, while Mrs Smith told him: "A body can thole a wheen o'troubles when ilka morn she can look at a bonny view like that in the licht o' God's sun".[1] That was an incident of which Archie told many times, for through it he was given the vision of God's working in the world for one parishioner, and of how he revealed the beauty of what he was doing for her, despite the distresses of where she stayed. Both the Congregation and Choir and Minister knew something of the vision of God's working in the beauty of Orkney, but also they were aware that in Kirkwall God had raised up many people to build and keep standing in the town, through many centuries, a magnificent Cathedral, filled with great beauty and strength for countless Orcadians, as well as for visitors from all over the world. Could this vision be conveyed to a vast seeing and listening TV audience? Could the psalmist's vision of "strength and beauty in his sanctuary" be passed on to them, both to their eyes and their hearts?

Our conviction was that this could be done, and that the TV cameras and lights, and the Choir, and the Congregation, and the Readers, and the Minister, would all play their part. Despite "The Dilemma of the Preacher"[2]–sometimes small numbers here and there, some people with none too clear a grasp of the Christian Faith, others ignorant often about the content and authority of Scripture, not least, many possessed by the scientific viewpoint which sees no need of a divine word or message for the living of their days–despite all these things, a good number of us believed that the TV Service hymns to be sung, and the prayers to be offered, and the lessons to be read, would prove meaningful for many; at the same time the Minister felt that he would be led to certain texts which would convey to a large number of viewers and worshippers both the beauty and strength of the St Magnus Cathedral building, and of the Gospel of God in Christ. When the broadcast took place, though it could have been otherwise, "The day spring from on high" visited the Cathedral, and there was light for us in more ways than one, as there had been in an earlier time for Mrs Smith of the Pleasance, Edinburgh.

I might be allowed to set down part of the Sermon on this TV Morning Service of June, 1980, having given you first the Lessons, and then Texts for that Sunday:-

Lessons   From The Old Testament–II Kings 20 vv 12-15 (NEB)

From the New Testament–St John 17 vv 1-5; 20-26 (NEB)

Texts   Then Isaiah asked, 'What did they see in your house?

(II Kings 20, part of v 15) (NEB)

'The glory which thou gavest me I have given to them, that they may be one, as we are one' . . . . (St John 17 v22). (NEB)

Sermon   "The living God is the God who questions you and me. He has sharp and penetrating questions for his people in every age. Our first text this morning contains one such question, though it is the prophet Isaiah who, on this occasion, puts it to King Hezekiah of Judah, for he had just been visited after illness by envoys from the King of Babylon. "What did they see in your house?" asked Isaiah. To which Hezekiah replied, "They saw everything, there was nothing among my treasures that I did not show them".

"What did they see in your house, in the great house of your Cathedral?", the living God asks those of us who belong to Orkney. But in addition he asks, "What did the visitors and viewers see there", in what has been called "The mightiest monument to the Norsemen in the West". We can surely reply that it was our privilege to show them some of our treasures.

The treasures of this ancient and beautiful Cathedral, founded here in 1137 by Earl Rognvald, include the stonework itself. The massive stone pillars of the nave, with its soaring arches, have been much admired, as have the polychrome work of the 13th century west doors, and the South Transept door. Indeed the rich rose, pink and red colouring of the stones provide a warmth to the whole building which, of an evening, can glow in the rays of the setting sun, as they pour through the West window. Another treasure of this Cathedral is the stained glass depicting Kings and Earls and Saints from Celtic and Medieval times. Some are to be seen in the North Transept, which includes the St Magnus window. It is the great East window, however, showing Christ crucified and ascended, which, in the view of so many people, is the finest of all, and which draws the eye of the visitor, on first entering through the West door. The wood carvings of our Cathedral, as on the pulpit, are also very precious to us; especially so are the carved figures in the St Rognvald Chapel at the Cathedral's East end. In the centre on the wall stands Earl, later St Rognvald, a Norwegian, holding his Cathedral; on his left, is his father Kol, with plumbline and plan, as the Cathedral's architect; while on the right is Bishop William, the earliest resident Bishop of the Cathedral.

Yet splendid though these treasures are, is that all that is to be seen here? Have our visitors and viewers only to be shown our material possessions? That could have been the fault in Isaiah's mind of Hezekiah. He showed his visitors only his ephemeral financial, and material treasures; he failed to show them the glory of his God. The living God asks of us today, "What did they see, those visitors and viewers in the great Cathedral house of Orkney?" Did they see, not only the achievements of craftsmanship and skill but also the Gospel or Good News of the glory of God?

That really was the subject of this sermon which spoke about 'the Gospel of the Glory of God on the Cross,' 'in the Ascended Christ's Living and Continuing Work in the World' and 'in You and in Me'.

At the risk of wearying those who are not members of St Magnus, it seems appropriate to remind the congregation of some of the comments from those who had viewed the Cathedral in these broadcast services, and had valued them. Here are some received from different parts of Ireland, England and Scotland.

From the Morning TV Service

From Hampshire: "Thank you very much for that delightful and impressive service, you conducted in your beautiful Church . . . Harrington and Effingham are still running in my mind".

From the Isle of Wight: "Christian greetings from an island off the south coast of England to an island off the north coast of Scotland. I'm writing to say how much we enjoyed the service from your impressive St Magnus Cathedral . . . we thought the singing was of a high standard . . .

From Lancashire: "I'm pleased that such an instrument as the television is in existence, which enabled me and others to listen to your inspiring service".

From Helensburgh: "My wife joins me in warm thanks for a splendid and up-lifting service. The choir in red robes added a colourful touch to the glorious Cathedral, and how they sang! . . . "

From Perthshire: "We would like to say how up-lifting, relevant, and natural the television service was . . ."

From Edinburgh: "Today I have been thinking a lot about the fine service from St Magnus Cathedral which I was privileged to see last night . . . I felt I was worshipping with those present in the Cathedral . . . I felt up-lifted and helped by the service . . . many thanks to you and the choir who helped so wonderfully. I shall long remember the service broadcast from St Magnus Cathedral"

From the 'Songs of Praise' Service:

From Inverness: "I should like to congratulate all concerned on the simply beautiful 'Songs of Praise'. It was the best I have ever heard, with magnificent singing, and I felt proud as an exile that it was seen all over the country . . ."

From Dublin: "This is to tell you how deeply touched I was with the 'Songs of
                   Praise' tonight"

From Cumbria: "Like a few thousand more I enjoyed 'the Songs of Praise' from
                   your most lovely Cathedral. The singing was superb, and the
                   whole atmosphere one of great beauty . . ."

From Aberdeen: "We liked the choice of hymns, and the singing was excellent. It
                   was a very meaningful service indeed . . ."

From Milton Keynes: "All the people interviewed had an interesting story and
                   testimony to their faith–in itself most refreshing these days. The
                   camera work did, I am sure, do justice to the magnificent
                   architecture, and the Island as a whole. The choice of hymns was
                   excellent and they were beautifully sung. In all ways this was a
                   beautiful Songs of Praise–for myself the best I have yet seen"

From a Choir   "Warmest congratulations to the congregation and to the Choir and
Mistress in   their conductor and to the organist at St Magnus Cathedral for "the
Hampshire: wonderful singing last night. It was the best we have heard . . . the
                   whole thing was marvellously inspiring, and God bless you all, and
                   thank you . . ."

Broadcast services from St Magnus, not all were TV, reached out beyond
Orkney and there is evidence that they were fruitful for not a few people. More
followed in 82, 85, 87 and 90 but the local recording done in the Cathedral, and taken
out to those not able to come for different reasons to the services is much appreciated
also. 'BBC', 'Bert's Broadcasting Company' operates on a certain Sunday each
month, and it is still at work in 1999. Such services are recorded mainly by one of our
elders, Bert Rosie helped by his wife Anne. Many would wish to thank them both.

3.   Recent Restoration Work in St Magnus Cathedral

What was needed to be done in the Cathedral maintenance or restoration was
constantly kept under review by a Sub-Committee of the Orkney Islands Council.
This was chaired by the Council Convener, and had the Chief Executive as its
Secretary; the Lord Lieutenant, The Architect and the Minister of the Cathedral were
almost always present, as were a number of the Orkney Islands Councillors. It is only
possible here to give a selected account of what was seen to be required in the years
1980-85–namely the restoration of the Cathedral bells and more briefly, the new
lighting.
        Our Cathedral has three historic bells which are still in use today. These were

the gift of a Roman Catholic Bishop–Bishop Robert Maxwell in 1528. They were made in Edinburgh in the Sixteenth Century. The largest bell (1450P) was cracked in 1671 when lightening struck the spire. Then the tower timber was set on fire, and the bells fell to the floor. The town's people however brought in to the Cathedral loads of earth so that only one bell was required to be sent away to Amsterdam for repair in 1682. But in 1982, 300 years after this repair of one of them, they were all removed from the Cathedral of St Magnus, and were sent to the foundry in Loughborough. Part of the work to be done was the turning of the bells to present unworn surfaces of the sound bows to the blows of the clappers, so that the sound could remain the same as it had been more than 450 years ago. The way of ringing the bells by foot pedals and hand ropes was retained. There was a long debate in the Cathedral Sub-Committee of the Council, after experts had examined the bells and had given their report with certain suggestions as to what to do with them. I recall very early one morning climbing up to the bell tower in the Cathedral to stop three men who were about to disconnect the bells, so that further discussion might be held with Mr Graeme Lapsley–our then able Chief Executive and a man generous to the Cathedral. Eventually, after 'phone contact with the bell foundry final instructions were given, and the bells were lowered to the floor and sent south.

The Year of the Bells

So 1982 was for some in St Magnus "The Year of the Bells", and what happened to them was used to illustrate the theme that year of the Christmas Eve Service in a packed Cathedral. Some members or parishioners will be interested to hear something of what was said on that occasion for, among other things, certain details about the bells were recalled.

"In past months the Cathedral bells have been taken down, repaired in the bell foundry in Loughborough, and replaced here in their bell chamber, so that once more their distinctive sound can be heard by the people of Kirkwall". The whole episode of the repairs of the bells can be seen as a powerful parable of the Good News of Christmas which is the subject of this sermon.

Text . . . "and his name shall be called Emmanuel", (which means 'God with us') (St Matthew 1 v23) R.S.V.

I   "The first stage of this year's story of our Cathedral bells began with their cursory examination by certain experts "frae sooth" who shall be nameless. One suggestion was that these magnificent bells could be put in a museum–and for what? Wait for it! In order that there might be installed in this small Norwegian Cathedral a carillon of bells such as can be found in an English Cathedral! Once this inept view was rigorously turned down by the Orkney Islands Sub Committee, new instructions were eventually given to the bell founders about the renovation of bells. These were lowered to the crossing floor of the Cathedral, and then brought to the West end of the building. This stage in the saga of the bells repairs was that of revelation. What had so long been invisible became visible, and right down amongst us.

In the Good News of Christmas we discover the revelation of God become man, of the seemingly often distant God now amongst his people in the person of Jesus of Nazareth, of God really within the child of Bethlehem. The question has often been asked, "Is this story true?" How do we know that the child of Bethlehem and the man he became was God incarnate? Here is how Sir John Betjeman puts it :-

> And is it true? And is it true,
> This most tremendous tale of all,
> Seen in a stained glass window's hue,
> A Baby in an ox's stall?
> The Maker of the stars and sea
> Became a Child on earth for me?[3]

But think of the story of our bells. How could a stranger know that the bells lying there some months ago on the floor in the Cathedral really were those of St Magnus? The stranger could only know by examining these bells; when he did so, he would have found, as many did, that they were stamped with the arms of Bishop Maxwell: the inscription on the other two bells are similar to what is on the largest one: "Made by Master Robbert Maxvell, Bischop of Orkney, the yaer of God MDXXVIII, the yaer of the reign of King James V. Robert Borthwick made me in the Castel of Edinburgh" So it is with the revelation of God in Jesus. We believe it is true when we look at the life of Jesus Christ, we find on close examination that that life is clearly stamped with an amazing sacrificial love both for God and man, full of forgiveness and patient suffering service for friend and foe alike. Here in the life of Jesus, born in a manger and crucified on a Cross is the great stamp of the eternal self giving love of God himself and this love, set free in the world by the mystery of the resurrection and the gift of the Spirit, is meant for you and me, to bless and keep us full of hope and faith all our earthly days, however hard or difficult our circumstances may be. For Betjeman, the Incarnation, the coming down to earth of God in Jesus was true–I trust it is true for all who in the Church hear God's word, and at the Lord's Supper or the Holy Communion take the bread and the wine of our Lord's own institution: -

> "No love that in a family dwells
> No carolling in frosty air,
> Nor all the steeple-shaking bells
> Can with this single Truth compare –
> That God was Man in Palestine
> And lives today in Bread and Wine".[4]

II   The second stage of this story of the Cathedral bells was the response of the people to their being visible on the Cathedral floor. Many came in from near and far in Orkney to see them and examine them. Photographs were taken and from different angles.

The Good News of Christmas includes the response to the mystery of the child in the manager. Scripture records the journey of the shepherds and the wise men, and also the angels were around with their promise and thanksgiving and this brings us to what our response is to be: sometimes to sing with joy and alertness the Christmas carols; sometimes to wonder anew in silence at the humility of God in his down coming to earth in a little child; yet again to share in the faith of the Church which has clung to the light and strength of God's presence in the weakness, and in the rejection of the child, for whom there was no room in the inn. Through the long centuries people have come to this Cathedral in the darkness of sickness or disappointment or great anxiety for themselves or others, and they have been able to cling, with the family of the Church, to the infant of Mary, to the outcast and the stranger who yet became the Lord of all. To such was given often Christ's spirit of new hope and energy, and their flickering faith has been renewed. Sometimes at Christmas our reaction has gone before these responses, for we have reached out to give ourselves, and our wills have been energised in the service of others.

III   But the 1982 story of our bells is not finished until we remember how they were put back into the bell tower, where they could be struck again, and when their pealing notes could travel far beyond the Cathedral; some days out to the ships in Kirkwall Bay, or up to Wideford Hill, or into the hospitals, or into the homes of so many of our people where some were often delighted to hear them. But it will be Christmas Day in a few moments and joyful bells will sound out again in countless places, far beyond Orkney's shores. God's great bell of Jesus Christ's manhood was made to be struck, not least on the Cross, by the hammer blows of evil men; yet out of their sin has come the strange yet wonderful music of the divine love, forgiving and saving for us all.

There is a deep and challenging thought; for we have to go this way too. As our lives become bells for the world's striking, as we absorb into ourselves, courageously sometimes, humanity's evil, and struggle to battle with the material needs of others, or with their equally vital need for faith in the God revealed in Jesus, so it is that the Master Musician can bring, even out of lives such as ours, the music of creative power and of transforming and renewing love for ourselves and others.

Our Lord was born into this world not to bring gloom and doom, but rather to fill you and me with all the splendour of his own life and love and great joy, that it might flow out to others.

"Hail, the heaven-born Prince of Peace!
Hail, the Sun of Righteousness!
Light and life to all he brings,
Risen with healing in his wings.
Mild he lays his glory by,
Born that man no more may die,
Born to raise the sons of earth,
Born to give them second birth:
        Hark! the herald angels sing,
        'Glory to the new-born King'."
The Lord bless to us this preaching from his Holy Word and to his
Name be praise and glory–Amen

The Renewal of Lighting in the Cathedral

These words were written in the *Cathedral Magazine* of August, 1983: "As
many of you will know, new lighting is being installed in the Cathedral. This was
something that was urgent as the old wiring put in many decades ago had begun to
cause trouble. Those who had to put on lights on Sunday evenings, or at other times
were getting shocks, and there was a danger of fire in the large switch box in the
room off the South Transept. The new wiring has been carried out by a Kirkwall
firm–P A Sutherland Ltd–and it has been an excellent job . . . Although there are
now many musical concerts held in the Cathedral, especially at the time of the
yearly St Magnus Festival in June, the primary function of St Magnus Cathedral is
the worship of Almighty God in accordance with the ordinances of public worship,
used by the Church of Scotland. The fact that St Magnus is a Parish Church of the
Church of Scotland is incidentally clearly recognised in the agreement between the
old Town Council of the City and Royal Burgh of Kirkwall and the Church of
Scotland General Trustees: "The Cathedral Church of St Magnus is to be made
available as and for a Parish Church in connection with the Church of Scotland and
in particular, as the Parish Church of Kirkwall and St Ola". This commitment was
taken over and has been cordially carried out by the present Orkney Islands
Council, who are now the owners of the building on behalf of the people. In
addition to the above it should also be noted that "the maintenance, repair and
decoration of the interior of the Cathedral together with the placing of monuments
in the Cathedral" remain, as hitherto in the control of the former Kirkwall Town
Council, in the sole charge and control of the Orkney Islands Council. And so the
new lighting, now being installed (and almost completed) within our Cathedral is
the decision of the present Orkney Islands Council. The consulting electrical
engineers who have been concerned with this new scheme are Kenneth N Munro
and Associates of Glasgow . . .

The Kirk Session of the Cathedral are very appreciative of the new wiring and lighting installation. . . They are concerned with the Orkney Islands Council to show up the beauty of the Cathedral in a dignified and reverent way, always remembering that the Cathedral is first and foremost still today, what it has been for many centuries a house of God, dedicated to the glory and the worship of the Father and the Son and the Holy Spirit . . .

As many members of the Cathedral will know, Her Majesty Queen Elizabeth, the Queen Mother, has graciously agreed to come to Orkney on Wednesday, 24th August, 1983, at 4.30 pm to inaugurate the Cathedral's new lighting. She will attend a short service at that time".

4. The New Form of the St Magnus Fair - A Corporate Annual Way of Fundraising for the Cathedral

A yearly opportunity for this corporate raising of funds for St Magnus was begun in the seventies, but it has been carried on, and developed in the early 1980s. A huge number of Kirkwall's community organisations take part in this, yet they often have had help from far beyond Kirkwall and Orkney.

The St Magnus Fair stalls are set up in the Kirk Green outside the St Magnus Cathedral West Door. Stalls like these go back at least to the old Lammas markets of the 18th and 19th centuries. Merchants then came to Kirkwall with horses and cattle as well as with wool and linen and other goods. These all undertook to be peaceful traders, though Kirkwall had set up a Lammas Market Guard. At any rate from 1972 when the St Magnus Fair began in a new form, the stall holders were almost all Orcadians and their friends. Though Fair activities often went on beyond the site of the opening day, this took place usually outside the west door of the Cathedral. Then there were present the Fair Convener, and whoever was performing the opening ceremony along with certain other dignatories. It is interesting that the first St Magnus Fair was opened by the late Lord Birsay who did so much to help the people of Orkney and its Cathedral. Equally important in the early years of the Fair was the Revd Harold Hope, the Socpristen of Finnas, near Bergen, who brought to us the sum of £12,000 which had been raised by public subscription in Norway for St Magnus, for we must not forget that for many centuries St Magnus Cathedral had been in the control of the Archbishop of Nidaros (Trondheim). Among the notable people, mostly from outwith Orkney, who had kindly opened our Fair up to 1985 are: Sir John Betjeman, The Poet Laureate; The Earl of Wemys and March, President of the National Trust for Scotland; The Very Revd Dr John McIntyre, Moderator of the General Assembly of the Church of Scotland; Lord Grimond, then Liberal Leader and MP for Orkney and Shetland; the Bishop of Trondheim Designate; the Norwegian Ambassador: not least in 1980, Her Majesty Queen Elizabeth, the Queen Mother. It will help to give an idea of the large number of people co-operating in the Fair if the names of corporate stall holders are given.

Bottle Stall . . .	Tourist Office
Bakery Stall and Teas .	Council of Churches
Good as New Stall .	St Magnus Young Women's Group
Produce Stall . .	St Magnus Appeal Committee
Bric-a-Brac Stall . .	Townswomen's Guild
Baking Stall . .	SWRI
Side Shows . .	Scouts and BBs
Sweets & Ice Cream :	St Magnus Sunday School
Wet Sponge Throw .	Orkney Rugby Football Club
Lemonade & Crisps .	BBs
Hot Dogs . . .	Round Table
Housey Housey . .	Royal British Legion
Side Shows . .	Chamber of Commerce
Humpty Dumpty Amusement	Orkney Young Farmers

These are taken from the 1987 St Magnus Fair opened by Mr Edwin Eunson, OBE, Convener of the Orkney Islands Council. Further Fair activities include the Children's Train (Rotary); the Floral Dance in the Cathedral (Flower Arrangement Club); The Battle of the Peerie Sea (Coastguards); Concerts in the Orkney Arts Theatre; The Night Oot; and the St Magnus Fun Gala (Swimming Pool). The amount raised by the St Magnus Fair for the Cathedral maintenance has steadily risen and the Fair Convener and his committee have had to cope with a huge amount of work. Orkney and its Cathedral owe many thanks to these Conveners and their secretaries (Mrs Kelday, one of the longest serving and excellent of these). In particular it is fitting to pay tribute to Lt Col Gary Gibson, the present Convener. Colonel (now Sir Robert) RAAS Macrae, from whom the idea of the Fair came, was the first Convener. After this, Brigadier S P Robertson took over the convenership and he did so much to further this co-operative venture, often doing local broadcasts for it, as does Gary Gibson.

The Orkney Islands Council has given immense support to this yearly Fair under the present kind Chief Executive, Mr Ron Gilbert. Charles Millar BEM, one of his employees, and his men always set up the stalls and do so much more. While the first Fair raised well over £1,000, recently the St Magnus Fair has gathered in over £8,000 with very little expenses. It must also be noted here that the Orkney Islands Council gives £50,000 each year, now more, towards its Cathedral's maintenance, for there is in certain years expenditure of well over that sum, (this past year over £200,000 for the restoration of the Spire). It must also be said that there are two major Cathedral Financial Funds operated by the Society of the Friends of St Magnus Cathedral, which was set up in 1958. One of the Society's main objects was the raising of funds to ensure the preservation of the building. The Convener of the Friends is now Orkney's Lord Lieutenant and the Vice Convener is the Cathedral Minister; the Patron, as has been said, is Her Majesty the Queen Mother.

Last year 14th August, 1996, the Fair was opened by a very generous American supporter, Mrs Lawrence Stahl, and there were items in the Fair, not to be found earlier, while the Kirkwall City Pipe Band played in Broad Street at certain times in the evening. On Sunday, 18th April, 1996 there was a Songs of Praise in the Cathedral.

We now pass to certain other activities in the Community which did not change. They had been established before I came as Minister, and Cathedral members took their part in them.

5. The Kirkwall Council of Churches

One such important area of corporate worship and action was the Kirkwall Council of Churches. This had been set up in 1965 when the Inauguration Service was held in St Magnus Cathedral. The Lord Provost, Baillies and Councillors of Kirkwall Town Council were present and praise was led by the Salvation Army Band. Office Bearers from the different congregations were at the door; the Preacher was Lord Birsay and the offering went to Christian Aid.

The basis of the council "shall be that of a fellowship of churches which confess the Lord Jesus Christ as God and Saviour according to the Scriptures and therefore seek to fulfil together their common calling to the glory of the one God, Father, Son, and Holy Spirit". The Council's objects were:-

"a) To draw the Churches represented on the Council into greater understanding and unity
 b) To enable the Churches more fully to share in the ecumenical movement
 c) To enable the Churches to bear a more united witness in the community and to serve it more effectively
 d) To give such expression to their common faith and devotion as may from time to time be found desirable".

It was also decided that the Council would be associated with the British Council of Churches.

The work of the Kirkwall Council of Churches was shared by the two Church of Scotland Churches as well as by the Kirkwall Roman, Episcopal, Congregational Churches along with the local Salvation Army. Lay representatives of each participating Church made an important contribution in worship as in action and in discussion. There were the usual significant activities of a Council of Churches–regular participation in corporate worship during the Week of Prayer for Christian Unity in January, in the St Rognvald Chapel of the Cathedral, while in Holy Week the services were held each evening (other than Saturday) in different member Churches. During this week there was usually a guest preacher on an ecumenical basis. We were glad to welcome men like Neville Davidson, George MacLeod and Roland Walls, while also, we had Murdo Macdonald, George Reid, Ian Cowie and Maxwell Craig. Teachers from the Divinity Colleges also were much appreciated:

James Torrance and Chris Wigglesworth. In 1987 the year of our 850th Cathedral Anniversary we were pleased to have Henry Sefton. There were other regular corporate activities carried out each year, not least what was called our Autumn Assembly when 'the Kirkwall Community's or Orkney's Future' was considered–sometimes with questions to a panel of speakers. On other occasions, the subject took the form of a speaker or speakers from the World Council of Churches Assembly. In the 1970s we were given excellent insights into the World Council of Churches meeting at Nairobi by The Revd Dr Bill Johnstone and Mrs M. Hart. Their presentation took the form of "the Nairobi Road Show", but this was followed in the 1980s by "an enthralling and informative account of the recent meeting of the World Council of Churches at Vancouver, peppered with humorous anecdotes", the main speaker was The Revd Professor Duncan Forrester.

Sometimes in Holy Week, Ministers of one denomination were welcomed as preachers in another: for example, the Minister of the Cathedral, in the Episcopal Church. Also one year the Roman Catholic Church was given unanimous permission by the Kirk Session of the Cathedral to hold their services every Sunday Morning in the Cathedral at a time prior to the Cathedral morning service. Restoration work was necessary at that time in the Catholic Church building. It was also thought helpful at a later stage of the Council, despite St Magnus Cathedral being a Presbyterian Church within the Presbytery of Orkney, that the Catholic Church should be given an opportunity to hold their Mass, in the Cathedral, followed by an ecumenical discussion in the St Rognvald Chapel later on. Mass was therefore held by the Kirkwall priest one evening in the Cathedral nave.

In a recent book called *An Earthful of Glory*, which contains prayers, liturgies and meditations, and which celebrates the whole of creation in its beauty and brokeness, the writer, the Revd Dr J Philip Newell, perceptively points out some of the dangers of the present day Church. One of these is that in it "we in the Church had ceased to use our full vision . . . In our praying, and thus in our living, there is an inner seeing to be recovered that enables us to know the immediacy and interwoveness of the spiritual within the matter of our lives and our world . . . In order to be freed from the imprisonment of a hellish secularism, we need to receive a consciousness of the holy angels of God all around us and undergirding life".[5] In the Ecumenical Church also it is possible to become so shut in within its worship and debating that God's presence in the world is neglected, and his very needy people there forgotten. We were guilty of this in some ways but we tried to avoid it in the Kirkwall Council of Churches by corporate action in Christian Aid week each May. It was frequently a struggle to get sufficient collectors to go round the houses in Kirkwall, but the Roman Catholic Church and the Salvation Army often led the way in this matter. It was not easy to get up early in the morning and go round certain doors with envelopes and then with help sometimes, to collect them later in the week. However, such action revealed amazing generosity on the part of some householders, encouraging us to continue in this service.

The projects of Christian Aid, to which the money collected went, were regularly set before members of the Council and a good many others, in the form of a film showing Aid work overseas.

6. Co-operation With Church of Scotland Missionaries and the Kirk Session

Another area of continuing work for the Cathedral in the early 1980s was participation in ministry to missionaries of the Church of Scotland serving abroad. Mr George Burgher took over about this time as Cathedral Session Clerk. He had been a Teacher but had become the Secretary of the National Farmers Union in Orkney. George did excellent work in the Cathedral as overseas representative. As early as 1973 he wrote in the magazine about our Missionary Partner Plan. This is an important area of the Cathedral's witness about which nothing has been said so far so it is relevant to quote what he wrote about the objectives of the Partner Plan: "First to LEARN more of the work of missionaries overseas, and to ensure that missionaries are encouraged in their work by receiving letters from us; it is important to WRITE to the missionary partner, and any individual or Church organisation willing to write a letter should contact me; thereby it is hoped that by gaining more knowledge of overseas work and missionaries, congregations will be encouraged to GIVE more to help with their work. Finally congregations and individuals are encouraged to PRAY specifically for their overseas partners".

"I trust that we as Home Partners can achieve these objectives". George went on to make a significant contribution as Session Clerk, as the former young Clerk, Mr Billy Hadden–also an Orcadian–had done before him. Ministry to missionaries overseas meant our receiving from them. Some came to Orkney or wrote about their work in the *Cathedral Magazine*: for example the Revd Nick Archer from Malawi, the Revd Dr Chris Wigglesworth from India, and later on in the 1980s, Miss Margaret Keltie a dedicated teacher in Malawi.

Still one more continuing sphere of the work and leadership in St Magnus Cathedral in these years was the Kirk Session and there took place an important change, for certain ladies of the congregation accepted this leadership for the first time in the Cathedral's history. Their diligent work has certainly been of immense value in the elder's district, and for the well being of the congregation. The Kirk Session at this period also had to ensure the continuance of the ministry of music in the Cathedral, and this was done through the appointment of the late Richard Hughes MA FRCO, then Principal Teacher of Music at Kirkwall Grammar School, to be organist and choirmaster in St Magnus, while David Drinkell BA ARCO (later FRCO) became his assistant in the Cathedral. David had a good assistant in Robin Cheer, eventually our organist. Further the Kirk Session was active in another vital area of action in St Magnus in the early 1980s–Youth Work, among the teenagers in Bible Class and Youth Club. Young elders had been teachers of the Bible Class and

Youth Club for some time. Orcadian members of the Cathedral will remember the excellent leadership provided by Ann Clark and Ken Milligan–Ann sometimes producing with the young people, helped by Jimmy Dewar, an Orcadian teacher, dramatic plays. Fraser Murray an elder elect, took on responsibility for the Bible Class, while the Youth Club, it will be remembered, in 1982 became the Spectrum Club and was very well led by Robert Grieve (an elder) and by his wife Sheena.

These years, 1980-1985 were those in which the Minister of the Cathedral was often South at many Conference Centres, when he was Vice Convener and then Convener of the In Service Training Committee of the Church of Scotland, in the Board of Education.

Notes

1.   E Templeton - 'A Life of Archie Craig' - God's February - 1888-1985 - p30.

2.   A C Craig - 'Preaching in a Scientific Age' - SCM Press (1954) - pp7-28.

3.   John Betjeman - 'Church Poems' - Christmas - John Murray - p41.

4.   Ibid - p41.

5.   J P Newell - 'An Earthful of Glory' - SPCK - Introduction - pp2-3.

Chapter XII

Further Events in the Life of the Cathedral

A New Cathedral Order of Service: A Professor's Gospel Sermon:
The Meaning of Christian Worship, it's Crisis, and the Need for
Renewal

I have always been interested in what some of the best teachers of the Christian Faith have said to students about the Christian Gospel. When I was starting my period of ministry in St Thomas' Church, Leith, I was much helped by Archbishop Ramsay talks (1960) in the Sheldonian Theatre at Oxford, for these were published in the next year, in a small book called *Introducing the Christian Faith*. In my last stage of ministry in St Magnus, I was once more helped and inspired by what another Christian teacher, Bishop John Taylor, had said to the same university of Oxford, and in the same Sheldonian Theatre, about 25 years later, in 1986. His addresses to the students were published later that year, and were called *A Matter of Life and Death*. One of the chapters in John Taylor's book is called 'More Dead than Alive' and while he sees deadness in a wider context than the Church–eg "There is a frightening amount of deadness around in our Western society these days",[1] he makes it quite clear that this infection had spread into the Church. The Bishop saw that the worst sin is apathy "lack of response, the total antithesis of that aliveness and awareness which is my theme in this book. And if there is salvation as the Christian gospel claims, it has yet to come to us as the remedy for this particular scourge, and bring the half-dead to life".[2] I feel in these last years that the question must be raised in relation to the congregation of St Magnus. Were there yet many who were 'half-dead', not really awake and responsive to the Gospel or Good News of the aliveness of Christ both in the Church and in the world? I could not help remembering John Taylor's words: "But for most of the time the church, whatever branch you look at, is humiliatingly disappointing and a major obstacle to belief in God".[3] On the same theme these are the words of another Anglican Bishop - "The Lord has a controversy with his people" (Hosea 4 v1). "That is a great encouragement to me, because it seems quite clear to me that again and again the behaviour of the church is one of the greatest arguments against the existence of God. One finds that one cannot do without the church, but nearly two times out of three one finds that one cannot do with it either. I have formulated this into what I call my ecumenical slogan: 'Even the church cannot keep a good God down' and I believe that to be a profoundly biblical observation".[4] But can we really believe such things about the people of St Magnus? I could certainly not say that about many of our members, for their response to belief in Christ was both to be seen in their faithful worship, and in their sacrificial service in the world, in family life, and in their work, and in their meeting needs, material and spiritual needs, as they helped others to become more alive to exciting things around them and in Christ's Kingdom.

And yet were those who came to the Cathedral Sunday by Sunday being given sufficient opportunity to articulate their witness and questions at some point in the Service? They could voice these things at the coffee time afterwards, or they could pursue the minister to the vestry, or the reader at some later stage. Yet on the whole this did not often happen. Could not people be given the chance, both to witness and raise their questions, and to participate more dialogically in their Cathedral, learning not only from the Minister, but from one another in a group smaller than the usual 250 or 300 + at a Morning Service?

1.   A New Morning Service: Smaller Groups

This important matter was raised in the Cathedral's Kirk Session certainly in 1987, if not before that time. The Cathedral elders rightly did not want any immediate radical change in the normal Morning Service, but when the proposal was made that there should be two Morning Services–the first one at about 9.45 am, followed by the Sunday rehearsal period for the Choir at 10.30 am, and then by the usual Morning Service with robed Choir at 11.15 am–when this was suggested, it was eventually thought to be worth doing, at least for a short time of several months. One or two elders were very keen to see this new Service begin. They felt it would give younger members the opportunity to hear something of the Gospel, in a less formal setting, and then to bring forward questions or doubts or convictions in relation to the Christian Faith, or to other relevant community or Cathedral matters–eg the Lord's Supper. It was also agreed that the children and youth of the Cathedral, not least members of the Junior and Senior Sunday School and the members of the Bible Class would attend the early part of the Service, then go to different sections of the Cathedral and the Vestry for their class sessions. At that point, usually the Minister, sometimes an elder or member, would speak, followed by dialogical contribution and/or questions coming from members present. One of the Elders, Jack Ridgway, British Airways Controller at Kirkwall Airport, now sadly no longer with us, thought rightly that it would be good to tell the congregation about the nature of this new first service. So he put the suggestion on paper, explaining what was to happen at 9.45 am most Sunday mornings, though the service was not held after the schools were given the holidays. Jack was a person of strong views, but he was able to publicise new ideas, and he certainly explained very well this new service in the St Rognvald Chapel (Cathedral's East End). He told what the difference was between it and the normal service at 11.15 am, for this first service would be prepared for by more than the Minister (or Ministers); it would be largely participatory by elders and members; and not least on most occasions it would be dialogical, not only between Minister and people, but between elders/members and members. This service was not always prepared for, as it should have been. But often elders/members came to the Cathedral manse on a Saturday evening when the theme for this first service could be gone over. This was particularly helpful when discussion might be difficult initially. However once these Services began, it clearly was what a number of young individuals or young marrieds found interesting and stimulating. The Minister also learned much not only from the points made by those at the Service, but also by their taking the prayers and the readings from Scripture. Some of the most exciting first services were those which were attended by people from other denominations. One day when Roman Catholic sailors came from their boat in Kirkwall harbour and told us what they felt believing in Christ and God meant for them, that was extremely valuable for those of us from the Church of Scotland then present. The praise at this service was often taken from the "Songs of God's People" though it was felt that the great psalms and paraphrases, and the hymns of the Church Hymnary (Third Edition) should not be forgotten. This was a time too when the Minister could have an interview with a local politician or with a visitor to the Cathedral, or to Orkney from the South.

My successor, the Revd Ron Ferguson, has also found this first service valuable and he has developed it in more ways than one, not least sometimes in promoting group discussion in smaller numbers than previously. It is now ten years since this service's initiation, and it was a great privilege to have been asked recently by Ron, to return to it, and speak there about belief in God, based on the Apostles' Creed. The Service has not really brought on the problem that was feared, a great reduction in the 11.15 Service; many people are still very much in favour of a service where there is normally little congregational verbal participation apart from the praise and the prayer responses and fixed prayers. This first service, in part because of smaller numbers being present who very much represented the younger people of the congregation, including young adults, was essentially a teaching service where great convictions given by the risen and ascended Christ through the Holy Spirit to his Church could be considered afresh, and their meaning probed and better understood. Each generation has to grasp for itself the mystery of God's truth and love revealed in his Son. Only then will they be able with vision to "be thankful unto him, and bless his name, for the Lord is good, his mercy is everlasting and his truth endures to all generations" (Psalm 100 v4 and 5). The main Service of the Cathedral, however, remained at 11.15 am where there was frequently a well filled nave, as also the South Transept, with a robed Choir of 20-24 to lead the praise of God.

2.   *A Professor's Sermon*

From time to time the Cathedral has been able to welcome to the Services distinguished guest preachers, and historians from the South. In May, 1986, we had a visit from Professor Yule, Professor of Church History in Aberdeen University. He spoke to us about the nature of God, as revealed to Moses at The Burning Bush, and in the full disclosure of Himself in Jesus Christ, in the mystery of His Cross and in the continuing wonder of his risen and ascended life. The Lessons he chose for his Service were Exodus 3 v1-5 and St John 17 vv1-6, and he quoted these words of St John at the start of the sermon: "Father, the hour is come; glorify thy Son, that thy Son also may glorify thee".

The following are the main points of what Professor Yule said, in his own words:

"The hour is the hour of the Cross, and glory, the presence of God on earth. So Jesus says, you will know the name, the character of God because I go to the Cross. On the Cross you will see the glory of God . . ."

"How different from us; we talk of a glorious sunset, of a glorious spectacle, of glorious technicolour–John says the glory of God is seen on the Cross, we think we know about God–but do we?"

"In the story of the Burning Bush, Moses asks God 'What is your name?' 'What is your character?' And God says: 'I am whom I shall show myself to be.' (There is a future tense in the Hebrew)

God says in effect:

'You will know who I am by what I shall do.
The One who rescues from slavery in Egypt and Babylon.
The One who is utterly reliable despite Israel's lack of faithfulness.
The One who not only creates the heavens but calls his sheep by name.
Totally unexpected, totally reliable.'

Then the astonishing thing happens: God Himself comes to us in Jesus. He becomes our brother. We now can see Him in the only medium we could grasp. But even so, blinded by our conception of God, we failed to see the living God when he came to us".

* * * * *

"St Mark's Gospel is the story of Jesus, the Son of God whom nobody recognises–neither the scribes, the pharisees, Jesus' mother and brothers. While Peter who confesses Him the Christ, thinks of Him as the Christ who will conquer, not suffer. Yet Christ–and He alone is the one who delighted to do God's will–goes the way of the Cross in love to the Father, and forgives his enemies in love towards man . . . If He had come down from the Cross, as we in that situation undoubtedly would have done if we had been able so to do, what would we have got? A magician; not the living God.

What does our Lord do? He descends into hell and hell equals the feelings of complete separation from God. The more one loves God, therefore the more hellish is hell. Our Lord so identified Himself with us in our lostness that for our sake He takes to Himself our sense of separation from the Father, and so His cry of dereliction - 'why has thou forsaken me?' - is his descent into hell for us. Far from sending people to hell, the truth is that we drive ourselves there because we cut ourselves off from God–and in His love He came down beside us. But in hell Christ is still the man of faith, 'Father, unto thy hands I commend my Spirit', and so hell is defeated. A man is no longer in hell when he can cry to God.

'Truly this man was the Son of God' (Mark 15 v39) - so he was seen by the pagan centurion when he views the Cross. Now God has fully shown His name–His character:

> He is the One who stands beside the helpless and the hopeless
> He is the One who stands in the place of the sinner and the outcast
> He is the One who loves us despite our appalling selfish idolatry
> His love, in Wesley's phrase, is "immense, unfathomed, unconfined".'

It may be said that we have quoted enough of the Professor's sermon, yet his conclusion may be allowed:

"What follows from this?"

"1. There are no 'ifs' in the love of God. He really and truly loves us in a way we can barely glimpse. He doesn't say, 'When you do this or that, then I'll love you . . . God loves us before we are contrite and this love enables us to repent, so that our whole life can become one of grateful repentance, as Luther said, and we get rid of more and more idols. In joy we can now lift up our hearts and cry 'Abba, Father' - 'dearest Father'.

2. The love of God is marked on us in baptism. Christ says in effect: 'You are the ones for whom I died and rose from the dead. You are united to me and forgiven. Now join with me and go the way of the Cross in love for my children. So get up each day and say 'I have been baptised'. The day is different because of it.

3. Turning the way of the Cross means sharing in God's love for all mankind in all its need.

4. Pray for someone for whom no one else will pray unless you do; pray for their welfare. Share in God's concern to let all the lonely sad people who feel unforgiven, and people with no purpose in life, know of the love of God. . .

5. Whenever unity of the Church is mentioned in the New Testament it is done

in the context of Christ's death on the Cross eg–cf Ephesians 2, Colossians 1, and here in the final prayer of Christ for us–as both we and they are in Christ, we belong to each other -

'That they may be one as I and the Father are one,
That the world may believe that thou hast sent me'

i.e. a loving community that reflects the love of God in the Incarnation".

These words of Professor Yule let many of us face with new strength the preparations for the 850th Anniversary of the Cathedral in the coming year, in co-operation with the Kirk Session and congregation and the Orkney Islands Council. I believe that they encouraged particularly our Session Clerk who had been appointed recently. He was Reg Bond,[5] in the view of the Cathedral's Kirk Session he was sure to prove a good successor as Session Clerk to George Burgher, and would provide his own kind of lay leadership and initiative. Briefly Reg was a man who retained his soldier's qualities to the end of his life. He was active for his Lord in prayer, and in action in the Cathedral, Community and Presbytery. In the latter he became Home Mission Convener, and was soon going down to Edinburgh to the Church Offices. He interviewed some of the ministerial secretaries there, in what, in his joking way, he called the 'Kremlin', and where he discovered what he called 'The Razor Gang', at one time the Union and Readjustments Committee! Reg was in charge of most of the seating in the Cathedral during the Queen's visits, and soon afterwards, of the Queen Mother's and of the King of Norway's visit, and he made a very good job of it all. Sadly we did not have Reg Bond long with us as Session Clerk. He died in 1988 in Aberdeen Hospital his wife with him there. His daughters (two of them) were also there, as was the Minister.

He, and the Revd Harold Mooney, the Cathedral Historian, and the Revd David Williams, Presbytery Clerk, did a great deal for St Magnus Cathedral in their life time in Orkney.

Like other Ministers I am grateful for elders; many of these were much older than Reg and are no longer with us. Some years ago now a special dinner was held in a hotel to honour those who had been more than 30 years in the Eldership, and I still have a photo of all who attended, though only the then Session Clerk and myself survive. Their names will be well known to many Orcadians. So I will be permitted to name them: Duncan Bain, Jimmy Cooper, Alex Doloughan, John Flett, Jim Gourlay, Bill Groundwater, Bob Milne–all comrades in fighting the good fight of faith.

3.   The Meaning of Christian Worship: Its Crisis and the Need for Renewal

To return to the principal Morning Sunday Service what is the purpose of this, which begins with 'Let us worship God'? In the former Bishop of Durham's words, "Now we need to go on to ask: "What does the Church exist for?" My short answer to that is: 'To celebrate and promote worth in the name of God the Holy Trinity' . . . "Worth is what God sees in us . . . Worth is what God offers us. He is actually and practically, in a down-to-earth way, offering us a share in his life of eternity. . . The worth that God offers us is the worth of sharing with other loving and living people which can go on infinitely developing and multiplying into the infinity of God. This is the worth that God entices from us. . . This is the worth that God is determined to share with us by loving us through sin and death. That is the good news. That is what the gospel is about, and that is why the gospel involves the cross and salvation".[6] But all this flows from Jesus Christ, for the worth of God is in Christ before it is through Christ for us and in us. To put the purpose of our worship in more Christological terms: it is to celebrate joyfully in Word and Sacrament the living God, who sent his Son Jesus Christ, into the world not to condemn but to save, and as ascended Lord to reconcile humankind to Himself through the power of His Holy Spirit. So it should be with glad thanksgiving that the members of a Church or of a Cathedral gather together on a Sunday, the day of their Lord's resurrection, and remember what has been done for them by Jesus Christ. He who was once crucified for all is now at work in the world according to his promise, and is within his people with the gift of his own sacrificial life and spirit, with the gift of his joyful faith in the Father, and of his amazing and forgiving and saving love, and with his unfailing hope for humankind.

Is this how it really is with our people in their Church or Cathedral, with those called out from their homes to celebrate God in the last years of the 1980s, and to meet with his son, Jesus Christ, the living Christ, with great joy, Sunday by Sunday?

Yet there is a <u>crisis</u> in relation to Christian worship, and this has been recognised for a long time already. It was being noticed even in the late 1960s. The report on 'Worship in a Secular Age' produced at the Fourth Assembly of the World Council of Churches (1968) has these words: "There is a crisis of worship and behind it a widespread crisis of Faith". Such a statement is more true now than then in Scotland, as well as elsewhere in Britain, despite a theologian having written: . . . "in every act of worship, it (the Church) experiences afresh the miracle of the coming of the Risen Christ to be with His followers".[7] Yet people often cannot recognise the assembly of their local Church or Cathedral as the place where, through Word and Sacrament, the risen Lord is encountered, and in him, God Himself, so what happens at a Morning Service can indeed be mocked as we come towards the end of the millennium. Part of the problem was put like this in the 1970s: "He (the theologian) has to understand man's exit from a sacred universe and his entry into a secular universe".[8] We live in this kind of world now which means one in which nature and society's functions are to be explained not in terms of the divine but of the human. For example farmers do not seek blessing on their ploughing or sowing; they just make sure they have a good tractor and seed and fertilizer. Humankind has come of age and man is in control of nature.

It might be said that too much is being made of the crisis of worship but the signs of its presence are clearly with us today. There is the sign of 'leavetaking': Jurgen Moltmann has written "What is the purpose of the Church? Many people today are asking this question. For some the question is a matter of leavetaking. . . This apathy no longer manifests itself primarily as partial identification with the church but increasingly as complete non-identification".[9] Moltmann is speaking out of the German situation, but who can deny that many Church of Scotland congregations report a similar leavetaking? There is also the sign of prayerlessness in the faithful attenders. This is not saying that these never pray, but rather that in many congregations a regular prayer life has gone.

Dr Paul Verghese in *Worship in the Secular Age* wrote: "most people have given up trying to pray, including large numbers of pastors, theologians and priests".

Yet again the crisis of worship can be found in what can be called the sign of dumbness. Many Church members are not prepared to articulate their faith and are reluctant to speak about it.

One more further evidence of this crisis is that in many parts of Scotland, the local Church appears to be, and sometimes is, a small geriatric community. Young people do not find it easy to be at home in such a gathering, especially when they find the language and the form and content of the worship, hard to grasp, and in which to share.

Many years ago Dr Lee wrote: - "It is in the minds not of the old, but of the young that we read the sure prophecy of approaching revolution".

In the light of this crisis of worship and of its signs clearly before us in the late 1980s, can we dare to speak of renewal? Or have we to engage in leaving the ghetto of the Church to go out into the desert in the world, as Charles Davis said it was necessary for him to do in relation to the Roman Catholic Church?[10] But has the Church not got in every age a Christological Centre? Has the living and ascended Christ not still power to renew his Church? What was written before in the 1970s is true for us now in St Magnus Cathedral, and for the smaller community Churches in our Presbytery: "The Christ of our Faith is a Christ full of grace, and according to the Gospel He is the one who seeks out the poor and the lost and the weak and the struggling. Hence, if indeed it is true that in many places the Church of Scotland congregations are poor, and often lacking in vitality and in hope and love, in so far as they know their poverty and needs and have only a little faith to seek His help, Jesus Christ is not one who will turn away from them. He will stay with them according to His faithful promise. "Where two or three have met together in my name I am there among them" (Mt 18 v20). And if Christ is in the midst, have we not every right to believe in His power to renew the Church, to which He can give grace to trust in Him, and for which He still intercedes? When the local congregation gathers for the public worship of God, when the Word is read and preached, when common prayer and praise are offered, when there is good fellowship, even though there could be a more frequent sacrament, who is going to say there has taken place no manifestation of God in Christ? And if the Risen Lord has encountered His people, however weak and deviant the world may reckon them to be, who is going to limit the result? Who is going to assert that He is incapable, even with men and women of weak faith, of bringing new life into the ghetto of His Church and of moving out His people into His world?"[11]

He is able by his presence among his people at worship, to create a new awareness of the supernatural character of Christianity. Sharing in that is not just the teaching of a higher morality. He can bring home to us the deep nature of our Faith, that through our Lord Himself, our humanity has been restored, and that, through the Spirit he gives us in our penitence and self offering, we can really share in his Sonship with the Father, and in his closeness to God, and in his divine glory in the world. Christian worship now and in the future millennium is still 'the recapitulation of the history of salvation'. That means that it is in Christ before it is through Christ. And what is recapitulated or repeated and confirmed is the dying and rising life of Jesus Christ. That is what he accomplished by God's Spirit in his life on earth. He gave it away in compassionate service and healing, and in teaching and preaching, revealing God and himself. Then finally he gave his life away on the Cross in obedience to God's will, breaking down the barrier between man and God. The veil in the temple has been torn down and humankind made available to the Father through the never to be repeated sacrifice of his Son. God raised his Son so that in heaven he continues to pray for his people pleading his eternal sacrifice, and on earth he pours out his Holy Spirit enabling his Word and Gospel to be proclaimed and his Holy Communion to be received. In worship therefore both of the Word and of the Sacrament we learn with Christ to die and rise again, stroking out self and being enabled by the Spirit to receive the life of our Saviour into the whole of our existence. This death and resurrection which is given to us by the living Christ can be grasped in Services of the Word, though better at the Lord's Supper. We go there joyfully to meet with this same Christ, and by faith we can hear his voice in different ways, though in the Church of Scotland tradition it is often in the sermon. "In Christ's new order", it has been written, and for all who believe in it, worship means meeting together with <u>him</u> and hearing what <u>he</u> has to say to us. We do not have to make any secret of our preacher's fallibility and our own spiritual deafness . . . we gather here with expectation because we believe he can and will take up the preacher's stumbling words into his service, and enable us to hear through them his own word to us. . .

When Christ speaks to us, he tells us the truth about our lives–truth that goes home, truth that commits. When Christ goes into the church and teaches then worship becomes a living, breath-taking experience".[12]

Yet if in the Service of the Word, the congregation is to share in the death and resurrection of Jesus Christ, we have both to hear his word, and to be given an opportunity to respond to it not only with our ears but with the offering of ourselves together. This brings me to the climactic point in the Service of the Word.

But is the Word read and preached really the climactic point of the Service? Many people in congregations would say that it is, within the Church of Scotland. According to this view, the people are meant to go away, each one, with the Gospel message ringing in their ears, and live it out in the coming week. Yet there are others who see the climax of the service differently. They, in no sense wish to play down the place of the sermon; the preaching of the Word is for them the Word of God, but they see an order within the Service of the Word, which is in the central tradition of Reformed worship, and which carries the worshippers forward to a climactic point beyond the sermon in praise, self offering and fellowship. This order is also a logical order in their eyes; approach to God leads to hearing the Word of God, which in turn leads to response to that revealed Word in thanksgiving and service. "It may be remarked also that this worship follows the biblical order, where knowledge of God is the result of the divine initiative, to which man responds by self committal to God, entering through Christ into a holy fellowship. 'We love, because He first loved us.' That is the sequence of this worship: the revelation of God in holy Scripture and the response of His children in the fellowship of the great prayer".[13]

If the transformation of life is a reality within the service of the Word through the presence of the risen Lord, how much more in the service of the Word and Sacrament". But the theology of the Eucharist we shall consider later on.

Notes

1.   J V Taylor -' A Matter of Life and Death' - SCM Press - p20.
2.   Ibid - p21.
3.   Ibid - p76.
4.   D E Jenkins - 'God, Jesus and Life in The Spirit' - SCM Press (1988) - p42.
5.   Colonel Reginald Bond MBE, BA, FBIM.
6.   D E Jenkins - Ibid - pp76-77.
7.   J J Von Allmen - 'Worship - Its Theology and Practice' - Lutterworth Press, London - p27.
8.   J G Davies - 'Every Day God' - SCM Press (1973) - Part one - Chapter 1 'Exit from the Sacral Universe'.
9.   J Moltmann - 'Theology and Joy' - SCM Press (1973) - p76.
10.   cf C Davis - 'Temptations of The Church'.
11.   H W M Cant - 'Liturgical Review' - Church Service Society (C of S) Vol V No 1 (May, 75) - p25.
12.   J W Leitch - 'The King Comes' - SCM Press (1965) - p19.
13.   W D Maxwell - 'Concerning Worship' -Oxford University Press (1948) - p38.

Chapter XIII

The 850th Anniversary of St Magnus Cathedral
(1137-1987) and The 850th Anniversary Services

However much the light of steadfast courage, sacrificial forgiving service, and continuing wisdom, had been received from others within the Cathedral, and not least, from people like Reg Bond and many more (among them sisters in Christ) there was to be a yet greater pouring out of light, for Cathedral and community alike, in the 850th Anniversary Celebrations of St Magnus Cathedral.

Some thought had already been given to this celebration as early as 1984 and 1985, but in 1986 a letter was written from the Kirk Session to the co-ordinator for this, appointed by the Orkney Islands Council, and to the Council's Chief Executive. Some extracts from this letter are relevant: "Purpose (a) The celebrations are to mark, with joyful thanksgiving before God, 850 years of Christian faith, fellowship, service and worship, as seen in the life of the Bishops, Ministers, Elders and people of St Magnus Cathedral, and as reflected in the stonework, the stained glass (many pictures depicting the Orkney Earls and Norwegian Kings), the rich symbolism in wood, and in the historical documents, within the building and related to it. (b) To celebrate also the Cathedral's origins and place in the religious life of Scandinavia (particularly Norway), Scotland, and in and beyond Europe. Duration–The celebrations should commence in Easter 1987, if not before, and should continue until St Rognvald's Day, (Cathedral Founder) 20th August".

Reg Bond always believed that the troops in a battalion should know, as far as possible, what was to happen in the future, so these words were written by him in the *Cathedral Magazine* to give a fuller description to the members of what was planned for our Anniversary Year.

"The celebration of the Anniversary will begin on New Years Day, with our Minister throwing up the 'Ba',[1] to the large crowd, mainly of Orcadians, waiting for this to happen in Broad Street, outside the Cathedral West Door. Holy Week services, from Monday, 13 April, will be led by the Revd Dr Henry Sefton of Aberdeen University; St Magnus Day comes about the middle of the week, and there will be a special Anniversary Service (invitations are to go to the members of the Orkney Islands Council, to all the Presbytery Churches, to the Kirkwall Council of Churches, and to the members of the

Society of the Friends of St Magnus). At the end of April the Renaissance Singers will be in Orkney, giving we trust some of the music of the earlier centuries of the Cathedral's life. During May there will be the now well established Folk Festival. In June the St Magnus Festival of Music and Drama (about a week in duration) will include some specially written pieces for the Festival–for the BBC Scottish Symphony Orchestra, and for the Edinburgh Quartet (some musical concerts of the Festival always take place within the Cathedral itself). A Medieval Banquet is planned for July. Towards the end of the month there will be an International Conference dealing with the life and importance of Orkney in the 12th Century, when the building of the Cathedral commenced.[2] The Norwegian Training Ship, the *Christian Radich,* which was in attendance at the 800th Anniversary of the Cathedral, will again be in Kirkwall for a few days.

The climax of the celebrations will be the dedication of the new stained glass window in the Cathedral, (in the presence of Her Majesty the Queen, who will unveil it), and soon after that in the same month, August, there will be a gift of the Tapestry from Hordaland in Norway, by King Olav V of Norway to the Queen Mother, who will receive this as Patron of the Friends of the Society of St Magnus on behalf of the people of Orkney.

Details of these events are still to be finalised, but they will be supported by a Children's Pilgrimage from the parishes of Orkney (following the route taken by those who brought the body of St Magnus from Egilsay to Birsay, and then to Kirkwall, to St Olaf's Church. Later it was put in the East end of St Magnus Cathedral). There will also be a Riding of the Marches as well as a Son et Lumière presentation of the Cathedral's history".[3]

Certain details can be given now about the new stained glass West window, about how it was chosen and about the artist. It was selected by a small local committee–Colonel Robert Macrae, the Lord Lieutenant of Orkney, Brigadier Sidney Robertson, Lt Col Edgar Gibson, the Head Art Teacher at the Grammar School, and the Minister of the Cathedral–from work made available to it on slides. The artist who was chosen, was a Scot, Mr Crear McCartney, a school teacher from near Biggar, Scotland. His design for the window was put on display in the Kirkwall library. All who wished to subscribe to it were invited to do so as individuals or as members of the congregation. Many subscribed in memory of their loved ones, and these names are now in a book below the window itself. All the money required for the window was quickly subscribed.

1. Light from Holy Week

Something further requires to be said here about the April celebration events, for they were excellent windows through which God gave penetrating light into the Cathedral and into the Saints, Bishops and people associated with it.

The Holy Week Services were indeed such a window and the sermons at these were much appreciated. "The Minister and Kirk Session of St Magnus Cathedral wish to thank the Revd Dr Henry Sefton, Master of Christ's College, Aberdeen for coming to Orkney in 1987 . . . Dr Sefton was Holy Week preacher at the services held in the Cathedral but arranged by the Kirkwall Council of Churches . . ." (Introduction to the Sermons).

These–called *Sermons in Holy Week* - were collected together and published later in 1987. There are five Chapters: 'Christ and the Church', 'Christ and the State', 'Christ and the Home', 'Christ and St Magnus' and finally 'Towards Jerusalem'. All of them are extremely relevant to St Magnus Cathedral, and contain the writer's perceptive view of it. We have only time to say something of Dr Henry Sefton's vision in, 'Christ and the Church.' Henry mentions not only the vine in the Old and New Testaments, but also both the symbol of the vine and its reality within the Cathedral. He was aware of this symbol as he spoke, above the heads of the people in St Rognvald's Chapel roof. But it was not a broken and an empty Vine, it was a Vine with its fruits, with its grapes. Henry pointed out that for long centuries this Vine had been hidden away from so many people, but had recently been discovered again.

But our preacher also saw in the Cathedral the reality of the Vine, the Vine, who is Jesus Christ risen from the dead, and he is doing his work there still, joining his people to himself for they are branches in himself, enabling them to listen to his words, to receive his gifts of Baptism and Holy Communion, to produce his fruits of praise and prayer and service, and of love and joy and peace, and of ever deeper faith and hope.

All this does not mean that there are not branches in danger of falling out of the living Vine of Christ. Some can be cut off and become dead wood. Henry stressed this point: "we are the branches of a Vine. If we are cut off from the Vine, we are useless. We are fit only for burning. If we become separated from Christ we are useless. We cannot approach God. Only in and through Christ can we come to the Father. It is only in Christ and through Christ that we can be said to live in any significant manner. Apart from Him our lives are useless".[4]

Yet there is another Tree which was seen in the Cathedral–the Tree of the Cross. To this tree also the Christian has to be joined. Christ cannot be left alone on his Cross; he does not simply give us the gifts of his crucial words and commands, he comes to us with the gift of his Cross, often the gift of sacrifice, scandal and pain. Yet through it, he gives us forgiveness for our breaking apart from him and from God our Father; he takes our place being separated from God on this tree and his expression of this is the cry of dereliction. So Jesus Christ awakens in us a new passion and desire to stroke out ourselves, and receive his Spirit of thanksgiving to the Father, and of strong courage and thirst to serve others in his name, even those whom we see as our enemies.

I have no doubt also Dr Sefton saw the Cathedral East window, with the Cross there as elsewhere in the building. With these piercing words, and with a description of the Cross, he ends his first sermon:

"I am the Tree, you are the branches–Yet we must be associated with that tree too. We must allow ourselves to be a reproach, a stumbling block, and scandal. We must have a share in the cross. We dare not leave Christ on the cross, for apart from him we are nothing. We cannot come to God, but with and through him. Apart from Christ we are nothing, we are useless. We are only fit for the bonfire.

"Jesus says - 'Abide in me and I in You'
Faithful Cross above all other
'One and only noble Tree
None in foliage none in blossom
None in fruit compares with thee".

The Easter Communion followed these services on the Sunday in the Cathedral. The Ascended Christ came to our people yet again with the gift of his Holy Spirit, to reveal his Cross, and to find entrance for his sacrificial life and prayer into the lives of all who that day were seeking his saving and renewing presence.

2.   *Light from The Easter Conference*

Another important Spring event in our Anniversary Year, was the Easter Conference from 18th–21st April. The Chairman was Mr R D Kernohan (Editor then of *Life and Work*) and the conference programme had the following subjects and speakers:

'The Medieval Bishops of St Magnus'
        Professor I B Cowan, Glasgow University
'The Sixteenth Century and the Movement for Reform'
        The Revd Dr Duncan Shaw–Moderator Designate of the General
        Assembly (Church of Scotland)
'The Eighteenth Century Church in Orkney'
        W P L Thomson, Rector of Kirkwall Grammar School
'Some Aspects of the Nineteenth Century Church in Kirkwall'
        Revd H W M Cant–Cathedral Minister
'The Church in the Post Permissive Age'
        The Revd R Ferguson–Leader, Iona Community
'Twentieth Century Life and Worship in St Magnus Cathedral'
        The Revd H Mooney–formerly Minister of Deerness and Tankerness,
        Orkney
'The Task of the Church in Today's World'
        The Rt Revd Professor R Craig, Moderator of the General Assembly,
        Church of Scotland

The invitation to this Cathedral Conference included these words: "Celebrate with us its given Light, through the centuries, from Medieval, Reformation, and later times to the present". Eventually a book was published containing all these lectures, called *Light in the North*. It had a Foreword by our Lord Lieutenant (then Colonel Macrae): a very necessary section on 'The Origin and Context of St Magnus Cathedral', by an Orcadian, Howie Firth, (a distinguished student also in mathematical physics from Edinburgh University and a writer and broadcaster). A brief introduction to the Conference was written by Edwin R Eunson OBE, Convener of the Orkney Islands Council since 1978.

There have been many who, in different centuries, have caused the light poured out from St Magnus, and by its saints, leaders, and people, to be recognised and seen. I believe that this very much happened in this April Conference. Colonel Macrae wrote in his Foreword: "It may surprise some that so many wise and distinguished men and women came to Orkney in 1987 to honour the 850th Anniversary of the founding of St Magnus Cathedral with their eloquent and learned words. *Light in the North* is the record of their coming–aptly named, for so it has been down the ages".[5]

This has been a light bringing book to many who have been able to read it; all the chapters in it bring insight about the Cathedral, or about many who have been associated with it. I want to make reference only to the first preparatory lecture in the book, called "The Origin and Context of St Magnus Cathedral",[6] by Howie Firth, and in particular want to set down what is quoted, by itself, at the beginning of his chapter, from a distinguished Orcadian historian. "There is something in their Church", wrote Storer Clouston as a young man, "that none of the respectable townsfolk have the slightest suspicion of–something alive that vibrates to the cry of the wind and the breaking of the sea, and the little human events that happen in the crow-stepped houses".[7] The Ministers and many of the people of Orkney have often thought about their Cathedral, and about what it has brought and still brings to them, but this was the first time that the blessings of the Cathedral had been put in this way. "There is something in their Church . . . something alive," what indeed is this? Storer Clouston in the article where this phrase is found, explains. It is a spirit that indwells the Cathedral, though it has ranged around in many places before, "then it looked for a fitting home where it might live when it could no longer find a home in the people so it built the Cathedral, and there it silently dwells today".[7]

But as important, this indwelling spirit is a remembering spirit: When it first began to look down from its windows upon those men going about their business in the sunshine and the rain, it saw among the little creatures some that were well worth remembering . . . There was Rognvald himself. The very stones of the Cathedral recall him for us, and his uncle, Magnus. Howie Firth makes this point well in these words: "The warmth of the building makes it indeed, as in Storer Clouston's words quoted earlier, 'something alive, seeming to carry something of the personalities of Rognvald and Magnus in it, and inspire a similar kind of affection".[8]

The spirit of St Rognvald has continued his work, for it vibrates in the homes of many ordinary people, energising them to go on building up, or restoring or beautifying the Cathedral he vowed to build. Mr Eunson, the Orkney Islands Council Convener, tells how the Cathedral was threatened in different centuries: in the 17th century by the Earl of Caithness, though Bishop Law intervened to stop his destructive intent, and in the 19th century by the move to abandon the Cathedral–'The Stone and Lime Disruption'–and build a new church, but a Government department, thinking the Cathedral was theirs, carried out restoration. Mr Eunson continued: "Finally, about fifteen or sixteen years ago, a survey shocked all who loved the Cathedral with the information that the West gable was cracked and was in danger of collapsing on to the Kirk Green".[9] All this is something Howie Firth noticed: "Whenever its fabric is in danger, someone comes to its aid–to prevent destruction or to stimulate restoration . . . And for each of these crises and people who emerge above the current of history, there are a myriad of individuals who have done something that, however large or small, required of them to give their best, making or giving, or fetching and carrying, in which their piece of work fitted into the overall pattern, like one of the many pieces of stained glass in a window".[10]

This aliveness of the spirit of Rognvald is so often hidden, yet it still shines and vibrates in the little human events of the people in their homes. It is relevant to describe it as the light of sharing gifts.

Ministers or people in the congregation or connected with it have sometimes vivid memories of this. I will always recall with astonishment and gratitude the lady who put a roll of notes into my hand. Within it I counted afterwards one thousand pounds. It was "for the Cathedral", she said, "in whatever way it was thought right by the Treasurer and Kirk Session to bring something to it or to beautify it in some way". And there have been others in recent years who have given smaller or larger sums for a specific cause for which an appeal has been made. Some years ago a lady told me that in grateful memory of her husband's generous life,–a man who loved Orkney and its Cathedral not least–she would like to give a handsome piano. Its rich melody is now often heard at a Sunday Morning Cathedral Service. Some gifts destined for the Cathedral have been months, if not years being prepared. In the ministry of my successor, the Revd Ron Ferguson there has been given a magnificent Communion Table Cloth, beautifully embroidered in so many places. Also there has come the gift of a splendidly carved oak candlestick, in which a candle is lit every Sunday Morning Service, and which speaks of the faithful departed, including Rognvald and Magnus. The gifts to the Cathedral are far too numerous to mention, though those of robes, of a lectern bible and pew bibles, or hymn books or bible markers come to mind. Also many gifts have poured in from Norway and elsewhere, from far beyond the members of the Cathedral. However we cannot forget the huge sum of money (£60,000) gifted by the late Sheriff Thoms (who is commemorated in our East window) for a major restoration of the Cathedral (1910–1933), nor can we forget the more than a quarter of a million pounds donated in recent years to restore and rebuild part of the Cathedral, and prevent it falling down at the West End. And we will always remember the gift in our Anniversary Year of our new stained glass West Window, unveiled by Her Majesty the Queen, and donated by countless Orcadians who wished it to be a memorial to their loved ones, and a shining light for all to see, now and in generations ahead, within the Cathedral, and in a wonderful way also, of an evening outside it.

The vibrating spirit of Rognvald, and of Christ through Him, did more than energise the sharing of gifts to the Cathedral in many homes, it also made possible the receiving of gifts from the Cathedral. And of this too so many respectable townsfolk had no suspicion. What were these gifts? They were of different kinds "Many benefits to a community flowed from the establishment of a cathedral. Those who would serve there needed to be trained to the highest standards. There would have been a music school, and it has been suggested that Rognvald himself may have founded it, and that the Cathedral was the reason for the establishment of the grammar school in the town".[11] In addition the light of truth was encouraged in the Cathedral and beyond it, through the teaching staff provided. The Revd Dr Duncan Shaw, in his chapter in the 16th century tells of how Bishop Reid helped in this way by re-organisation of the Cathedral Chapter. He was also the Bishop of Orkney who made a "bequest of money for the founding of the University of Edinburgh, and the Reid Chair of Scots Law, in fact, now indicates the connection between the Bishop of Orkney and the community of Edinburgh". This light of truth is also clearly found in the later chapters. "The tradition of clarity of thought is brought, further on in the book, into the present day by the Revd Ronald Ferguson and by the Rt Revd Professor Robert Craig, each tackling the great issues of our time and building up a strong rational base of principles from which to chart a course of action. Thus the pattern of the Church setting the foundation for the order of society continues into our own time, as it did in the vision of Constantine, of Charlemagne, of the Norman Dukes, and of Rognvald".[12] Yet again there was brought about the possibility of new trade and travel, for Rognvald could be seen as having created a "major new international trading centre at Kirkwall with harbour, market place, and Cathedral".

Howie Firth's chapter tells us too about the impact of the Church in the Cathedral. This could be put in different ways but the author sees it in these words: "From a busy market place, and the often intense day to day matters of island life, a door only a few short steps away leads to a still place in a turning world, where the solid pillars stand firm on the rock they are founded on, and where the human eye and spirit can rise upwards through the harmony of the building".[13] We cannot think about what St Rognvald achieved without at the same time being mindful of St Magnus. Can we also speak of the vibration of his spirit in the Cathedral and in the little human events of the crow stepped houses?

The Revd Harald Mooney wrote: "Many a petition, in days that are gone, was addressed to 'Guid Manse', as he was called. People delighted to call their sons Magnus: so much so that in Caithness Orcadians used to be known–perhaps still are–by the nice name–MANSIES". And yet today Magnus is often seen as a figure from the past who has got miraculous power associated with him. That was the way it was, with the first residential Bishop of Orkney, Bishop William. As George Mackay Brown reminds us: "People sick in mind or body, began to flock to Magnus' tomb in Birsay, and extraordinary cures were reported. At first William, Bishop of Orkney, disapproved of such vulgar credulity, but later his eyes were opened–literally and metaphorically–to the presence of something rare and strange and new in the life of the islands; a sweetness and a light unknown before".[14] This light it is remembered penetrated into the mind and heart of Magnus' mother, Thora, in her gracious reception at her table of her son's murderer, Earl Hakon. But what about today in the year 1999? What do Orcadians really think now about Magnus, even though many know the stories concerning him, and where he is remembered and honoured and buried? G M Brown makes his thoughts clear for us about Magnus in the view of his people and of himself. "The Orcadians, if they thought about Magnus Erlendson, considered him to be a queer fish, one of those medieval figures, clustered about with mortifications and miracles, that have no real place in our enlightened progressive society. For me, Magnus was at once a solid convincing flesh-and-blood man, from whom pure spirit flashed from time to time–and never more brightly than at the hour of his death by an axe-stroke, in Egilsay island on Easter Monday, 1117".[15] Here in Magnus, even if respectable townsfolk had no idea of this, George in his small house in Stromness finds 'something alive' which vibrates in himself. He sees it in Magnus' death most clearly, the vibrating of an amazing accepting and forgiving love for his enemies as well as for his friends and the source of this comes, as George well knows, from the light and life of Magnus risen Master, Jesus Christ, and it was that light which drew him to the mystery of the Mass, and make him in his autobiography quote these words of George Herbert:

"Love bade me welcome; yet my soul drew back,
    Guilty of dust and sin . . ."

but also the words from the same poem–"The Temple: Love".

"You must sit down", says Love, "and taste My meat".
    So I did sit and eat.

So it was wonderful to G M Brown that he, a mere writer of words, should become like the farmer or the fisherman, penetrated by the Spirit and life of the Father and the Son. So Magnus was after all a Catholic, and this came home to G M Brown "Was this Magnus a Catholic or not? In western Europe in the twelfth century there were only Catholics. And the Cathedral in Kirkwall had been built by Catholic masons, for the offering of the Catholic Mass".[16] This points us forward to the new west window of the Cathedral which, in part, tells about what Presbyterians call the Lord's Supper, where our Lord's life shines out with its shining light from the Cup.

But we must speak now about the royal services in which Orkney and her Cathedral was honoured, first by Her Majesty the Queen, and then, some weeks later, by Her Majesty the Queen Mother and by King Olav of Norway.

The 850th Anniversary Services - 9th August and 19th August, 1987

In 1987 there were two Royal Services in St Magnus Cathedral. The Morning Service, the occasion of the unveiling of the Stained Glass West Window–a Memorial Window of Thanksgiving–by Her Majesty the Queen, took place on Sunday, 9 August, at the normal time of 11.15 am. Another Service, on the occasion of the visit of their Majesties, Queen Elizabeth, the Queen Mother, and King Olav V of Norway, was held on Wednesday, 19 August, at 12 o'clock. It is fitting that we should speak first about the Service in the Cathedral where our Queen was present. When Her Majesty came to Orkney in this Anniversary Year, she had duties to perform other than what was done within the Cathedral, but the centre piece of her Orcadian visit, in August, '87 was the unveiling of the West Window in the historic building of St Magnus. There were many presentations made to Her Majesty–for example at the Airport, not least of the Convener of the Orkney Islands Council, Mr Edwin Eunson, and of Mrs Eunson–before she arrived at the steps of the Cathedral's West door where the Minister was introduced to her by our Lord Lieutenant, Colonel R A A S Macrae.

In relation to the Service itself, Praise included Hymns 138, 362, 115, 333, 521 and 505, while the Choir sang the Anthem, O Thou The Central Orb of Righteous Love–music by Charles Wood. Prayers were said by Father H Bamber S J, by Bishop Andreas Aarflot, Bishop of Oslo, and by the Minister. The Lessons were Psalm 48, read by Colonel Macrae, 1 John 3 vv11-18, read by Mr Edwin Eunson, and the Gospel, St John 8 vv12-20, read by Colonel R J Bond. In his sermon, the Minister took as his theme: "The windows of God's creation and redemption, through which he wills his light to shine". *The Orcadian* recorded that Mr Cant said that here in St Magnus God's light and love has been streaming in for 850 years to forgive and renew peoples lives, lifting them up into new faith and love and hope, and great rejoicing, generation after generation. Later in the Service, the new window was unveiled, the Minister saying - "Your Majesty, we invite you to unveil the Memorial Window of Thanksgiving". After this the Cathedral bells were rung, then Colonel Macrae and Mr Eunson came forward to the Lectern. These words were spoken by our Lord Lieutenant: "In the name of all who have contributed to this window and of those whose names are written in the Book of Remembrance, I ask you, as representing the Council and the People of Orkney, to receive this Memorial Window of Thanksgiving".

To this Mr Eunson replied: "We accept this gift as a sacred trust, and shall guard it reverently, in honour of God's blessings of the preservation of this Cathedral, and of 850 years of Christian worship and life therein, and in thanksgiving for the faithful lives in whose memory the window has also been gifted".

Mr Eunson then asked the Minister to dedicate the window.

These are the words of dedication: "In the faith of our Lord Jesus Christ, I dedicate this Memorial Window of Thanksgiving to the glory and praise of God, and in memory of his servants–In the name of the Father, and of the Son, and of the Holy Spirit, Amen". Then this prayer of dedication was said: "Glorious art thou, O God, Father, Son and Holy Spirit, ever to be adored in all the congregations of thy people, who love the habitation of thy house, and the place where thine honour dwelleth. O Holy God, who giveth to all things their beauty and their fitness, we beseech thee to consecrate this window to the beautifying of this Cathedral, to the blessing and edifying of its people, and to the glory of thy great Name. We pray that all who behold the fair colours of this window, in this generation, and in those which are to come, may by thy Holy Spirit be filled with thoughts pure and lovely, and be drawn to the vision of heavenly things. Increase in them the purity of heart whereby they may behold thee, and confirm them more and more to the image of thy Son, so that where sign and symbol may have passed away, and that which is perfect has come, they may behold the things thou hast prepared for them that love thee . . ." The Lord's Prayer.

Many introductions were made before Her Majesty left the Cathedral, including certain Cathedral Office Bearers, also the Architect, the Organist and some members of the Society of the Friends of St Magnus. It is important to remember too that Mr Crear McCartney (the window artist) and Mrs McCartney were presented to Her Majesty near the Pulpit, from which the new window could be clearly seen. The Queen was particularly interested in the inspiration behind the work in the window, which took one and a half years to complete. Mr McCartney remembered this some years ago: "I was looking here through the window, when the mist suddenly lifted and sunshine streamed through, giving a sunburst effect. That was the moment the idea of a stained glass window came to me". Mr McCartney said that the Queen was very impressed by the new window and he added: "Her Majesty expressed the hope that there would be sun with which to illuminate it before the end of the summer".

Mr Martin Farrelly, the window installer, and Mrs Farrelly, and Mr Alan Stout, the Cathedral Mason, and Mrs Stout were also presented.

Before leaving the Cathedral, Her Majesty, was invited by the Minister to sign the Memorial Book and the Visitors' Book; thereafter the Lord Lieutenant presented a gift to Her Majesty, of an Orkney Chair, from the Society of the Friends of St Magnus, and conducted her to where outside the West door, she was welcomed by members of the Children's Pilgrimage. This brief note about it may be helpful here:

"During 1987, the children of Orkney are making a Pilgrimage for St Magnus to mark the 850th Anniversary of the Cathedral, founded in his name. As a lasting souvenir of the occasion, and as the children's gift to the Cathedral, each Parish or Island has contributed a sea washed stone which, when cut and polished, will be used to embellish a font, to be placed in St Rognvald Chapel. From Egilsay, where Magnus was martyred, relays of children have progressed round Orkney by sea and land, Parish by Parish, by way of the Saint's resting place in Birsay to arrive at last in Broad Street, before the Cathedral of St Magnus, in the presence of Her Majesty the Queen".

Following her watching the children leaving the stones before her in the wooden casket, representing that which had carried the bones of St Magnus from Egilsay to Kirkwall, Her Majesty was entertained to lunch in the Town Hall, where grace was said by the then Dean of the Chapel Royal–The Very Revd Professor R S Barbour.

The other Royal Service, on the Wednesday of August 19th 1987, was held in the presence of Her Majesty, Queen Elizabeth the Queen Mother, and of His Majesty, King Olaf V of Norway. This was once more an Ecumenical Service like the earlier one. The Bishop of Trondheim, Bishop Bremer, shared in the worship, while Dr Dramdal, Convener of Hordaland Regional Council, addressed the congregation from the Lectern. It was helpful for many worshippers that Norwegian and English was spoken, and that there was celebration not only of the Cathedral's Norwegian origins but also of the close connection of Norway and Orkney through many centuries. Hence it can be no surprise that inside the packed Cathedral there were members of the Orkney-Norwegian Friendship Association, as well as members of the Orkney Islands Council along with those of the Hordaland Regional Council. The Service Readings also saw Orcadian and Norwegian co-operation: The Orkney Islands Convener reading the lesson from Zechariah 8 vv3-8 and 20-23 - 'The Vision of a New Corporate Life and Fellowship Among the Nations'; The Epistle was read by Dr Dramdal–Ephesians 4 vv1-6–'The Togetherness Which the Spirit Gives'–while the Gospel, St John 17 vv18-23–'The Unity for which Christ Prayed' –was heard from the Bishop of Nidaros (Trondheim). In his address to the congregation, Dr Dramdal spoke of the old links between the two districts which had been in place long before formal twinning links were established in 1983. He then spoke of how artists had continued to draw inspiration from the Norse period, and explained that the Tapestry symbolised the strong links between Norway and Orkney.

Prior to the dedication of the Tapestry by the Cathedral Minister in the small aisle of the choir, His Majesty King Olav V addressed Her Majesty Queen Elizabeth the Queen Mother with these works: "I ask you to receive this Tapestry, the gift of the people of Hordaland" "As Patron of the Friends of St Magnus, it gives me great pleasure to accept this beautiful tapestry on behalf of the people of Orkney" was the reply. The Minister was asked by King Olav V to dedicate the Tapestry, and his words of dedication were: "In the faith of our Lord Jesus Christ I dedicate this Tapestry to the glory and praise of God–In the name of the Father and of the Son and of the Holy

Spirit–Amen". There followed the Prayer of Dedication. Lights revealed a long white tapestry in many ways resembling a sail. The Tapestry designer and weaver, Mrs Kari Dyrdal was presented to the Royals, and King Olav discussed the design with her.

Here is part of the reflections of Col. R Bond, the Session Clerk–printed in the 1987 September issue of the *Cathedral Magazine*–on the 850th Anniversary Celebrations:

"The Easter Conference was intended to follow the Life and Worship of St Magnus Cathedral from its foundation through the change of the years, and then under God's guidance, to form our vision of its life into the Twenty First Century. The programme was completed and, according to reports, successful. Now it is up to each of us, who have any connection with the Cathedral, to work out what is our personal responsibility in this matter . . . Norway contributed to the celebrations: We had visits from three ships: Did you notice that all the off duty personnel of the *Christian Radich*, and the *Statsraad Lehmkuhl*, and most of the passengers and crew of the *Jupiter* joined in worshipping God in the Cathedral?. . . Stanley Cursiter (at one time Queen's Limner in Scotland) and Edwin Muir, whose centenaries are co-incidental with the Cathedral's 850th Anniversary, often bring out the ongoing strength of God's purposes. We have been privileged to see a representative collection of Stanley's paintings, and to hear excellent presentations by the Arts Society and the Festival of Edwin's life and works. A breath-taking thrill came over those who were worshipping at Morning Service with Her Majesty the Queen, and saw the unveiling of the light, the colours and the designs of the new Memorial Window. And did not the silences during the Service move us just as much as the words which were spoken? The participation of ministers from other denominations was a foretaste of the ecumenical tolerance and combined Christian witness which has since become the commitment of the Roman Catholic leader, Cardinal Hume, as well as many Protestant leaders. But going back to the window, were you not just as struck when it was illuminated from inside during the Son et Lumière. I hope we see and hear George Mackay Brown's pageant again next year . . .

Everyone likes to see the Queen Mother in Orkney for we hold her in great affection. This year she came on one of our few sunny days, and it was a unique privilege–even if we could not see the actual ceremony–to have been present when King Olav V of Norway asked her to receive the Hordaland tapestry. Were two crowned heads ever together in the Cathedral on any other occasion?

The Riding of the Marches, revived last year to commemorate the granting of the Charter by King James III, took place this year in the wettest rain the skies can produce: but everyone seems to have enjoyed taking part in it. The thought crossed my mind that if the Cathedral still owned all this land and property, we would have no financial worries!

But I do not want to end on this material note. The challenge of the celebrations to each of us, especially members of the younger generation, is to make sure that the life and worship and witness of the Cathedral have an ever increasing influence in our community in the coming decade and century".

After the celebrations were over they were seen to have been very happy and memorable within the Cathedral and outside. Thanks were expressed by the Minister and Kirk Session to the Orkney Islands Convener, members and officials, for all their help and generosity. They also expressed their great appreciation of the work of the Co-ordinator, Mr John McDonald, and of the very valuable secretarial contribution of Mrs Sandra Leslie. The Minister expressed gratitude to the Choir and the Organists for leading the praise so splendidly at all the major services, and to the Elders for all their extra visits to their districts. He also thanked Stanley Sinclair, the Church Officer, and John Windwick the Custodian, for all the extra time and help they gave during the preparation for the Royal visits to the Cathedral services. The Cathedral will always be indebted to Colonel Bond, The Session Clerk, who had the none too easy task of ticket distribution, as well as other weighty matters, while Mr I T W Sloan, the Clerk to the Board was involved also with the seating plans and his help too was invaluable.

Along with many other Orcadians, the Session and people of the Cathedral wish to pay tribute to the work done by the Lord Lieutenant, Colonel Macrae. Without his achievements the Royal visits would not have passed off in the happy way they did, and whose idea it was, that the new window was uncovered in the way it happened in the presence of Her Majesty the Queen.

Notes

1. For details of the 'Ba' Game see J D M Robertson's excellent book 'Uppies and Doonies'.
2. The details of the subjects and speakers were later published in "St Magnus Cathedral and Orkney's Twelfth Century Renaissance' - Edited by Barbara E Crawford, St Andrew's University.
3. There will also be on display, near the Cathedral, historical documents (some Kirk Session Records, going back to the 17th century, as well as Communion Silver: Some chalices from the 17th century also).
4. H R Sefton - Chapter on 'Christ and the Church' - p7.
5. Foreword to 'Light in the North' - R A A S Macrae - p1.
6. H N Firth - 'Light in The North' - The Orkney Press - Edited by Cant and Firth - p5.
7. 'The Magnus Book' - Storer Clouston's Article on the Cathedral.
8. 'Light in The North' - Ibid - Edited by Cant and Firth - p21.
9. E R Eunson - Introduction to the Conference in 'Light in The North' - p24.
10. 'Light in the North' - Ibid -21-22.
11. Ibid - p17.
12. Ibid - p17.
13. Ibid - pp17-18.
14. G M Brown - 'For The Islands I Sing' - John Murray - London - p9.
15. Ibid - p52.
16. Ibid - pp52-53.

Chapter XIV

A Prospect of the Future Church, in the Millennium

A Developing Ecumenical Church

For more than two decades I was a member of the Kirkwall Council of Churches, yet it was always sadness to us that important Christian groups in the town were not full members of the Council–for example, the Baptists, and the Christian Fellowship, and the Plymouth Brethren. It may well be that, though the Kirkwall Council of Churches failed to achieve a more fully developed membership, this will now better happen through the wider ecumenical dialogue and worship of the Local Churches Working Group which is looking at ways of preparing for the Millennium Church in Orkney. There may also take place new ecumenical developments in certain parishes throughout Orkney, to a greater extent than at present; these could bring fresh insights and service to the Church of Scotland Churches. Not least Church growth together in Orkney could focus on one of the most important aspects of the Church of Scotland's present failings, its mission, at Presbytery and Congregational level, to bring into Church fellowship and witness not least those who have entered the teenage years. Yet while the Millennium Church may reveal itself to be increasingly ecumenical, this cannot exclude an examination of the state of what is still called the Church of Scotland. By over 40 years in this Ministry I have been led to see both its darkness and its light. Ministers, elders, and members have no doubt contributed to these realities in various ways, yet to be confronted anew by these things could be helpful and beneficial.

I   The Darkness of the Church

This dark divide which R S Thomas portrays in his poem 'The Minister'[1] and his people, has been seen in the Church of Scotland in the past, and it could penetrate into the Church of the future. It was seen in his own Church, and in other lands like Africa and America, by the Very Revd Dr George MacLeod. "What has gone wrong in American religion is the terrible cleavage between Church activity–never more prosperous than today–and any realistic sense of God's sovereignty in history, and His demands upon us in His now unified world".² "Barring a thin red line of Christian protesters in the last three centuries . . . The Church simply has not made the nexus. It has concerned itself with 'getting the Gospel right first'. Thus we are where we are".³ Further on George writes: 'What concerns me is the large number who, admitting social obligations, in fact stand short of implementing it!' At any rate, George MacLeod, in his speaking and writing, believed that it was always necessary for the Christian to be going forward, and he quotes these words of Dr Phillips' paraphrase of the Epistle to the Hebrews: "Let us not lay over and over again the foundation truths–repentance from the deeds which led to death, believing in God, baptism and laying on of hands, belief in the life to come and the final judgement. No, if God allows, let us go on".⁴ So in the present and future Church we cannot be imprisoned in God's word of forgiveness and in the fundamental convictions of the Christian Faith without being moved out and on to a deeper understanding of and thanksgiving for the Father's love for his people, and to seeing the things around us, which include service to the needs of men and women. Many Christians now–and I believe in the future Church–will know that if Christianity begins in a uniting fellowship with God the Father, through the Son, it leads on and ends up in action in society and in the world.

The sometimes pressing darkness of the Church is hard to summarise, but it can be put like this: The ministers, elders, leaders, and members, can forget what they have received from God, Father and Son and Holy Spirit, they can fail to recall they have been forgiven and have within them Christ's life and spirit, God's reign in their hearts, for they have become his children by a rebirth of spirit. They forget that they are surrounded in their congregation by their brothers and sisters (though not all of these are aware of this) and are called to bless the Lord and not to forget his benefits, "who forgiveth all thine iniquities, who healeth all thy diseases, who redeemeth thy life from destruction; who crowneth thee with loving kindness and tender mercies; who satisfieth thy mouth with good things; so that thy youth is renewed like the eagle's.⁵ Thus the forgiven person is energised afresh and made strong to mediate Christ's forgiveness and new life to those around him or her. This leads on to another side of the Church's life.

II   The Light of the Church

a)   Shining in Jesus Christ, Incarnate and Crucified and in whoever Believes in Him, and Receives Forgiveness

We are sometimes asked and this will be asked of those who belong to the Church of the Millennium: "What does the Church give to those who approach it and enter it?" The Church gives external things to individuals and families at certain times. It provides marriage and baptism and funeral services when the people of the congregation and parish ask for them. But even in doing these, the Church is asking people to receive inwardly what is said and done. But further, the Church in its Sunday Service proclaims the Word of God. That Word has often been called a judgemental and challenging Word, but it can also be called a receptive Word, a Word to be received by those who hear both negatively and positively. Yet this Word is ultimately a Gospel, it is good news about what Jesus Christ, the Son of God the Father, has done for us, and about what he seeks to do within us, and within the Church and the world. If light brings judgement upon us, it also brings energy and growth and new direction in so many places, so it is not surprising to find the Gospel of Jesus Christ put by himself in these terms: "I am the light of the world; he that followeth me shall in no case walk in darkness, but shall have the light of life". Both the Father and the Son are wonderful light givers. The Father gives the Son to the world - 'Thanks be to God for his inexpressible gift", says St Paul, and St John says: "God loved the world so much that he gave his only Son". But the Son gives to his Church, and has given it, and will give it far beyond the Millennium–namely his Spirit, the legacy of Jesus Christ–which is nothing less than his own light which brings new life and love.

So in the present and in the future Church, the shining light of God's reign over evil and sin is not confined to Christ incarnate and crucified, for it penetrates into the earthy life and times of the person who receives and accepts his or her forgiveness. A perennial part of what the Church will always have to say to the modern listener will be about how the dry rot of sin, of separation from God and man, found within humanity, has been overcome in the life of Jesus Christ, but supremely on the Cross, and that forgiveness is offered to all, and can, when rightly received, bring a new heart and a new master to every humble believer. In my study in Orkney there is a picture of Salvador Dali's Crucifixion. "The picture dominates the room, as the figure of the Christ, nailed to His Cross, dominates the picture. The picture means much to me not only because it was the kind gift of my Youth Fellowship in St Thomas' Church, Leith, but also because of its powerful message. Christ on His Cross has His face hidden, and the viewer only sees the top of his head as He looks down upon His world. There are three small figures near boats in the foreground, and these always remind me that Jesus Christ died for each one of these fishermen, as He died for you and me.

Really to believe that Jesus Christ died for us each one, to take away our sin, what does that mean? It means first of all that we are given a new heart. The believer in Christ finds that for him Jeremiah's prophecy of a new heart is fulfilled. Believing in Christ's dying for us, we find that there is within us a heart full of love, a love that seeks to express itself in praise and prayer, in worship, and in service".[6] What happened in John Wesley's life can be appropriately remembered here: "In the evening I went very unwillingly to a society in Aldersgate Street, where one was reading Luther's preface to the Epistle to the Romans. About a quarter before nine while he was describing the change which God works in the heart through faith in Christ, I felt my heart strangely warmed. I felt I did trust in Christ, Christ alone for salvation; and an assurance was given me that He had taken away <u>my</u> sins, even <u>mine</u>, and saved <u>me</u> from the law of sin and death".[7] Thus to be forgiven is to have our true nature restored, and our commitment to love God our Father, and humanity, made possible in new ways, and strengthened.

The position of the person who has been forgiven by God through Christ in the Spirit's power is well described by saying that he has to carry in life both the vertical and horizontal beams of Christ's Cross. Who carries which beam has been put like this: ". . . we have dismembered the Cross. Churchmen carry about the vertical beam, our forgiveness in Christ, and unconsciously escape the turgid demands of its corollary in horizontal obedience. (Or do we do it consciously when we glimpse the measure of the cost?). While the world (oh so moral and well meaning!) carries round the horizontal, forever seeking right relation with neighbour man or neighbour nation, trying to get itself straight without the Bible knowledge of man's condition that humbles, and about the Christ that alone can totally exalt . . . It is precisely the conjunction of the vertical and the horizontal, that, in every sense, makes the Cross. And it is the Cross that alone can save".[8] Both these beams are difficult to keep together, but it is often the horizontal side which can prove far too much to carry for the follower of Jesus in the world. The Revd Dr Archie Craig gives an excellent illustration of this in his struggle to befriend a rebellious parishioner, called Harry Galloway, in his first and only parish.[9] Archie felt that despite all his efforts to help him–sometimes Harry seemed to be his enemy–and to be in touch with him with the same kind of love as he had received from his Saviour, he had failed to show it to him with convincing power.

II   *The Light of the Church*

b)   *Shining in Jesus Christ Ascended and Giving His Spirit To Enlighten and Empower*

Most Christians can identify with Archie Craig and realise that they too have failed in seeking to shoulder properly service to others. But this brings us to another part of the shining light of Jesus Christ; it brings us to him risen and ascended, ever available to his people, especially when they are frequently overcome in the struggle to worship, or in the battle to be his soldiers in the forgiving and sometimes suffering service of those near to them, or far from them. So the reign of God does not only reach men and women by way of the incarnate and crucified Christ, through whom they have received forgiveness, it can reach them through the ascended Christ, who encounters them with his Spirit, and asks them to do things in obedience to him. Both my New Testament professors in Edinburgh and in New York were aware of this, but this is how Professor John Knox in Union Seminary (New York) puts it in his book on St Paul, when his words focus on the living Christ: "Paul's thought about Christ the person always moved from the 'Christ who lives' to the 'Jesus who died', always from the one known to the one remembered. It is the present living reality which comes first to his mind when he speaks of Christ . . . They speak of "Jesus whom God raised up", Paul speaks of "Christ and him crucified" . . . when we read the phrase 'Christ and him crucified' we think first of the human Jesus, of his life of devotion and service, and our minds then move forward to the cross; but when Paul wrote the phrase, he was thinking first of all of the risen exalted Christ, and his thoughts moved backwards to the cross . . . 'For if while we were enemies we were reconciled to God by the death of His Son, much more, now that we are reconciled, shall we be saved by his life'; The "life of Christ" is, not the remembered life that preceded his death; but the life which followed it–the present life of the Son of God".[10]

Reaching out to others in prayer or in ways of practical helpfulness, and doing this in a consistent way is often not a delightful duty but an overwhelming task. Hence we require to call upon the power and the mobility of the ascended Christ who can come to us with his Spirit. "He leads captivity captive; releasing us that we may be chained to Him. But do we adequately convey in addition that 'He gives gifts to men': The Holy Spirit: the gift of all good things to them that ask Him? Or, in another figure, do we convey the intoxicating offer of St Paul that not only is Christ at the right hand of God, but that we with Him are there already? We still pray 'through Jesus Christ our Lord'; but is the proximity of this relationship apparent? Is the fact that "with Him we are ascended and continually do dwell" part of our consciousness?

Not only are we renewed in spirit by our penitence, but empowered by unfeignably believing the whole Gospel. It is identification with Him as High Priest that assists us to see Him as King of the situation to which, from our worship we return. If our consciences are really to be cleansed from dead works to serve the living God, we must portray a living High Priest and not just the memory, however central, of a transaction on the Cross".[11] If it is true that Christians can forget the saving power of what Christ did on the Cross, even more so can we forget the ascended Christ who has taken us with him to God's right hand, and whose will it is that we should be for ever with him, and can always discover that his power and presence is available to us when we turn to him and call upon him in his Spirit. This is the amazing powerful reality which Professor John McIntyre taught in certain of his lectures and books, and not least in his Communion Address on "The Availability of Christ". It is also what my New Testament professors, Scottish and American, both had realised, and it is what George MacLeod taught in Iona and elsewhere, and it is spelt out in what he wrote in his chapter 'Christ as High Priest in the Midst of the Congregation'.[12] "It is the vision of the everlasting and thus present High Priest that allows us to go on". This brings me to the vertical beam of the Cross at work in the Church.

III   God's Reign Over His Church

a)   *Going on in Sunday Services of the Word and in Daily Worship*

We have to remind ourselves now, and as we look forward to the future, that the Church has been called "the Community of the Voice of God". Shortly after my time at New College, one of its professors wrote these words: "We cannot see Jesus, for He has withdrawn Himself from our sight . . . but we <u>can hear</u> His <u>Voice</u> speaking to us in the midst of the Church on earth . . . Jesus Christ was the Word of God made flesh, the still small voice of God embodied in our humanity, and it is that same Word and that same voice, that is given to the Church in the Bible. It is by that voice that the Church in all ages is called into being and upon that Word of God that the Church is founded. The Church is, in fact, the Community of the Voice of God, for it is the business of the Church to open the Bible, and let the voice of Christ speaking in it and through it be heard all over the world".[13]

But this Voice, as Professor Torrance knew well, is not simply one of judgement and condemnation. That is what 'The Minister' in the poem seemed to be saying to his people, and Job Davies was looking for something more to be told to him and his people:

"Take a word from me and keep your nose
In the Black Book. . ."

"Don't be too hard on them, there were people here before these and they were no better".

But if he had done that truly he would have remembered God's mercy and forgiveness as well as his judgement. He would have thought again that the Church was always meant to be for its people the place of upbuilding, both for himself and for all who came, a place where the gracious Father listened patiently to their stumbling prayers knowing that there were amongst them so many people like 'The Minister' and Job, and of Jacob and David. He would have recalled that while judgement can have a part in this upbuilding, it requires to be accompanied with the forgiving love which comes from the Father and the Son. He would have remembered his own distance from God and his desire to make a new start:

".. . I made a vow
As other men in other years have done,
Tomorrow would be different . . ."

He required to be told these words quoted in an earlier book of Professor John Knox: "I have said that membership in the Church is a sharing in memory and the Spirit; it is also a sharing in love, that is, a sharing in the <u>receiving</u> of love, a sharing in <u>being</u> loved–and being loved in a unique way, which overcomes our loneliness and estrangement, and with our brethren makes us sons again in our Father's house. We are speaking of this actual experience of sharing in love when we speak of the Atonement".[14]

Upbuilding of congregations is continually going on in different ways Sunday by Sunday, when the voice of God is heard within the worshipping people. It can be heard through the praise and the prayers and the fellowship of the members but it will still be heard powerfully in the preaching of the Word provided that this had been prepared for by the prayers, not just of the minister but of his people also. These can be said in what has been called 'The Prayer Meeting' but this can be done by the members of a congregation taking the prayers in a smaller service Sunday by Sunday, or by themselves.

The business of going on in worship must be related to activity in work and relationships outside. If it was possible for the farmers in R S Thomas' poem soon to 'unlearn' what had been given them in their rural church by their moving on to their business in the market, it is also the kind of thing that Christians can do in many places and when Christians are mentioned, ministers and church leaders are to be included with members. How often what is said or sung in a service can pass over us, and we have made a good job of unlearning scriptural truth in a short time, and yet there can be the other side, for words from a hymn or psalm or scripture or prayer or from what the Minister was given to say, can lodge in our minds and hearts and wills, and can energise us in the following weeks (or years!)

But we have to go beyond Sunday worship to what happens day by day. Here again the vertical must be related to the horizontal. Minister and elders all know this a battlefield in which they often have to retreat as failures. For how do we keep in touch with "Christ and him crucified" in a family or as an individual? Good relationships are a way in which God's reign works here, yet there are the little books about prayers and the practice of the presence of God in ourselves, which are a witness to struggles in these matters. But if we are to keep the vertical and horizontal lines of our Christian life together, we have to try and have some Scripture reading brought together with our view of what is happening in our part of the world or beyond it, and of what we have to do with the day ahead. And in all this we also keep in mind our closeness to Christ, and his knowledge of us and of our situation, and of the availability to us of his guidance and saving power, through his Spirit's reaching down to us. It is good to use a series of readings of Scripture for the days of a week.

These are obtainable in what are called Lectionaries (eg in the Church of Scotland's booklet called *Pray Together*) and are often to be found in a Church or Christian Fellowship or in a Bookshop. Thus, through the readings for the day, and through thought about what needs to be done in the hours ahead often in relation to the family or neighbours or the work situations or crises near or far, the Father's grace and help will be sought. This has frequently been seen as the ascended Christ's openness to us, and our lives will be directed for the future with the Spirit's pervading presence. This is the kind of 'going on' required for so many Christian people, now and in the future of the Church. The Revd Dr J P Newell's book, *Each Day and Each Night*, has a useful Lectionary for each day (apart from Sunday) and has proved a great help for the individual–or for more than one person, as my wife and I find each new day.[15]

III God's Reign Over His Church

b) Going on in Eucharistic Services

If the reign of God can reach the people of the Church now and into the future through the Word and prayer, it does this best corporately in the Eucharist. Here God's reign comes in a powerfully saving, and visual way, as in the Church of Scotland, for the bread and wine is often given to members by the elders and passed on by members to one another. It took many of us who had been ex-Servicemen some time before we grasped that at the Eucharist we received more than an individual remembrance of his death and pardon for us. We learned these words of the Revd Professor J K S Reid: "we shall not rightly say that the object of Eucharistic remembrance is the death of Jesus on the Cross in and by itself. The words themselves forbid this limitation. Our Lord tells his disciples to do this, not in remembrance of his death but in remembrance of him. He who is remembered is of course he who died, but he is not less certainly he who, being dead is alive for evermore". So this living Christ comes to us, not simply to an individual, but binding us together with his forgiving love, and strengthening us for relationships within and without the congregation. The corporate significance of the Eucharist can be amplified. The people hear together something in the sermon of the grace of God, of his forgiving love in his Son; they hear it too in the Great Prayer which tells of what Christ has done, but they can also make an offering of themselves at the end of that prayer. The following is an example:

"And here we offer and present unto Thee ourselves, our souls and bodies, to be a reasonable, holy, and living sacrifice; and we beseech Thee mercifully to accept this our sacrifice of praise and thanksgiving, as in fellowship with all the faithful in heaven and on earth, we pray Thee to fulfil in us, and in all men the purpose of thy redeeming love; through Jesus Christ our Lord, by whom and with whom, in the unity of the Holy Spirit, all honour and glory be to thee, O Father Almighty. World without end. Amen". And as we offer ourselves together to the Father through the Son, so we also receive together, as we hold out our hands for the bread and wine, and we then go out into the world to witness and serve. So many congregations miss out in adumbrating this social significance of the Eucharist in the Liturgy. Yet the Eucharist can stimulate a corporate effect outside the congregation as well as within it. There is a good illustration of this in the story of St Magnus . . ."The actions of Everyman, once the bread of divine wisdom is in his body have an immense importance; what he does and says and thinks reverberates through the whole web of time. Men not yet born will be changed, either for good or ill, by his speech and the things that his hands find to do. . . A man can therefore direct his purified will into the future for the alleviation of the pain of the future. . . The man whispered and the whole web of history trembled".[16] In that little church in the island of Egilsay in Orkney at the Easter Mass, Earl Magnus whispered his self offering even to death to his risen and ascended Lord, receiving the broken bread–Christ's sacrificial and forgiving life–and the whole web of history trembles. For one thing through the dedication of this one martyr, the fighting and the burning and the hatred in Orkney ceased, and the light and peace and good order began to shine there, and far beyond Orkney's shore. At any rate, if the Eucharist has indeed this dynamic and binding influence both within and without the Church, then "the Church of Scotland must now depart from its long infidelity to its own origins and restore a more frequent sacrament".[17] In the future in the Millennium Church it is hoped that the meaning and social significance of this Eucharist will be studied more patiently and carefully in leadership groups, not least in Kirk Sessions and that it will be practised more often in smaller groups as well as on the great occasions of the Christian year. For the Eucharist is filled with the dynamite of the reign of God.

III   *God's Reign Over His Church*

c)   *Going on in Home Visits*

In the parable of the Hidden Treasure, Jesus told of how it was unexpectedly found by the man ploughing his field. Often, probably, he had done this, but one day his plough struck a sunken box or chest. He stopped and opened it, and to his joy and amazement found it was filled with precious things–gold and gems beyond his dreams. Yet how near that treasure had been to him for so many years! That is the kind of discovery which can be the good fortune of an elder or Minister on entering a home in his congregation. How close to him often and yet sometimes so unexpected! A Minister can go to a home sometimes, not very eagerly (even wearily!) but there he hears about the family in a renewing way, and what they say to him makes possible and relevant the gift he can bring next time, or the nature of the prayer he feels he can say then not only for them, but in their presence for others (sometimes he will ask permission if he can say the prayer). So there can be giving and receiving for minister or elder and people. What Professor Manson said about the mystery of the Kingdom becomes a reality, but not only is there a doing of God's will in terms of coming to the home with love and prayer, but the goal of the reign of God, the conquest of the gap between God, the Father and his people, and between humankind is achieved, and brought into immediate and joyful relationship in that family. That is the other side, the profoundly important side of God's reign over evil and doubt, beyond the actual doing of the Father's will by minister or elder in coming to enter the home. Some ministers almost always read a portion of Scripture, but there are times when Scripture words or promise can be included in the prayer which can frequently be informed by what the Minister learns from those in the family circle. Hence the prayer will not simply be the Minister's, but in a very real sense the prayer of those in the family both for others and for themselves. and yet the prayer can be Christ's prayer in the Spirit's power, "For God has sent the spirit of his Son into our hearts whereby we cry 'Abba', Father".

The reign of God, however, means more than worship, so there is at times in a home opportunity given to speak about the Church, and about what can be done there by members to make it grow, both in commitment and even in numbers, especially in relation to the entry into it of younger members. Often in a visit the Minister meets these younger people and their friends, and they can stimulate discussion, sometimes in a critical way, but also in a seeking and positive way. There are days when the Minister is given by such conversation, the names of people often baptised, he can see afterwards. These can be invited on occasion to come, with or without a friend, to an enquirer's class concerning Church membership. What Professor Milligan has written on the Church's work for herself is important on this matter. "Important as the sacred writers knew their message to the world to be, they never failed to exhibit the conviction that it was even more important to the churches; that, while they had no doubt to convert unbelievers, it was still more imperatively required that they edify believers and carry them on to perfection; and that the different members of the Body needed to be completed into one, each working well in its own place, and all working smoothly together, before the Church could successfully accomplish her mission. . . And hence to take only one noteworthy example from the writings of St Paul, when that Apostle tells us of the object which the ascended Lord had in view by the gift of His various ministries, the conversion of the world is not mentioned. Everything has relation to the Church. Apostles, Prophets, Evangelists, Pastors and Teachers are given 'for the perfecting of the Saints unto the work of ministering, into the building up of the body of Christ' ".[18] It might seem from all this that every ministerial visit to a home was easy and co-operative. This is not so, and there could be, seemingly, little response. But that did not mean giving up the visits to members in their homes, for sometimes resistance can come from misunderstanding or lack of diligence on the part of minister or family member. In any case there is more than one way of a Minister seeing his people. Greater use of elders is sometimes possible, through their generosity in gathering members of their district in their own home, when the Minister also can be present.

It could be said that the relation of the reign of God to the visiting of homes by a Minister is the kind of subject a senior minister could discover in his talks with, or instruction of assistants. This did not happen at a theological level in my experience, nor in that of many other assistants to whom I have spoken. Hence the issue could be considered afresh by the staff in a divinity college, and the reign of God could be developed not least in relation to mission.

IV   God's Reign Over His World

a)   Discovering more of this Treasure in Nature

Despite what has been written earlier about the working of God within the Church in home visits, God's reign through the ascended Christ is over the world as well as his Church. Once more what was written by the late Professor Milligan is relevant: "The Church must be animated by the belief that she is elect not for her own sake, but for the world's; and that her life is to be a priestly life in the name of the Heavenly Father, for the spreading of that 'kingdom' which, bringing men to God, brings them also to one another, and lifts them up into that sphere of the holy, the beautiful, and the loving which is as yet consummated only in the Great High priest in heaven".[19] Our Lord was clearly aware of the beauty of nature, and it is good that so many who seek to be his followers today are like him in this way. They are unlike Elias Morgan in R S Thomas' poem, for he said:

> "But I didn't even know the names
> Of the birds and the flowers by which one gets
> A little closer to nature's heart"

We can be glad indeed that so many of our people are aware of nature's beauty and strength, that they know that seasons come when God's renewal of the earth can be seen, and that humankind is not always enclosed in 'God's February' when it is harder to perceive that he is still at work. And if we have those about who can see more in nature than its savagery, so with human nature, they can perceive there the working of the Spirit, of his love joy, and peace, they can recognise that, as the

Psalmist knew, it is 'God that hath made us and not we ourselves;' and they do not fall into the ways of Elias Morgan who

> ... "Let his mind
> Fester with brooding on the sly
> Infirmities of the hill people"

The response of nature and freedom and recognition to the love of God is dealt with in Chapter 5 of Dr Vanstone's book - *Love's Endeavour, Love's Expense.*

IV *God's Reign Over His World*

b) *Discovering also the Treasure in Society*

But most of us have society around us, as well as nature and human nature, and this too can be seen as the discovery of the riches of God's reign. "The usual question, 'what shall we do?' must be answered with the unusual question 'whence can we receive?' People must understand again that we cannot do much without having received much".[20] This is a good thought for Minister and people and others to have in their minds when they want to think about the corporate groups within society, such as schools or councils or large clubs of some kind. These can be for the Christian, gifts of God to be received with thanksgiving. It is easy to see the faults of a school–the deficiencies of some member of staff in it can flash before our eyes–but in reality how often teachers are well trained, and have as their main objective to teach their pupils well, and to be their friends where they have opportunity. A school is also a place where a Minister can receive much wisdom from staff and pupils as well as contribute something to it. Is it not the same with the local council or a large group like a branch of the Royal British Legion, or the Rotary Club? Like the school in a parish, these groups within society are not entirely full of those who are filled with the Spirit, but how often their lives have been once more God's gift to us. In a Council we can find people of integrity and with a strong passion, in the midst of much debate and difficulty, to pursue justice and compassion for those by whom they have been elected, and whom they feel called to serve. The ascended Christ with his enlivening Spirit has been amongst them, and through this councillor or convener, or that paid official, can illumine and stimulate their community, or can invigorate a guest or visiting chaplain. There in that place there has been a "re-humanising of the area and content of our salvation" - Much to the people's surprise, it is realised again and again that, just as in the Royal British Legion and in the Rotary, the apex of Divinity is to be found in glorious humanity, in seeing and meeting human need. Such society groups can be renewing and refreshing for those seeking to follow Christ, and we remember that their communities are not given us to be condemned, but rather to make us look critically at ourselves or at our Church community, and for us sometimes to be inspired by the giving generous society which can be there. So we read: "To rest in God is to be lost in community that we may be found in Him. A fullness of the times has come when obedience to Christ as the new community is the only way to be comforted of Him as the new Man. . . I claim this community will not be recovered by the congregation, and therefore not proffered to the world for its acceptance or rejection, till we re-humanise the Message: recover for men the Vision of a Man in Heaven and fall down with them in awe at the knowledge that the apex of His Majesty resides in His most glorious humanity".[21]

These society groups of which we have been speaking, have, we find, splendidly discovered the humanity of Christ in many ways at the horizontal level, but some within them are puzzled about the vertical level of the Christian faith. Because these say there is no God, or that they are very uncertain of his existence, and of the living character of his Son, they cannot understand about the cry 'Abba', Father, sent into a man or a woman's heart and mind. At this point we must remember in the present church, moving towards the Millennium, what we have been given, world wide and local. There is still something for our citizens to receive and there is a Christian community to enter. God is not a silent God, he has been speaking and will continue to do so, through the people of our communities and in their groupings, but this will not usually mean that he had evacuated the Christian fellowship he has gathered through his Son and the working of his Spirit. On the contrary, even when that community has become very small, and is neglected, or even persecuted, the river of his presence is still there, though it may be hard to find, and may require the faith of the psalmist to say "The Lord of Hosts is with us and the God of Jacob is our refuge" (Psalm 46)

It must be remembered that in local churches, large or small, there are still inspiring and courageous receivers, for the moment often silent, yet who know that they have God, Father, Son and Holy Spirit, to believe in, a community of faith and hope and love to which they belong, and something to work for–the reign of God over evil. Such believers also know that they have so much more to be given by the Saviour they have come to know, who will strengthen them more for witness and service when the time comes.

V   The Reign of God

A Burden to be Carried or Sails for our Voyage?

In the present and the future church, in its worship of the Word, and the Eucharist, or in crisis and home visits, or in recognition of and service to nature, human nature and society, God's reign can be seen at times as another weight to be carried, and it can indeed appear as a hard thing to accept, even though it be regarded as the will of God to be done or his love to be pursued. Yet God's reign can also be recognised as a gift from God our Father, embraced by Jesus Christ his son, and passed on to us in the Spirit's power.

It is a precious treasure near at hand to be discovered, and the pearl of great price to be obtained. It is there in the homes and lives of our people, and in its fullness it is the potential for every human being, though it is so often covered over each day. Above all, the reign of God is best found and seen in the light of the Church, present and future moving towards the Millennium, especially in the Christ within it, once incarnate and crucified but now the ascended Lord, who has the great passion to come to us with his Spirit, and the persistent desire to penetrate and rule our lives with the mystery of his will and love. For he is himself the embodiment of the reign of God, and his purpose is that we should discover it and receive it and share in it and convey it to others, And if this reign can reach out through Jesus in the flesh and crucified, and declaring for us his forgiveness, it can also come to us through our ascended Lord, who cannot really be separated from Jesus crucified, but who encounters us sooner or later showing us his Cross and asking us to bear it like the Jesus of Calvary.

The Church we know now contains, and the Church of the future will contain it–namely the passion of God our Father to be with us and in us through Jesus Christ his Son, giving us blessings and light and life beyond our imagination. What we are asked to do is to come and see it and receive it in increasing measure. This great image and truth is to be discerned in the west window of St Giles Cathedral, not far from New College, near to the top of the Mound in Edinburgh. This window is dedicated to the memory of Robert Burns, and takes its inspiration from one of his best known and loved poems, 'O my luve's like a red, red rose.' "At the heart of the window is the red flower or flame, an image of the love that is at the heart of life. The realm of creation and the world of humanity are depicted as streaked through with terribly dark lines of wrong and confusion, but still deeper are the strands of golden light that issue from the rose and are interwoven through all things. At the centre of life and at its beginning is the fire of passion. . . The gospel is given not primarily to tell us that many of our passions are dark and destructive, for we more or less know that about ourselves. Rather the truth which we have forgotten, and which the gospel is given to recall us to, and thus to liberate us with, is that we bear within ourselves the passion and creativity of God".[22]

Being ever mindful of the grace of God, Father and Son and Holy Spirit, who wishes to bestow upon all the blessings of his reign over evil, sin and death, and to give us eternal life with the faithful of all ages, may the present and the future and Millennium church member constantly pray "God, be merciful to me a sinner,' and yet saying it with hope, for there is a Man in Heaven".[23]

Notes

1. R S Thomas - 'Selected Poems' - 1946-1968 - Bloodaxe Books Ltd, (PO Box 1SN, Newcastle on Tyne) - pp19-33 ('The Minister').
2. G F MacLeod - 'Only One Way Left' - The Iona Community - p24.
3. Ibid - p26.
4. Ibid - p29.
5. Psalm 103.
6. H W M Cant - 'Preaching in a Scottish Parish Church' - The Kirkwall Press (W R Mackintosh) p107.
7. L F Church - 'Knight of the Burning Heart' - The Camelot Press - pp95-96.
8. G F MacLeod - Ibid -p37.
9. 'God's February - A Life of Archie Craig' - E Templeton - pp33-36.
10. John Knox - 'Chapters in a Life of Paul' - Abingdon - Cokesbury Press - pp130-131.
11. G F MacLeod - 'Only One Way Left' - Ibid - pp102-103.
12. Ibid - pp97-119.
13. T F Torrance - 'When Christ Comes and Comes Again' - Hodder and Stoughton -London - p27.
14. John Knox - 'The Church and The Reality of Christ' - Collins - London -p109.
15. J P Newell - 'Each Day and Each Night' - Wild Goose Publications/The Iona Community.
16. G M Brown - 'Magnus' - The Hogarth Press - p141.
17. 'People With A Purpose' - The 40 File 1972-1978 - p12.
18. W Milligan - 'The Ascension of Our Lord' - MacMillan & Co - p281.
19. Ibid - p290.
20. Paul Tillich - 'The Protestant Era' - Nisbet - p85.
21. G F MacLeod - 'Only One Way Left' - pp53-54.
22. J P Newell - 'One Foot in Eden' - SPCK - p53.
23. G F MacLeod Ibid - p163.